232

796·8

Don Gresswell Ltd., London, N.21   Cat. No. 1208

D1330594

Sport, society and politics

General editor
John Williams

Already published
Hilary Mcd. Beckles and Brian Stoddart *Liberation cricket:
West Indies cricket culture*

Forthcoming
Peter Donnelly *Contested terrain: a cultural history of mountaineering*
John Nauright *Rugby and South Africa*
Keith Sandiford and Brian Stoddart *The imperial game*
Jennifer Hargreaves *Sporting heroines*

Boxing and society

An international analysis

John Sugden

Manchester University Press

Manchester and New York

distributed exclusively in the USA by St. Martin's Press

Copyright © John Sugden 1996

Published by Manchester University Press
Oxford Road, Manchester M13 9NR, UK
and Room 400, 175 Fifth Avenue, New York, NY 10010, USA

Distributed exclusively in the USA
by St. Martin's Press, Inc., 175 Fifth Avenue, New York,
NY 10010, USA

British Library Cataloguing-in-Publication Data
A catalogue record for this book is available from the British Library

Library of Congress Cataloging-in-Publication Data
Sugden, John Peter.
    Boxing and society: an international analysis / John Sugden.
      p. cm. – (Sport, society and politics)
    ISBN 0-7190-4320-4. – ISBN 0-7190-4321-2
    1. Boxing–Social aspects–Cross-cultural studies. 2. Boxing–
Political aspects–Cross-cultural studies. I. Title. II. Series.
GV1196.8.S84   1996   96-29445
796.8'3–dc20   CIP

ISBN 0 7190 4320 4   *hardback*
        0 7190 4321 2   *paperback*

First published 1996

00 99 98 97 96   10 9 8 7 6 5 4 3 2 1

Printed by Biddles Ltd, Guildford & King's Lynn

Contents

Acknowledgements

There have been many people over the years who have given me invaluable assistance in the development of this book. I would particularly like to thank Andy Yiannakis and Bob Broadhead, who held my hand in America, Joanna Head, who inspired me in Belfast, and Greg Darby, who kept me together in Havana. Alan Bairner's and Alan Tomlinson's combined critique and editorial expertise were likewise invaluable. Thanks are also due to my family, who put up with my long absences and moody reflections, and to friends such as Billy and Norman for their unfailing support. Finally, there are the boxers, trainers, managers and corner men whose openness, generosity and indefatigable spirit never ceased to amaze me.

Introduction

This is a book about the sociology of sport, but, as a culmination of a decade and a half of work which dominated the formative years of my adult life, it is also a book about me. During the course of this project, when people learned that I was writing a book about boxing they usually asked whether I had been a boxer or whether I at least was a fight fan. The fact is, before I set foot in the boxing club which features in chapter 3 I had never seen live boxing and boxing had been one of the few sports that I had little conscious interest in. It was not that I took a moral stance against boxing. Indeed, I suspect that I have long since had a dormant interest in the ring. After all, I came from an industrial sea port city where it is expected that men should learn to 'use themselves' and where fighting and avoiding fighting were integral to the male adolescent experience. While I never attended one, through the conversations of my father, uncles and grandfather, I recall that every Friday night there was a boxing show at the stadium which, until the late 1960s, was a popular event for dockers, sailors and factory workers from Liverpool. Boxing was a seminal feature of the popular culture of my father's generation and, albeit in markedly different ways, it provided some symbolic bench marks in my own coming of age.

I grew up in the era of the Beatles and Vietnam, but it was also the era of Cassius Clay's metamorphosis into Muhammad Ali. I watched a small black and white screen in the corner of the living room as he danced, jabbed and stung his way to boxing's highest pinnacle. As an eleven-year-old I was included when the nation collectively jumped out of its seat when 'our enrey' (Cooper) put the champ on his backside in London in 1963. At fourteen I sat in the same room in 1966 to watch England win the soccer World Cup and Clay demolish Brian London in three brutally short rounds. Like many others I gradually became hooked as Clay became a totem for a dispossessed generation as his egotistic rhetoric became peppered with statements on social justice. His conversion to Islam was a moment of confusion for those brought up in a culture within which blacks are seen as inferior and Arabs are villains. Nevertheless, his incarceration following his refusal to fight in Vietnam ('no Viet Cong ever called me Nigger') gained him as many fans as he lost. We were all euphoric when, after his release from prison, he regained his title after the classic 'rumble in the jungle' with George Foreman in Zaire in October 1974. Once more Ali reigned supreme until 1978, when, over two fights with Leon Spinks, he lost but then regained his title. Then, after a two-year lay-off he took on a former sparring partner, Larry Holmes, and was humiliated in Las Vegas. Ali was finished, the Beatles had split up and Vietnam was a bitter memory.

I concentrated on soccer, trained to be a PE teacher and began to wonder what I was going to do with the sociology and politics degree which I had picked up as a by-product of my embrace of university life. When an offer of a scholarship to teach sports while studying the sociology of sport at the University of Connecticut came through a former tutor, I jumped at it. It was while I was based in the United States that the seed that grew to become this book was planted. I had reached the stage when I was searching for a suitable topic for a PhD dissertation. Most of my undergraduate sociology and much of my postgraduate work had focused on the unravelling of grand theoretical debates, the value of which I had begun to question. At the same time I had been exposed to a variety of research methods in courses which gave prominence to the epistemology of positivism and quantitative data gathering and analytical techniques; these I grew to suspect as being quite limited as tools for sociological interpretation. Disillusionment both with grand theory and survey research led me to reconsider the work of the Chicago School,[1] which in turn led me to an appraisal of qualitative methodologies in general and the development of grounded theory in particular.[2] I became convinced that the generation of interpretation and theory was a task that had to begin in the field, and I resolved to learn how to be an ethnographer. I was now a man with a method but, as yet, I had no questions to ask or answer.

As part of my duties as a graduate assistant in the Department of Sport and Leisure Studies I was often asked to help with research projects which had little or nothing to do with my own interests. My head of department was approached by a local boxing promoter and was asked to do some preliminary research into injuries in boxing. It was decided that rather than targeting the sport's top professionals, this research should begin at the grass roots of boxing. I clearly remember sitting in the head of department's study, looking out of the window at the foliage and lush grass cloisters of one of New England's nicest rural campuses, as the decision was taken to dispatch me into one of Hartford's notorious ghettos to make contact with the lower reaches of the boxing fraternity.

The funding for the full-blown project on boxing injuries never materialised. However, almost from the moment I set foot in the Memorial Boxing Club in the Burnt Oak housing project I realised that I had found the research field which would perfectly complement my preferred methodology. The essence of good sociology is making sense of the mysterious. Here was a social universe which was buried deep within a subcultural envelope about which I knew next to nothing and

---

[1] A tradition of urban sociology/anthropology rooted in the works of Robert Park and his contemporaries based at the University of Chicago in the 1920s and 1930s.
[2] For a more detailed discussion of these methodological issues see the Appendix.

about which there was virtually nothing written.[3] For the next two years I led a dual existence: in the semi-rural idyll of the University campus as John Sugden, the anonymous college postgraduate student; and in Hartford's ghetto and in the basement gym as 'Doctor John',[4] the idiosyncratic English ethnographer and the boxing club's odd-job man.

Thus my affair with the noble art began in earnest. The main yield of this period of field work was my PhD dissertation (1984) which, on completion, was dispatched to a major publishing house to see if they were interested in it. They said they were but that they would require a significant rewrite. Until the current, more substantial work materialised, I regretted that I did not follow this offer through. At the time I had just been appointed to my first full-time lecturing post and I was up to my neck in new work. Also I now realise I was suffering from a hitherto undiagnosed condition, post-doctoral depression – I was sick of the sight of my dissertation and the thought of rewriting it brought on fresh waves of nausea. Thus it sat on my shelf gathering dust until I was finally persuaded to produce at least a summary for publication in a collection of essays on sport and society (Sugden, 1987). Unbeknown to me, it was this publication which would eventually lead me back into the field in search of the boxing subculture which provided the material for the second case study, presented in chapter 4.

At this time I was living and working in Northern Ireland and most of my research and scholarship was directed towards making sense of the complex relationships between sport, culture and politics in that troubled corner of Europe. Given the background that I have just described, it may seem strange that despite the fact that boxing has a significant presence in Northern Ireland, it was one of the few sports which I did not choose to focus on while carrying out research for a book on sport and society in Ireland (Sugden and Bairner, 1993). I can explain this only in terms of lingering post-doctoral depression. Then, in 1992, I received a call from a television producer in London who said that she was interested in doing a documentary on boxing from a social/anthropological angle and that because of Belfast's complex community structure she wanted to film it there. She went on to say that once the idea had been formulated she had conducted a literature search which had yielded my article referred to above. The grounded and interpretative style transmitted by this piece was precisely what she favoured and so she became determined to track me down and enlist my help in preparing the programme. However, she was astounded to discover that I actually lived and worked in Belfast!

For the next twelve months I worked on the programme, necessitating a considerable amount of field work in north Belfast, the detail of which appears in

---

[3] I began this work in 1979, at which time there were only two short pieces with any sociological content written about boxing in the US ghetto (Weinberg and Arond, 1952; Hare, 1971). Neither of these had a strong ethnographic flavour.

[4] When I first entered the field I introduced myself as John and explained that I was working towards my doctorate. The locals merged the two pieces of information and henceforth I was referred to as Doctor John.

chapter 4 and in the appendix. The programme, 'Fighting for the Holy Family', was duly completed and was screened in 1994 as part of BBC2's 'Under the Sun' series, as well as being screened worldwide on National Geographic's cable television network. Throughout the research and the filming I had been able to draw on my US experiences to assist in terms of both method and interpretation. It was while I was writing up my field notes to be used as the basis for a journal article that I realised that the two ethnographies were linked and could form the basis of a more significant publication. However, I also considered that two case studies represented a narrow comparative base and thought that one more would strengthen the global presence of the book. I thought of places such as Sweden, where professional boxing is banned, or South Africa with its complex racial, class and community structure as possible sites for further research. However, given the time and the physical and emotional energies demanded by ethnography, the prospect of starting from scratch in a third 'new' culture was daunting.

At this point I remembered that while researching 'The Holy Family' I had briefly encountered Nicholas Hernandez-Cruz, the Cuban who was seconded to coach the Irish boxing team in the Barcelona Olympics. Cuba is the strongest amateur boxing nation in the world and I already had a familiarity with Cuban society and Cuban sport. In 1989 I had been invited to the University of Rhode Island to speak at an international conference on the theme of sport and world peace. Among the speakers was the former runner Alberto Juantorena, the legendary double gold medallist from the 1976 Olympics in Montreal. Like myself he had arrived for the conference a couple of days early. We were staying in the same hotel and we got to know each other quite well, to the extent that each morning we would go running together while spending the rest of the day exploring Rhode Island's Atlantic coast. Alberto is a highly placed official within the Cuban Ministry of Sport and after the conference he invited me to visit Cuba to study the sports system there. This I did early in 1990 and I returned with a study group in 1991. During my first visit Juantorena introduced me to Teofilo Stevenson, the heavyweight boxer who had won consecutive gold medals at the Munich, Montreal and Moscow Olympics. Nevertheless, when I co-authored a chapter on sport in Cuba (Sugden *et al.*, 1992), once more boxing was conspicuous by its absence. I resolved to put this right as I concluded that Cuba, with its boxing links with Ireland and its pre-eminence in world amateur boxing, should be the third case study for inclusion in this book.

Without providing a comprehensive social history of boxing, chapters 1 and 2 attempt to support the case studies which follow with at least a sense of history. This is based on the premise that nothing is new under the sun and that boxing in its various settings in the modern world is but the leading edge of complex cultural and institutional processes which are rooted in the deconstruction and reformation of dominant forms of social, economic and political life. Chapter 1 begins with brief discussions on the social location of boxing in ancient and medieval societies before concentrating on the 'golden era' of bare-knuckle prize fighting in Regency

England. The rise and decline of prize fighting on both sides of the Atlantic is assessed in the context of the social and cultural upheavals which accompanied the transition from feudalism to capitalism in England and in the USA. The sport's rebirth under the aegis of the Marquess of Queensberry's rules is considered and the re-emergence of gloved, professional boxing and its relationship with urban poverty in the early part of the twentieth century is explained. It is argued that by this time all of the social ingredients of the modern boxing subculture had been established.

Chapter 2 reviews the progress of prize fighting in the twentieth century, with a particular emphasis on the political and economic context which framed the development of modern professional boxing. For most of this century the nerve centre of boxing has been the United States and in this chapter issues such as immigration, race relations, war, organised crime and political propaganda are looked at in terms of how they influenced the careers of world-class fighters such as Jack Johnson, Jack Dempsey, Max Schmeling, Joe Louis, Sonny Liston and Muhammad Ali. This chapter also overviews the complex administrative and business relations which characterise contemporary professional boxing, tracing the multiplication of governing bodies and weight categories and the careers of some of the sport's most significant promoters, such as Tex Rickard and Don King.

Chapter 3 dissects the boxing subculture as it existed in the United States in the early 1980s and locates it as an integral feature of the ghetto. It concentrates on the rites of passage of young boxers who struggle to make something of their lives in the face of poverty, discrimination, violence and a whole catalogue of disadvantage. At the core of this case study is the relationship between urban poverty, youth culture and professional boxing. It is a paradoxical story which tells of both freedom and exploitation. The liberating discipline and bravery of the fighters and their passions and ambitions are set against the hypocrisy of the boxing entrepreneurs who are able to harness disadvantage and deprivation in order to secure the recruitment base of the professional circuit. It also reveals how, behind the evangelistic rhetoric of rational recreation, the gatekeepers of the boxing subculture are able to line their own pockets. This first case study confirms the history lesson that professional boxing and urban poverty need each other, regardless of the consequences for the fighters themselves.

Chapter 4 uses boxing as a window into the troubled soul of Northern Ireland. It focuses on the Holy Family, a boxing club located in a part of Belfast where, at the time this research was carried out, 1992–93, working-class Catholics were separated from working-class Protestants by empty streets, barbed wire, high walls and barricades. This is the breeding ground for paramilitary organisations and sectarian death squads. The case study reveals in boxing yet another paradox whereby arguably one of the world's most violent sports operates peacefully, in a cross-community context and in ways that defy the sectarian contours of working-class Belfast. As with the US study, it shows how, more than being an escape, for many youngsters the boxing club is a sanctuary within the ghetto: an oasis where the vicissitudes and vices produced by urban poverty, political conflict and violence are temporarily suspended through respect for the ring and its traditional values. Through the mouths of young fighters and their parents the chapter also shows how Northern Ireland's boxing subculture is sustained in contradictory ways by visions of hope and layers of hopelessness. Despite the self-proclaimed neutrality of boxing, this case study also shows how the sport has been a victim of Northern Ireland's political conflict.

Chapter 5 differs in style from the preceding case studies. Rather than focusing on a single club it locates boxing broadly in the context of contemporary Cuban society, using the sport as a basis from which to explore the condition of a nation which, until the late 1980s, was at the leading edge of international communism but which in the 1990s finds itself politically and economically isolated. In this respect it is as much about Cuba as it is about boxing. However, the recurrent themes of privation, struggle and exploitation are significant in the interpretation of boxing in Cuba and, albeit from a different angle, this chapter retains the comparative thrust of the book. It traces the historical development of boxing on the island, stressing the cultural influence of North America and how this helped to shape the island's sporting traditions in general and to establish boxing as Cuba's most popular sport next to baseball. The changing form of boxing is used to consider the impact of the 1959 revolution on Cuban society. Castro's personal interventions into and contribution to Cuba's sports system are evaluated and his appropriation of boxing is used to exemplify the strength of the links between sport and politics in Cuba. Finally, the impact on Cuba of seismic changes in the world's political economy, particularly the collapse of Soviet communism, is considered. The chapter concludes by arguing that until very recently, Cuba's long-standing boxing tradition coupled with a tolerable degree of economic hardship and an efficient sports system provided an excellent social base for the production of successful amateur boxers. However, as economic hardship goes beyond the margins of the tolerable and Castro's popularity continues to decline, the future of his regime and the sports system which he sponsors is being questioned.

The final chapter extracts and extends some of the conclusions drawn from the ethnographic material into the broader context of social theory. This theorisation is then used to inform the medical and moral debate over the future of boxing. Doubts are raised about the moralistic notion that there is no place for a sport such as boxing in a civilised society. The historical continuity of boxing is used to suggest that the sport may reflect a primordial but nonetheless significant aspect of the human condition. It is argued that social development both between and within nations is so stratified and uneven that the idea of an encompassing civilising process cannot be sustained. Instead it is concluded that rather than threatening 'civilisation as we (all) know it', boxing poses serious questions about a class-based version of civilisation – bourgeois hegemony. While recognising the essentially exploitative nature of professional boxing, it is argued that, given the global condition of urban poverty and ghettoisation, it does offer, albeit in complex ways, both sanctuary and succour to a handful of the world's urban dispossessed. Returning to the moral debate the book concludes that those wishing to ban boxing should redirect their efforts towards the eradication of poverty, for without the latter, as the Swedish case is used to illustrate, there is little appetite for the former.

I have emphasised how the links between the three case studies are the natural product of my lived experience. As such they are not contrived to tell a particular story with a beginning, middle and end. While there are important common themes which cut across all three, each study reveals different aspects of different societies at different stages of social and economic development and each should be considered separately before any comparative generalisations are made. However, I believe that the three case studies do provide a balanced view of the submerged world that exists beneath the ring. The study of the club in the US ghetto concentrates on the social processes which surround the occupational socialisation of professional boxers. In doing so, while the social welfare claims of the pro-boxing lobby are scrutinised, this aspect of the research concentrates on the essentially exploitative thrust of commercialised, professional boxing. The study of the Holy Family Boxing Club in Belfast is mainly about amateur boxing and is particularly concerned with the positive aspects of a sport which brings order, discipline and sanctuary to a group of young people living on the front line in a deeply divided society. The final case study, by looking at the sport in a country which is one of the last bastions of communism, is able to show how the core elements of urban poverty, status frustration and the need for self-expression transcend the boundaries of differing social systems to entice people into the ring.

Above all, the last thing this book claims to achieve is the construction of a grand sociological theory of boxing. Neither does it set out to provide a definitive answer to the debate over whether or not boxing should be banned. I have deliberately avoided adopting a moralistic stance towards the sport, but I believe that the case studies provide the reader with sufficient insight into what boxing means to those who are involved at a grass-roots level. As such, readers will be better informed should they choose to join the debate over the future of boxing. I hope I have provided sufficient grounded information for readers who are not happy with my own interpretations and conclusions to draw their own. I encourage them to do so.

1

Historical continuity and boxing

Circa 700 BC, Greece, Dares versus Entellus:

> Holding their heads held high, and well out of reach of blows, they began to spar in interplay of fist with fist, warming to the fight. Dares could rely on his youth, and his footwork was better. Entellus had the strength of his limbs and his massive bulk, but his knees were slow moving and unsteady; he shook, and a painful panting convulsed his vast frame. Often the boxers would strike dangerous blows at each other but miss; often a punch would smack against the hollow of a flank or land on a chest with a loud thump. Hands flickered fast round ears and forehead. Crack! sounded a jaw under a violent stroke. (Virgil, 1956: 132)

21 August 1807, London, Dutch Sam versus Jem Belcher:

> From the thirty-first to the thirty-sixth round it was evident to the spectators that Belcher could not win. The ferocity of Sam was tremendous in the extreme; he followed his opponent to all parts of the ring, putting in dreadful facers and body blows, dealing out death-like punishment, till his brave opponent fell quite exhausted. (Egan, 1812: 330)

7 September 1892, New Orleans, James J. Corbett versus Yankee Sullivan:

> He rushed in and planted blow after blow on Sullivan's face and neck. The champion, so soon to lose his coveted title, backed away, trying to save himself. He lowered his guard from sheer exhaustion, and catching a fearful smash on the jaw, reached to the ropes, and the blood poured down his face in torrents and made a crimson river across the broad chest. (Gorn, 1986: 245)

30 October 1974, Kinshasa, Zaire, George Foreman versus Muhammad Ali:

> The end came when Foreman who almost collapsed in his corner after the seventh, was pawing and being pushed away. Ali clipped him with a right, repeated the punch, and Foreman's legs unhinged. The champion pitched to the centre of the ring face downwards then twisted over as he fell. Foreman's red trunks were covered with resin as he looked vacant-eyed to his corner men. (Gutteridge, 1974)

This is not a history book. Excellent social histories of boxing have been written by Gorn (1986), Brailsford (1988) and Sheard (1990). Nevertheless, because the anthropological method which informs the core of this text is premised upon Raymond Williams' (1977) understanding of culture – that cultures are produced and reproduced by people acting within institutionally framed settings which themselves have been constructed through the meaningful action of previous generations – it is necessary to give this work a sense of history. In this regard, as a contemporary social medium, boxing, as it is practised in the United States, Ireland and Cuba, indeed throughout the world, at least in part, has to be located at the cutting edge of a social formation which has its roots in the very foundations of civilisation. Accordingly, the following summary social history should not be read simply as a preface to what takes place in and around the modern ring. Rather it should be understood as part of the deep texture of contemporary boxing subcultures.

The origins of boxing

Tracing the social origins of sport is a fascinating but notoriously difficult task. Sport is a cultural product and what passes for sport in one place and at one time may not be viewed as such elsewhere. Bullfighting, for instance, has an ambivalent status as a sport even in its traditional homes of Spain and Mexico. It hardly meets the unwritten conventions of sport in other parts of Europe and North America. However, less than 200 years ago bullfighting stood alongside bear-baiting, cockfighting and a range of other animal-based, blood-letting pastimes which were in the mainstream of sporting culture in Great Britain. Since then a wholesale revolution in sport and recreation has seen blood sports more or less completely displaced by a wide variety of individual and team sports, most of which would have been completely unrecognisable to the sports people of the early nineteenth century. The fact that bullfighting survives as a sport in Spain and Mexico can be explained only in terms of particularly strong social and cultural traditions which prevail in those countries.

In many ways bullfighting is more of a national ritual than it is a sport and should be viewed as an exception to the general rule whereby sports of the pre-industrial age have disappeared altogether, been forced underground or been so transformed that they bear little or no resemblance to their modern forms. There are a few activities, however, which continue to take place in the public domain, which are clearly recognised as sports in the modern sense, which have large popular audiences and which have more than a passing resemblance to sports which were popular in pre-industrial cultures. Boxing is one such sport.

If we define boxing simply in terms of two people fighting with their fists, given that people have fought in this way as long as history has been recorded, then we may conclude that alongside running, boxing is the most ancient of all sports.

Formalised versions of unarmed combat were regular features of secular and sacred festivals in the ancient cultures which flourished around the Mediterranean (Jewell, 1977; Gorn, 1986; McIntosh, 1993). During an epoch when physical prowess was directly related to self and community survival and when, behind sword and shield, the body was the most important military resource, it is not surprising that hand-to-hand combat featured both in military training and popular recreation (Elias and Dunning, 1986).

Versions of boxing and wrestling were common at the funereal rites of the ancient Greeks and were popular events at athletic contests and festivals, including the Olympic Games. The Romans drew heavily on the Greek cult of athleticism as they developed their own sports system, which reached its most perverse form with the gladiatorial spectacle. McIntosh has argued that during the height of Rome's imperial power there was a strong relationship between political authority, social status and the capacity to stage brutal games:

> The elaborate organisation of mass pursuit and slaughter of wild beasts, the throwing of condemned criminals and others 'ad beasts' – to starved and thirsty beasts of prey – and the multiple combats of gladiators, many of which amounted to the butchery of prisoners or slaves by experienced and trained killers, was deliberately set up by Augustus as an instrument of government and social control to bring to an end a prolonged period of civil strife and turbulence in Rome. (McIntosh, 1993:32)

Special academies for the training of gladiators were set up by Rome's powerful patricians, who recruited slaves to be trained in both armed and unarmed combat. These gladiator camps can be viewed as ancestors of the contemporary boxing stable. However, a Roman boxing match bore little resemblance to either its Greek predecessor or its modern equivalent. The blood lust of the crowds which thronged into the coliseums led to the adoption of the *caestus*, a thonged, metal and barbed gauntlet worn by boxers to enable them to inflict the most grievous injuries to the body and head of their opponents. The *caestus* and the gladiatorial spectacle of which it was a part disappeared, at least from the records, with the decline and fall of imperial Rome. Boxing as an organised sport re-emerged in Great Britain, one of Rome's former colonies, more than a thousand years later. Precisely why this was the case is uncertain, but there are some clues which help us to speculate.

Boxing in Britain

Of course, the influence of Rome in Britain did not simply vanish with legions, but lived on in a variety of institutional and cultural forms, including language, law and architecture. Certainly, the link between the techniques of war and sport remained long after the Romans left the shores of Britain. Skill on horseback, prowess with sword and lance and accuracy with bow and arrow were integral to both battle and sport in the middle ages. Wrestling and boxing were likewise viewed as important skills at a time when the forces of law and order were underdeveloped and self-preservation and the survival of one's kin might depend upon one's own physical prowess.

It was not simply the imminence of war or fear of physical assault which kept alive a tradition of armed and unarmed combat in the middle ages. Before the foundations of today's legal system were laid, there was recourse to trial by combat as allowed in Norman law, and this continued to stimulate a variety of forms of armed and unarmed combat. Moreover, the fact that such battles could be fought by proxy, whereby those in dispute could nominate somebody else to battle for them, meant that a class of professional champions emerged. What is more, given the dependent relationship between serf and master, it is also likely that these quasi-legal battles, which, more often than not, were fought over issues relating to the ownership and control of land, greatly excited the vested interests of the local yeomanry and peasantry, who would turn out in numbers to witness their master's and, possibly, their own fate decided in combat. In this regard the medieval tournament was often a mixture of trial by combat and pure spectacle.

Although there is a paucity of documentary evidence, we can be almost certain that whether it be through daggers, quarterstaffs or their bare fists, the lower orders developed their own, less formal system of trial by combat for settling disagreements. Eliot Gorn speculates that the relaxation of popular morality which accompanied the demise of Puritanism after the Glorious Revolution 'permitted the revival of rough sports' (1986: 23), including boxing, which may also have been inspired by the English gentry's rediscovery of Greek and Roman literature, which contained accounts of boxing matches. Whatever the reason, it is certain that boxing began to re-emerge as both a pastime and as a spectator sport in the seventeenth century. The French chronicler Sassaure witnessed this during a visit to England in 1727, observing two working men who, unable to resolve a dispute amicably:

> retire to some quiet place and strip from their waists upwards. Everyone who sees them preparing for a fight surrounds them, not in order to separate them, but on the contrary to enjoy the fight, for it is a great sport to the lookers-on, and they judge the blows and also help to enforce the rules in use for this mode of warfare. The spectators sometimes get so interested that they lay bets on the combatants and form a big circle around them. The two champions shake hands before commencing, and then attack each other courageously with their fists and sometimes also with their heads, which they use like rams. (Malcolmson, 1973: 42)

Undoubtedly, the fact that physical combat was viewed for several centuries not simply as sport but also as a legitimate means of resolving disputes and settling matters of honour was essential to the development of prize fighting in England in the 1700s. The year 1719, when James Figg, the 'Father of Boxing', was publicly acclaimed as Britain's first national champion, is generally accepted as marking the official beginning of boxing in the modern age (Gorn, 1986; Brailsford, 1988). No doubt there were boxers before Figg, but he deserves special attention as one of the first boxers on record to use skills in combat as the basis for setting up in business. Initially, he did this by opening booths at travelling fairs and festivals and challenging visitors to combat 'with cudgel, fists or broadsword' (Egan, 1812: 20). Figg's boxing booth appears in a famous Hogarth painting, *Southwark Fair*, and Figg himself is described thus by Pearce Egan:

> and the heroic Figg, of pugilistic memory, challenging any of the crowd to enter the lists with him, either for money, for love or a belly full! Figg was more indebted to strength and courage for his success in the battles which he gained, than from the effects of genius: in fact he was extremely illiterate and it might be said that he boxed his way through life. (Egan, 1812: 20)

Plumb (1974) observes that, because of advancements in printing technology and increased public literacy, culture began to emerge as an object of consumption in eighteenth-century England for a popular audience. A growing interest in sport, particularly boxing, stimulated the birth of sports journalism. Egan wrote regular columns for popular magazines and broadsheets such as *Blackwood's Edinburgh Magazine*, but it is his 400-page compilation *Boxiana; or Sketches of Ancient and Modern Pugilism; From the Days of the Renowned Broughton and Slack to the Heroes of the Present Milling Era* which contains most of his social commentaries. It was first published in London in 1812, during the height of the Napoleonic Wars, and by any standards *Boxiana* is one of the most remarkable books to be written about sport.

The contribution of Egan to the early social history of bare-knuckle prize fighting, or pugilism, is immeasurable. While he never set foot in the ring himself he otherwise participated fully in the subculture which sustained pugilism in its golden age. According to Reid (1971), Egan was never happier than when he was at a booze up or a sing-song with fellow sportsmen, which, unlike today's meaning of the term, referred to those who hunted or who followed and gambled upon horse racing and a variety of blood and combat sports. Egan both participated in and documented the activities and interests of the hectic social world of which he was a part. Above all this meant writing about boxing, boxers and the colourful social milieu which spawned them.

Egan wrote at the turn of the eighteenth century during a period of unprecedented social change. The rural-based feudal order was in its death throes, but it was yet to be fully displaced by urban, industrial capitalism. The population of what had formerly been market towns or small commercial and administrative centres was swollen with the influx of a pre-industrial labour force who had lost their agrarian function and a dilettante squirearchy who were no longer tied by customary responsibilities to their country estates. In short, this was a betwixt and between period, when the aristocracy played out the last act of their political authority while, almost hidden from view, a fledgling bourgeoisie gradually took over the reins of power and laid the political and economic foundations of the modern state. Popular culture during this period was generated by an urban/rural amalgamation of patrician and plebeian. It was this alliance which spawned and sustained pugilism during its golden era. Referring to this grouping as 'the Fancy', Egan described them thus:

> It was a union of all ranks, from the brilliant of the highest class in the circle of Corinthians [nobility], down to the Dusty Bob [chimney sweep] gradation in society; and even a shade or two below that. Lots of the upper house; the lower house; and lots of the Flash house. Proprietors of splendid parks and demesnes; inmates of proud and lofty mansions; thousands from the peaceable cot [slum dwellers] and myriads of coves [confidence tricksters] from no houses at all; in a word it was a conglomeration of the Fancy. (Egan, 1812: 66)

We learn from Egan that with the earnings generated by his efforts in the fairgrounds, Figg was able to open a booth at a permanent site in Oxford Street in the centre of London. Figg's Oxford Street booth was the forerunner of the modern boxing club. Showing initiative which predates all other sporting entrepreneurs, Figg commissioned his friend, cartoonist and artist, William Hogarth to design a business card which introduced Figg and advertised his profession. Figg's card read:

> James Figg. Master of the Noble Science of Defence. On the right hand in Oxford Road near Adam and Eve court. Teaches Gentlemen in the use of the small backsword and Quarter staff at Home or Abroad. (Brailsford, 1988: 5)

Figg's business card makes clear the market at which he was aiming: young gentlemen requiring instruction in self-defence. The young sporting gentlemen who followed boxing and who were attracted to Figg's booth are referred to by Egan as the Corinthians. They were an integral part of a class of urban aristocrats who, fleetingly, dominated public life and popular culture in the towns and cities of Regency England (Sennett, 1976). Having dispensed with the responsibilities of taking care of a tied peasant population and replete with a new-found commercial wealth, members of the aristocracy in increasing numbers separated themselves from their landed estates and came to the towns and cities in search of diversion and entertainment. They crowded the same social spaces and often came into conflict with one another. The continued existence of a medieval code of honour in combination with the underdeveloped state of the law, both civil and criminal, meant that retribution and restitution were regularly sought through direct action, often with deadly results at the end of a rapier, ten paces from a duelling pistol or with a skull fractured by a cudgel, backsword or singlestick.

Accordingly, self-defence and duelling skills became an essential part of a young gentleman's repertoire, particularly at a time when more and more of them were rubbing shoulders in the relatively confined public spaces of the city. However, there is no reason to believe that life was less precious then than it is now. In his Oxford Street booth Figg was able to capitalise on this potentially deadly market and, at the same time, to introduce boxing as a less lethal alternative to swordsmanship, pistol shooting and stick fighting. Writing of the relative merits of boxing over the dual, Egan writes:

> but what would rather that they should have had recourse to the manly defence of boxing than the deadly weapons of sword and ball [shot]; from which a bloody nose, or a black eye, might have been the only consequence to themselves and their families, and neither in their feelings or their circumstances be injured; reconciliation with their antagonist – faults mutually acknowledged – and perhaps, become inseparable friends ever afterwards. (Egan, 1812: 194)

In addition to a rationale for boxing as a medium through which to satisfy honour within one's own social class was the perceived need to develop combat skills as a deterrent to and protection from the lower orders. The agrarian and industrial revolutions had fractured the subtle and generally stable network of relationships between the upper and lower classes. Furthermore, the role played by an alliance of peasants and urban poor in the French Revolution instigated a moral panic among the English gentry, who developed a pathological fear of the 'mob' (Rude, 1980). The truth of the matter was that the increasingly urbanised 'squirearchy' had more to fear from rising crime than political insurrection. The arrival of an always poor, often idle and sometimes disorderly community of pre-industrial labour into the towns and cities of eighteenth-century England was a major source of dismay to their former masters, who had yet to develop a system of urban social control to replace the one which they had helped to dismantle in the countryside. As Gorn (1986: 27) comments:

> Street violence threatened peace loving citizens with assaults, robbery, gang attack and murder. Moreover the era was rife with revolutionary blood baths, wars of unprecedented ferocity, public executions, grinding poverty, restive labour, and repressive capital.

In the absence of a police force or its equivalent, self-defence, as taught in the likes of Figg's Academy, was a popular option for the city gent during the Regency. Moreover, irrespective of self-defence, sparring was increasingly seen as a vehicle for the development and maintenance of physical fitness for younger members of an upper class who became increasingly urbanised and sedentary as the eighteenth century wore on. It was based upon his experiences in Figg's school that in 1747 Captain Godfrey Barclay published the first book which could be categorised as sports science: *Treatise on the Useful Science of Defence*.

However, once established as a medium for fitness and defence, pugilism soon developed a dimension which went beyond any intrinsic or functional value. By and large the dilettante aristocracy of the eighteenth and early nineteenth centuries are more renowned for their hedonistic pursuit of pleasure than they are thought of for their contributions to physical self-improvement. Given a choice, they would rather watch other people fight and bet on the outcome of these contests than actually take part themselves. Boxing clubs rapidly developed as venues not just for gentlemen's sparring, but also for the staging of bare-knuckle prize fights.

Sporting and gambling were virtually synonymous for the Fancy. Extending their patronage of blood sports and horse racing, wealthy aristocrats sponsored individuals and groups of fighters in much the same way as they also kept stables of race horses and collections of fighting cocks. The pattern of these contests was straightforward. A challenge would be made, a venue agreed upon and the prize money put up by one or more wealthy patrons. As soon as the fight was declared, word would travel rapidly around the Fancy and heavy betting would ensue right up to the opening round and continue, with shifting odds, according to the progress of each fighter, round by round. The following passage from *Boxiana* reveals the connections between patronage and gambling:

> A match was at length made between Big Ben and Johnson for five hundred guineas. The former was under the patronage of the Duke of Hamilton. This battle, which had long been expected, excited considerable interest in the sporting world, and bets to the amount of several thousands were laid upon its decision. The characters of the combatants stood high – Johnson, from what he had done, was surrounded by friends, and the odds were seven to four in his favour. (Egan, 1812: 100)

As the rationale for boxing changed from self-defence to prize fighting so too did it become an increasingly violent spectacle. As aristocratic patronage of the ring increased, the capacity of the fighters to determine the limits of their own suffering diminished, and they were expected to fight with their last breath for their patrons' purses and wagers.

When Figg was proclaimed English champion in 1719 there were few rules associated with pugilism. In addition to punching, kicking was tolerated and wrestling holds and throws were permitted, as was the practice gouging – inserting fingers and thumbs into the opponent's eye sockets. By the end of the century the sport had been taken over by a fraternity whose passions revolved around blood, gore and a wager. While strength, nimbleness of foot and power and speed of punch were attributes in a fighter valued by the Fancy, being game and having 'bottom' (being lion hearted, resolute and, above all, long suffering) were considered to be even more important. The more prize fighting developed as a public spectacle and a gambling forum the more organised the sport became. This necessitated the introduction of rules which would ensure that all fights were governed by the same principles, and in 1743 Jack Broughton, one of the Regency's greatest pugilists and most successful trainers, introduced a set of rules which would govern prize fighting until the adoption of the Marquess of Queensberry's rules late in the nineteenth century.

As Brailsford (1988: 8) points out, Broughton's rules, which became established as the London Prize Ring rules, 'constitute the basic text in any history of bareknuckle fighting'. They were as follows:

That a square of a yard be chalked in the middle of the stage; and on every fresh set-to after a fall, or being parted from the rails, each second is to bring his man to the side of the square, and place him opposite to the other; and till they are fairly set to at the lines, it shall not be lawful for one to strike the other.

That in order to prevent any disputes as to the time a man lies after a fall, if the second does not bring his man to the side of the square within the space of half a minute, he shall be deemed a beaten man.

That in every main battle, no person whatever shall be upon the stage except the principles and the second. The same rule to be observed in bye-battles, except that in the latter, Mr Broughton is allowed to be on the stage to keep decorum and to assist gentlemen to get to their places; provided always that he does not interfere in the battle; and whoever pretends to infringe these rules, to be turned immediately out of the house. Everybody is to quit the stage as soon as the champions are stripped, before they set-to.

That no champion be deemed beaten unless he fails coming up to the line within the limited time, or that his own second declares him beaten. No second is to be allowed to ask his man's adversary any questions, or advise him to give out.

That in bye-battles the winning man to have two thirds of the money given which shall be publicly divided upon the stage, notwithstanding any private agreement to the contrary.

That to prevent disputes in every main battle, the principals shall, on coming on the stage, choose from the gentlemen present, two umpires, who shall absolutely decide all disputes that may arise in the battle; and if the two umpires cannot agree, the said umpires to choose a third, who is to determine it.

That no person is to hit his adversary when down or seize him by the hair, the breeches, or any part below the waist; a man on his knees to be reckoned down. (Egan, 1812: 51–2)

Even though Broughton's rules established bare-knuckle fighting as one of the world's first codified sports, they did little to reduce the brutality of the prize ring. There were no weight classifications and fighters with markedly different physiques, styles and levels of experience were often pitted against one another. The duration of a fight was potentially limitless and it was not unusual for a contest to go beyond fifty rounds, until one or other of the adversaries was either knocked out or fell through exhaustion. Egan's chronicle is full of accounts of the fate of hapless individuals who died during a prize fight or shortly thereafter. Given the likes of the following commentary, it is hardly surprising that serious injury and death were common:

Tenth – Bourke, full of pluck, set-to with great spirit, and close fighting ensued. Belcher losing no time, cut Bourke under the left eye; under the right; and another blow so dreadful in its effect between the throat and the chin, as to hoist Bourke off his feet, and he came down head foremost. Belcher also fell from the force which he gave it. Both on the floor, when Bourke squirted some blood out of his mouth over Belcher. (Egan, 1812: 136)

The naked brutality of such contests and the obvious risks to the combatants begs the question why would anybody take part? The answer lies in the prevailing social and economic conditions. Cities such as London and Bristol were like magnets to the uprooted agricultural population who were drawn towards the town in search of work and shelter. A fortunate few became apprenticed to a craft, trade or lowly profession, while others found employment as servants in the households of the wealthy. Many joined or were press-ganged into the army or navy. The vast majority, however, joined an itinerant, unskilled, pre-industrial labour pool from which, if they were lucky, they could find occasional employment as coal heavers, street porters, road diggers, iron workers, building labourers, stevedores and the like. Those less fortunate were forced to live out their miserable lives as beggars, vagabonds and thieves. Entire districts consisted of filthy slums, demoralised by crime, congestion, disease and prostitution (Bookchin, 1973). It was from such pre-industrial ghettos that the vast majority of prize fighters came.

By today's standards of racial and ethnic heterogeneity, Regency England was virtually a white Anglo-Saxon monolith. Nevertheless, there were some ethnic minorities, most notably immigrant Irish, diaspora Jews and a small number of African and African-American blacks, who tended to occupy the lowest positions in any social hierarchy. These minorities were over-represented in the early annals of boxing. This constituted a rehearsal of a trend which was to dominate the social stratification of boxing in the twentieth century inasmuch as these groups 'were especially drawn into the ring because of their lowly economic status and because it offered a chance to compete against Englishmen on an equal footing' (Gorn, 1986: 29).

Prize fighting captured the imagination of a large cross-section of the public like nothing else before. Its popularity grew to the extent that, as the nineteenth century approached, boxing booths and amphitheatres could not accommodate the capacity of those who clamoured to see celebrated pugilists battle it out. Increasingly boxing matches were held out of doors in alehouse courtyards and in nearby fields. Quite often boxing matches were held as part of larger open-air fairs and festivals and they were regularly held in conjunction with horse racing meetings. As a consequence, prize fighting came to be more and more available for popular consumption, particularly by the lower classes, from whose ranks the vast majority of prize fighters came.

The golden age of prize fighting occurred during a period when life expectancy was short and when a person could be maimed or even hanged for stealing a loaf of bread. The sports and pastimes which thrived in such an environment reflected the cruelty and brutality of the times (Elias and Dunning, 1986). Many of these sports involved tormenting or encouraging fights between animals such as bulls, bears, dogs, badgers and cockerels (Malcolmson, 1973; Ingram, 1995). Public floggings and executions were also established features of the urban entertainment calendar in the eighteenth century (Hay, 1977). To paraphrase Hobbes (1968), life for the urban poor was indeed nasty, brutish and short and in this context pugilism

17

would not have seemed particularly uncivilised as 'the bloodiness in the ring and the pit paralleled the bloodiness of society' (Gorn, 1986: 27).

It became fashionable for a fighter to adopt an alias or stage name, which was usually related to the kind of work he did or aspired to do outside the prize ring: Jarvis the Fighting Carman (sedan-chair carrier); Bill Love the Butcher, 'Knight of the Cleaver'; Big Ben the Collier; Hooper the Tin Man; Bill Stevens the Nailor (carpenter); Elias Spray the Costermonger (fruit and vegetable porter). Given the scarcity of work, the low wages and the generally low level of life opportunities, a career on the prize fighting circuit, no matter how short or how dangerous, seemed attractive. When Jack Broughton died in 1789 his legacy was worth £7,000, which is the equivalent of half a million pounds 200 years on (Brailsford, 1988). In addition to the purses to be won, successful prize fighters became local celebrities and often rubbed shoulders with the gentry who patronised the sport with increasing enthusiasm as the eighteenth century gave way to the nineteenth.

Because of their origins and notoriety within the ranks of the lower orders, the sponsored champions of the rich were, at the same time, the people's champions. When contests were organised in the open air, people flocked in their thousands to cheer on their heroes. In 1811, the fight between Tom Crib, then the champion of England, and Tom Molineaux, a freed slave from the United States, generated huge interest and was witnessed by Egan:

> Never was the sporting world so much interested, and for 20 miles within the seat of action not a bed could be obtained on the preceding night: and by six o'clock the next morning, hundreds were in motion to get a good seat by the stage, which even at that early period proved to be a difficult task. It is supposed that nearly 20,000 witnessed this tremendous mill. (Egan, 1812: 243)

On 26 May 1817, when Jack Scroggins fought Ned Turner in a field in Hayes on the outskirts of London, some 30,000 people were on hand to witness the battle. At that time the total population of Britain was slightly less than 10 million, which means that by today's standards this crowd is equivalent to more than 150,000 and would have filled Wembley Stadium twice over.

As the demand for prize fighting grew, so the production of pugilists became more organised and more reliable. While their patronage was essential, the gentry had little to do with the technical development of fighters. Once boxing became a public affair, the lower classes took an active interest in the development of their own, local champions. This was initially based around the semi-formal brawling which occurred in and around alehouses, in the services, at fair grounds, at horse racing meetings and other such public venues where much of the social life of the Regency period was lived out.

Sometimes a lower-class set-to would be witnessed by members of the sporting gentry and, if a fighter performed particularly well, he might be offered some form of patronage. It was by no means unusual for officers to select their favourites from the lower ranks of the army or navy, wherein conditions could be even harsher than in civilian life, and where organised fights between enlisted men were commonplace. These networks by which fighters were identified and through which they gained experience and recognition are well recorded by Egan, as the following passage reveals:

> Corcoran, upon his arrival in the Metropolis, commenced coal heaver; but which calling he soon left for that of chairman; and, owing to some trifling dispute, it was not long afterwards when he went to sea, where the rough elements gave additional vigour to his athletic frame; and, from the frequent specimens he at times had displayed, was considered for a mill, the first in the fleet, and was patronised by Captain Perceval. (Egan, 1812: 54)

As the system through which fighters were identified and recruited became more sophisticated, so too did the process through which they learned the crafts of pugilism. Often local battles were conducted under the supervision of established pugilists or those who had retired after successful careers in the ring. In ways which mirrored both the apprentice system of the crafts and guilds and the husbandry of the turf, they would take on promising fighters and train them as boxers. Almost all of Egan's biographies of boxers who featured after the middle of the eighteenth century contained a statement relating to the fighter's pedigree, such as, 'Edward Hunt, the celebrated pupil of Broughton.... George Meggs, he received instruction from Slack.... Jem Belcher, descended from the mighty Slack'.

This form of apprenticeship enabled otherwise anonymous roughnecks to refine their skills in reputable boxing establishments under the educated gaze of gentlemen of the Fancy, who, if they liked what they saw, would propose and finance a match. In this manner, the anarchic and sometimes brutal lower-class street culture of the city gradually became harnessed, by an alliance of small-time boxing entrepreneurs and sporting nobility, as the basis for a more or less rational farm-feeder system for the development of prize fighters. While the rules and the technical aspects of today's professional boxing are markedly different from those of bare-knuckle prize fighting, there can be little doubt that the subculture which sustains the former has inherited the social relations established by the latter more than 200 years ago.

However, even as pugilism entered its golden era in the first decades of the nineteenth century, the forces which would fashion the demise of bare-knuckle fighting were also beginning to appear. Throughout the eighteenth century, while segments of a dilettante, landed gentry were squandering the capital windfall which accrued from revolutions in animal husbandry, agricultural production and marketing, others, in alliance with the trading and professional classes, were investing this surplus into new forms of industrial production and, as such, helping to lay the foundations of a whole new social order. By the beginning of the nineteenth century this new, economically powerful class established a controlling influence over most political institutions. In addition, there was a perceived need to occupy the moral high ground and secure cultural domination.

As E. P. Thompson (1967, 1968) observes, in order for capitalism to flourish in England, once economic and political authority had been secured, it was necessary for this fledgling ruling class to be in the vanguard of a comprehensive cultural revolution through which the rhythms of popular life were reconstructed to complement the needs of industry and commerce.

The sporting calendar of the Fancy was more suited to the imprecise working patterns of pre-industrial England than it was to this newly mechanised and organised regime. Moreover, there was a moral dimension to the assault on the activities of the Fancy. An important element of the ideology which accompanied the development of capitalism throughout Europe was grounded in the puritan ethics of Protestantism (Weber, 1958). Hard work, self-discipline, thrift and abstinence were dominant features of an ethical code which applied not only to church matters and business, but also to everyday living.

As Brailsford points out, the zenith of the golden era of pugilism coincided and clashed with an upswell of cultural reform. 'It was an age for crusades – against cruelty to animals, child labour, excessive gambling and Sunday desecration' (1988: 94). The popular recreations of the masses in general and the predilections of the Fancy in particular were anathema to the ethics of both Protestantism and capitalism. The fact that tens of thousands of people would gather in a profligate context that included drunkenness and gambling to witness public displays of bare-fisted brutality was perceived as being both morally corrupt and threatening to the new social order. In short, as the century wore on, alongside public hangings and floggings, dogfighting, cockfighting and bear-baiting, prize fighting was increasingly viewed as uncivilised by those who occupied the moral high ground.

A warning of what was to follow had come half a century earlier. In April 1750 Jack Broughton, who had been very heavily backed by the Duke of Cumberland, lost a contest held in his own amphitheatre with Jack Slack after being blinded by a blow landed between his eyes. The sightless Broughton bravely fought on, but was easily defeated by Slack. The Duke of Cumberland, who, it is estimated, had laid bets of upwards of £10,000 on Broughton, was furious. In retribution he closed Broughton's amphitheatre and led a campaign to have prize fighting outlawed altogether. Boxing academies throughout the land were closed, but this only succeeded in forcing the sport outdoors. This event accelerated pugilism's popularity, as the sport became accessible to much larger numbers of people from all walks of life. However, although the golden age of prize fighting came some fifty years later, by forcing the sport into the open air, Cumberland's embargo drew the attention of the authorities and gave succour to certain sections of the upper and middle classes whose sensibilities were offended by prize fighting. In this respect Cumberland's action initiated a long process through which pugilism was outlawed and forced underground until, eventually, it disappeared altogether.

However, when boxing was first outlawed in 1750 both law making and law enforcement were, to say the least, ambiguous practices. Much was left to the whims of local magistrates and, in the absence of a recognisable police force, it proved virtually impossible to exercise more general control over popular recreations. The swelling urban population in the first half of the nineteenth century and the rising prospect of urban crime and disorderliness rendered this pre-industrial system of law and order untenable. Gradually new mechanisms for law and order were introduced by middle-class reformers, giving magistrates the instruments through which their authority could be enforced. The Metropolitan Police were formed in 1829, and by 1856 every local authority had to have its own police force. In addition, the Municipal Reform Act of 1835 left the way clear for the new middle classes to broaden their power base by taking over the running of local government. This gave them both the authority and the means to outlaw pugilism, which was deemed to be both antisocial and a threat to public order.

With the legal authority of the courts in one hand and the moral authority of the church in the other, the newly empowered middle classes conducted a systematic assault against boxing. Pugilism was an especially attractive target for bourgeois reformers because it brought together both of their class enemies: a decadent and dying aristocracy and an ill-disciplined, pre-industrial labour force. Undoubtedly, the success of their campaign was helped by the disorganised nature of the sport. Corruption within prize fighting played an important part in its demise. With gambling as one of the main reasons for staging contests, cheating and fight fixing became endemic. In the absence of a strong, centralised and well connected governing body, pugilism could neither police itself from within nor protect itself from the increasingly effective attacks of the reformers. The fact that the sport was tarnished by corruption and was also made illegal encouraged most of the gentry to withdraw their patronage of the ring. In addition, as the nineteenth century progressed, the ability of this stratum of society to continue to sponsor the prize ring diminished as its economic base was eroded. As the keystone of the following which sustained prize fighting was removed, the Fancy crumbled, leaving the sport exposed to the full force of the reformers:

> Denied the right to develop its own stadia or to regulate itself, pugilism, an outlaw and fugitive sport, could only pursue its cold and lonely road to oblivion. It had lived for too long outside the pale of respectability for there to be now any hope of gradual amendment. (Brailsford, 1988: 157)

Boxing in the United States

In England bare-knuckle prize fighting was forced underground in the 1830s and by the 1880s had virtually disappeared. For a relatively brief period during the nineteenth century, as bare-knuckle prize fighting went into decline in England, it enjoyed a period of growth in present and former colonies, particularly the United States. It is believed that boxing may have first been introduced into the southern states in the eighteenth century by slave-plantation owners who, having learned

21

the fundamentals of the 'sweet science' while being educated in England, would select slaves to fight on their behalf against slave champions from neighbouring plantations, both for entertainment and for gambling (Lardner, 1972).

As Gorn (1986) has pointed out, there is little hard evidence to support this view. Nevertheless, it is significant that the first two notable prize fighters to emanate from the Americas, Bill Richmond and Tom Molineaux, were both freed African-American slaves. It is also noteworthy that both men chose to seek their fortunes as pugilists in England rather than in the USA where, at the end of the eighteenth century, there was little tradition of prize fighting and the prospects for freed blacks in any profession in a society which still tolerated slavery were extremely limited.

Outside the southern states, there was a particular cultural resistance to pugilism in North America. It was viewed as a product of the corrupt former colonial master and was redolent of a despised dilettantism: 'Brutal, riotous, patronised by effete aristocrats and debased urban rabble, boxing symbolised the corruptions that a virtuous republic must avoid' (Gorn, 1986: 37).

Nevertheless, popular culture has a vitality and momentum of its own, and despite the protestations of republicans, once the material and social conditions which had generated boxing's golden era in England were replicated in the United States, it was inevitable that the sport would take root there also.

British and Irish soldiers and sailors had introduced forms of boxing to the northern states in the eighteenth century. The Europeans did not have to teach the Americans how to fight, but they needed to teach them how to box. After all, the Americans had defeated the British in the war of independence and had come a long way towards taming the wild west. They were possessed by a rugged frontier spirit which, among other things, found expression through resort to combat at the slightest excuse. But, as Lardner comments, a straight back and milling (rotating) fists were not always the recourse for settling disputes:

> To be sure Americans fought. They were more apt however to use the tools of their trade than the naked fist. River men afloat used boat hooks and belaying pins. The axeman used his axe or hobnailed boots. Coopers used hammers and if the contestants fought weaponless, they relied more on wrestling holds, kicking and gouging than on the clenched fist. (Lardner, 1972: 24)

However, as the English had discovered a generation before, duelling and related methods of resolving disputes could be injurious and were often deadly. The customs of the frontier became less appropriate as the United States' growing industrial towns and cities became more and more congested. Conflict and violence likewise increased, particularly among the lower orders, who had little access to legal means of retribution and recompense. Boxing offered a codified and less lethal means of dealing with personal insults, family feuds, libel, affairs of the heart, debts of honour and such like. Inevitably, these street-corner confrontations also attracted large local audiences, who would turn out to shout for and bet on neighbourhood heroes. In this way, as Gorn (1986) remarks, although prize fights were more structured than bar brawls and street fights, both forms of combat grew out of personal hatreds whereby public spectacles and private quarrels often became indistinguishable.

The strongest roots of prize fighting in the United States were laid by English and Irish immigrants who, fleeing poverty and persecution, were drawn in increasing numbers across the Atlantic throughout the nineteenth century. The establishment of urban communities around immigrant identities stimulated the growth of pugilism as a spectator sport. Many of the earliest battles were between expatriate English and Irish who harboured a traditional enmity for one another. Former English and Irish prize fighters, who had been forced out of the old country by anti-boxing reform there, found a ready audience in poorer working-class districts of New York, Boston, Philadelphia and New Orleans, where significant numbers of fellow countrymen had settled (Gorn, 1986: 46).

The social conditions for many Americans in the middle of the nineteenth century, particularly those who lived in the cities, were no better than those of the Victorian working classes in England. But, unlike in England, where the foundations of industrial capitalism had been constructed on the backs of an indigenous labour force, in the United States a domestic proletariat had to be bolstered by successive waves of cheap immigrant labour. Thus a pattern became established whereby first-generation immigrants occupied the lowest position within the ranks of the urban poor and were subjected to both deprivation and discrimination (Handlin, 1954; Higham, 1967). This was a very significant juncture in the social history of boxing in the United States. It was at this point, where urban deprivation met racial and ethnic discrimination, that the motivational impulse to step into the ring was generated.

As the nineteenth century progressed, prize fighting grew in popularity and the United States began to generate its own champions, some with obvious Old World links and others thoroughly American. Even though Yankee Sullivan hailed from County Cork in Ireland, as his fighting name suggests he earned his reputation as a pugilist in the United States. He was a hero to the hundreds of thousands of Irish settlers who had fled the great famine of the 1840s and swelled the population of the United States' burgeoning industrial cities. Just as he was an Irish-American hero, however, so he was a villain in the eyes of US nativists who viewed immigrants in general, and the Irish in particular, as threats to the livelihood and cultural purity of indigenous Americans (Higham, 1967). In 1849, when Yankee Sullivan was matched with Tom Hyer, the United States' first credible challenger, the bout attracted huge interest, not just because the two were good, evenly matched pugilists, but also because, in the eyes of the public, their fight symbolised the broader conflict between immigrant and native. As Gorn remarks, 'the clash between the two boxers was not just a test of physical superiority but a playing out of deep social, cultural and economic conflicts' (Gorn, 1986: 85).

To this day boxing in America has retained strong associations with the urban poor and ethnic identification and offers a reasonably accurate guide to what little progress a particular immigrant group has made in its attempts to access and become part of mainstream America. That the Irish dominated the annals of pugilism in nineteenth-century America while the English virtually disappeared from the ring is as much a testimony to waspish American nativists' resistance to the assimilation of the Catholic Irish in general as it bears witness to the skills and forbearance of particular Irish fighters. As Weinberg and Arond (1952) demonstrated, the fighting Irish eventually gave way to the fighting German, the fighting Jew, the fighting Italian, the fighting African and the fighting Hispanic. It is not so much that these groups, for a time, were gripped by the sheer pleasure of the prize ring. While this cannot be ruled out, given the brutal nature of the sport, particularly in its formative years, as Michner (1976) argues, it is much more likely that those who fought did so in an attempt to improve their lot in life:

> With a little practice, one could look at the Boston newspapers of any given era, and by seeing who was fighting whom, determine where the various immigrant groups were on the social ladder. Men fought in the Boston rings, not because they wanted to, but because it was the only way out. (Michner, 1976: 136)

As the following case studies reveal, the 'fighting a way out of the ghetto' thesis is an oversimplification. Nevertheless, by the middle of the nineteenth century, on both sides of the Atlantic, and increasingly in other parts of the world, urban poverty, racial and ethnic discrimination and relative deprivation had been established as the common denominators of prize fighting and subsequently professional boxing.

The zenith of bare-knuckle prize fighting in the United States came in the 1860s, immediately after the Civil War. This conflict had helped to spread the knowledge of and interest in boxing throughout the country on both sides of the Mason–Dixon line as hundreds of thousands of men, crowded in camps, created the ideal conditions for a good scrap, whether purely for sport or for settling disputes. There are several examples of boxing matches taking place between Confederate and Yankee champions in no-man's-land, causing impromptu truces in the midst of major battles (Gorn, 1986, 161–2). However, other popular sports, most notably baseball, also emerged strengthened by the social milieu created by the Civil War and this was one of several factors which contributed to the decline of bare-knuckle fighting in the United States.

Paralleling the growth of a prize fighting tradition in the United States was the emergence of the gymnasium movement, which used sparring among other exercises as a medium for the physical education of young, city gentlemen. As Adelman records of the gymnasium movement in New York City in the 1830s, the development of pugilistic skills 'were necessary and important means of self defence and that a gentleman would always use them appropriately' (Adelman,

1980: 560). Moreover, as Stearns (1987) points out, as the nineteenth century progressed the gymnasium movement became informed by an ideology of social Darwinism which suggested that the exercise of controlled aggression in sports was no bad thing for the physical and moral development of young gentlemen. Boxing, as Gorn observes, provided an ideal vehicle for this:

> Pugilism, then, was filled with meaning for turn of the century America. Blood-letting, merciless competition, and stern self-testing in the ring addressed the newly perceived need of middle- and upper-class men for more active life. Alive in every nerve, the boxer was in complete control of his body, negating by example the pervasive fears of over civilisation, nervous breakdowns and neurasthenia. The ring countered effeminizing tendencies, preparing men for a life of strife. (Gorn, 1986: 202)

However, gymnasium sparring was clearly different from the naked brutality of the prize ring, and the rising tide of opposition to pugilism from sections of the United States' middle class meant that the two disciplines became increasingly detached from one another. Nevertheless, as Adelman argues, the idea of boxing as a character-building enterprise was never lost and to this day this has 'provided supporters of the sport with an important justification and vital element in boxing's never ending search for respectability' (Adelman, 1980: 561).

Bare-knuckle prize fighting in decline

The timescale is slightly different but the cycle of rise, decline and rise again which characterises the demise of bare-knuckle pugilism and the formative years of gloved boxing was markedly similar on both sides of the Atlantic. Just as had happened in England thirty years or so earlier, precisely because it became so popular, pugilism became a target for middle-class reformers who viewed the existence of bare-knuckle prize fighting in the United States after the Civil War as an unwanted reminder of the decadent society which this conflict had been fought to vanquish. Prize fighting had been outlawed in the 1840s and more vigorous policing in the 1860s forced the sport underground where, with its administration outside the public gaze, pugilism was prey to the sharp practice of fraudsters and criminals. As was the case with their English counterparts, the US Fancy found it hard to defend a sport which, apart from its obvious brutality, became increasingly corrupt as its popularity grew. In the absence of a governing body to legislate for the ring and defend the sport against its manifold critics, in the New World pugilism began to wither away just as it had in the old country.

However, even as its demise was well under way, within the womb of bare-knuckle prize fighting the embryo of modern boxing was taking shape. Once more, it was social and political forces in England which initially led to the emergence of a new code of ring craft. There were two sides to the reform movement which pioneered the battle against pugilism and led to the development of a new and codified form of boxing. To begin with, as we have seen, there was the general campaign against the popular recreations of the pre-industrial, urban labour pool, of which the crusade against prize fighting was a part. Later, after 1850, once this phase of the Victorian cultural revolution was more or less over, attention was turned to filling the leisure void of the masses with activities which were healthy, educating and morally uplifting (Malcolmson, 1973: 172–3). Based on a revolution in physical education as it was practised in public schools, new, amateur sports progressively displaced traditional pastimes, first among the middle classes and eventually within the new, urban working-class communities (Holt, 1989).

Energies were directed towards reconstructing traditional sports so that they were rule bound, centrally controlled and administered, and subject to time discipline: in other words they were rationalised, in keeping with most other aspects of life in the new industrial age (Ingham and Beamish, 1993). Secondly, these reconstructed, rational sports and pastimes were imbued with a series of virtues and ethical principles which rendered them both physically beneficial and morally uplifting. Within this framework participation in vigorous sports came to be seen not as a vice but as a virtue, and muscular Christianity was born. On the surface, boxing, which had long since been labelled as the 'sweet science', and which had a high regard for physical fitness, seemed to be an obvious target for middle-class reform.

Ever since James Figg had opened his booth in Oxford Street in the early 1700s, the manly art of self-defence, or sparring, had been a popular pastime of the gentry. Once professional prize fighting was abolished, on both sides of the Atlantic, sparring was resurrected as an appropriate conduit for the physical and moral training of young gentlemen. In 1866, John Grantham Chambers teamed up with fellow Cambridge graduate John Sholto Douglas, the 8th Marquess of Queensberry, to found the Amateur Athletic Club, an establishment dedicated to training young gentlemen to box. Between them they suggested fourteen modifications to Broughton's rules which became known as the Marquess of Queensberry rules, which to this day govern both amateur and professional boxing, with only relatively minor alterations (Shipley, 1989: 81).

The extent to which the Queensberry rules made boxing a more civilised sport is very debatable. On the surface the introduction of gloves, a limited number of three-minute rounds, weight equilibrium and a standardised system for refereeing and judging gave the appearance of a safer sport. However, Gorn's (1986: 204) research suggests that descriptions of bouts under the Queensberry rules 'reveal no diminution of violence'. Gloves protected fighters' hands, enabling them to throw more and harder punches at their opponent's head. Under Broughton's rules, if they were tired they could go down on one knee and take a breather for a full minute before being required to 'come up to scratch' to start a fresh round. The new rules insisted they fought each round for a full three minutes until the bell went, they were knocked down or the towel was thrown in. In short, although

26

under the Queensberry rules the sport might have looked more civilised, in fact boxing became more dangerous.

Amateur boxing may have begun as a diversion for a privileged elite, but, as was to happen with so many of the other recreations of the middle classes, most notably association football in Britain and baseball in the United States, it spread rapidly among the working classes. In many ways, it could be argued that the middle-class loss of control over its own sports was self-inflicted through the work of middle-class reformers who saw amateur sport as an ideal vehicle to bring the message of muscular Christianity to the urban poor. Boxing did not need much space and in an increasingly crowded urban environment it could be easily facilitated in youth clubs, drill halls, workers' clubs and church halls. As Shipley observes, the working classes needed little encouragement to return to the ring. A long tradition of boxing remained deep in the cultural memory of the working class. The arrival of amateur boxing as an officially sanctioned alternative to street fighting was instantly attractive to the English working classes:

> This participatory sport was not imposed upon workers in industrial centres by employers, landlords, ministers of any church, or school teachers. The working class, which had enjoyed prize fighting and gloved contests for a century, observed the organisation of briefer contests which were less painful, and wanted to take part. (Shipley, 1989: 90)

As in Britain, in the United States during the last quarter of the nineteenth century organised sports grew at an astonishing rate, particularly among the middle classes, who made extensive use of a massive expansion in higher education to facilitate both academic and sporting interests. Denied access to college-based sports such as American football, the American working classes turned their attention to baseball and boxing.

Even in the earliest days of pugilism men made a living out of the sport as trainers to the elite and, in an era when the entertainment industry was enjoying an unprecedented boom, it was unlikely that boxing's potential as a money-making enterprise would be ignored. With its barely submerged tradition of prize fighting, boxing was one of the first sports to become openly professional under an amended form of the Queensberry rules. On both sides of the Atlantic improved working conditions, shorter working hours and gradual increases in disposable income created the context within which professional sports emerged. As Shipley (1989: 91) comments, 'boxing became a popular spectator sport when unskilled and casual workers became able to afford sixpence regularly each week for entertainment'.

Other than the Queensberry rules, what distinguished professional boxing from bare-knuckle prize fighting was that it had the appearance of being a developed form of amateur boxing, a sport which was considered to be legitimate within middle-class circles and which attracted huge numbers of participants from among the urban working classes. The ABA (Amateur Boxing Association) was formed in England in 1880 and, under its guidance, over the next thirty years amateur boxing developed a competitive structure which integrated local, national and, eventually, international participation. Amateur boxing was a sport in its own right, but it was also a training and proving ground for those who had ambitions to make a living out of the ring. Now, not only was professional boxing able to develop behind a veil of legitimacy, without significant interference from the authorities, but also it had access to a pool of well trained amateur boxers from which new recruits could be lured into the professional arena. Bare-knuckle prize fighting was dead, but with new roots its progeny was to grow to be one of the most popular and durable sports the world has ever seen.

As the nineteenth century gave way to the twentieth, the technical and institutional foundations of modern boxing had been laid. Regulations, governing bodies, structures of competition, weight classifications, rules governing equipment and so forth were all established and, subject to refinement and amendment, they continue to define the sport today. The link between the professional ring and amateur competition was likewise in place and the commercial viability of the former had been clearly established. Importantly, by the end of the nineteenth century, the layers of oppression and deprivation which pressed upon the vast majority of those who had stepped into the ring and which for centuries had sustained the subculture in which they were nurtured became crystalised within the ghetto.

2

The political economy of boxing
in the twentieth century

It is accepted that the Yankee Sullivan versus Gentleman Jim Corbett fight, held in New Orleans on 7 September 1892, was a watershed contest in the history of professional boxing (Gorn, 1986; Sammonds, 1990). To begin with, this was the first 'world championship' to be fought under the terms of the Marquess of Queensberry rules, requiring both boxers to wear gloves for a series of rounds, lasting three minutes each. As the nineteenth century wore on the naked brutality of bare-knuckle prize fighting had alienated middle-class audiences on both sides of the Atlantic. It was difficult to square Victorian notions of order and respectability with the relatively anarchic blood baths of the prize ring. Nevertheless, as the century entered its last quarter an ideological interweaving of social Darwinism, rugged athleticism and muscular Christianity encouraged the view that a suitably codified, controlled and gloved version of prize fighting was acceptable for both the physical training and vicarious entertainment of young gentlemen.

The dawning of a new era

The 1890s was a period during which leisure was developing from being the preserve of the elite to something for popular consumption. In this sense leisure must be understood in the context of an urban–industrial equation the central elements of which are work, free time and disposable income. In the latter half of the nineteenth century, through combinations of industrial development and working class/trades union campaigning, for sizeable numbers of workers, both the working week and the working day became shorter and wages improved. Consequently, more and more people were able to experience leisure and by the turn of the century sports such as baseball in America and soccer in Britain had massive public followings who were willing to pay to watch their favourite teams in action.

Likewise, boxing, with a long, if partially submerged, tradition of commercial development began to flourish as a legitimate business on both sides of the Atlantic. In the days of bare-knuckle prize fighting the money or 'purse' for which boxers fought was put up by wealthy patrons whose opportunity to recoup their outlays rested in the success of side bets which they would lay on the outcome of bouts. The close association between bare-knuckle prize fighting and gambling was the single most important factor which led to the sport's eventual demise. During the first half of the nineteenth century the patronage of the dilettante, for whom the wager had been a titillating diversion, was gradually replaced by the graft of the fixer, who would both raise purses and make matches in the full knowledge that through influencing the outcome of contests he could 'earn' far more than he invested.

While 'the corrupt, underworld scent always lingered' (Gorn, 1986: 242), in a new era of commercialised leisure more and more people became interested in funding and staging boxing matches because of the money which could be earned at the gate rather than as a vehicle for gambling.

By 1890 the custodians of the New Orleans Olympic Club were so confident of the future of boxing that they had invested in a purpose-built boxing auditorium close to the centre of the city. On the night of the Sullivan–Corbett fight 10,000 people converged on the stadium to witness what was widely considered to be the clash of the old, more brutish order personified by Yankee Sullivan and a new, more civilised world represented by Gentleman Jim Corbett. The full social spectrum of modern America was represented in the audience. Gorn demonstrates the cross-sectional appeal of the fight by quoting from an article published in the *New Orleans Times Democrat* on the day of the fight:

> The most intense excitement prevailed throughout the city, the streets were thronged with visitors of all classes, from the millionaire to the baker and the fakir. Politicians, lawyers, merchants and gamblers elbowed each other in all public places on comparatively equal terms. (Gorn, 1986: 244)

The openness and social inclusiveness of the Sullivan–Corbett fight contrasts with bare-knuckle contests, which were often staged clandestinely in back streets, on barges, in bars or rural areas, beyond the gaze of the law and patronised by society's most marginal elements. There was limited crowd control and those who turned up did so as punters (gamblers) rather than as paying customers. Gambling remained a feature of new-look boxing, but it began to appear less as the *raison d'être* for the activity and more as a sideline.

The interest aroused by the Sullivan–Corbett fight had spread far beyond the city limits of New Orleans. During a period of unprecedented social change, characterised by high levels of occupational differentiation, geographic and social mobility and rapid urban development, sport began to emerge as a medium of individual and collective identification. Shared knowledge of and emotional commitment to sports provided a community of interest which transcended occupational and geographic boundaries. A revolution in the communications industry made this possible and through newspapers and over telegraph wires

30

news of the build-up to and outcome of the fight was disseminated by an embryonic sports media across America and around the globe (Gorn, 1986: 245). This signalled the establishment of a relationship between boxing and the media which was to have a serious effect on the growth and development of the sport for the next hundred years.

Gentlemen's athletic clubs, such as the one in New Orleans, were key to this period of transition in the history of boxing. In addition to adhering to the Queensberry rules they formalised a range of weight categories which appeared to make the sport fairer and reduce the chance of mismatches. In the heyday of prize fighting there had been little attention paid to the weight of contestants. Understandably, the long-term result of this was that the best fighters were usually the biggest and strongest men around – hence Sullivan's other nick name, 'the Boston Strongman'.

For a short period in the middle of the nineteenth century prize fighters had been divided into lightweights and heavyweights. It was the athletic clubs which confirmed the rationalisation of boxing with the introduction of four additional weight categories: bantamweight; featherweight; welterweight; and middleweight. In doing so they not only greatly enhanced the sport's physical equity, but also significantly increased the size of the pool of those who looked towards the prize ring as a career. This changed the shape of boxing from a single mountain with one peak (the heavyweight championship) to a mountain range with a broad and common base with a number of distinctive pinnacles, each of which helped to stream the abilities and aspirations of boxers in the various weight categories as they grew and matured into their natural fighting weights. As well as opening up the sport to men of all shapes and sizes, this rationalisation, by increasing the numbers of potential champions, multiplied boxing's commercial potential. As Oats remarks:

> In theory, the finely calibrated divisions were created to prevent mismatches; in practice, they have the felicitous effect of creating many more 'champions' and many more 'title' shots. (Oats, 1980: 6)

For instance, the Sullivan–Corbett fight was part of a three-day boxing festival at which the audience witnessed no less than three championship bouts at lightweight, featherweight and heavyweight, as well as numerous non-championship contests at a variety of different weights on the under-card of each day's main event. It is estimated that, after expenses, the Olympic Club recorded a profit in excess of $50,000 as well as boosting the local economy with the influx of fight fans (Sammonds, 1990: 15).

As it turned out the fight itself was a mismatch. The older and heavier Sullivan was no match for the agile Corbett, whose whole repertoire was geared to the measured rhythms of the Queensberry rules. Corbett boxed an exhibition in the sport's new form for twenty-one rounds before felling Sullivan and leaving him out

31

for the count. In many ways it was fitting that it was Corbett's name which taxed the headline writers' imaginations on the morning after his victory. The newspapers of the day agreed that his triumph had been a victory for 'youth, skill and science ... over age, dissipation and brute strength' (Gorn, 1986: 245). Corbett symbolised much that was modern America – a confident and sophisticated urban society which was ready to shake free from the harsh and often brutish conditions which had characterised life both in the cities and at the frontier for much of the nineteenth century.

With its comprehensive new rules, weight classifications, governing bodies, specialist trainers and so forth, in certain ways it can be seen that the sanitised form of boxing which dominated in the post-Sullivan era complemented the ordered rationality of the new industrial age. However, as Sammonds (1990) argues, within this rational framework, boxing still reminded its audience of a simpler past, when attributes such as physical stature and courage had been the standards through which people were judged. In much the same way as the myths of the American frontier had been recreated in wild west shows and romantic novels for the consumption of disaffected and alienated urban Americans, boxing was presented as an antidote to the monotony and emotional stultification of modernity.

At the time of the Sullivan–Corbett contest, prize fighting – that is, fighting for a purse – was still outlawed in most of the American east. The New Orleans Olympic Club circumnavigated such legislation by organising sparring contests and exhibition bouts, even though it was common knowledge that sizeable purses were usually at stake. The spirit of puritan reform still burned in certain sections of society and legal attempts were made to prohibit such contests taking place, but with growing numbers of erstwhile respectable folk supporting boxing, the authorities often found themselves defeated in court. There would be setbacks for the legal status of the sport, but by 1900 boxing was clearly winning the legal battle to legitimise its place as one of the major sports of the dawning century (Sammonds, 1990: 14–29).

War games

The reputation of boxing was further enhanced by the build-up to and progress of the First World War. As the great European powers edged the world closer and closer to global conflict the physical fitness of the male population became the subject of increasing concern on both sides of the Atlantic. As ever, sport was pressed into the service of military preparation. Boxing was ideally suited to the task of whipping raw recruits into shape and honing them for battles which may still require participation in forms of hand-to-hand combat. Theodore Roosevelt, the President who oversaw the emergence of the United States as a world power, had sparred as an undergraduate at Harvard and had first-hand experience of the value of pugilism for military training when he used it as a means of toughening up

32

his company of 'Rough Riders' which he led as a cavalry colonel in Cuba in the Spanish–American War in 1898. Indeed, the presence of American servicemen on Cuban soil during the years which followed the end of the Spanish–American War did much to lay the foundations for the island's subsequent strengths in both baseball and boxing (Pettivo and Pye, 1994).

During the build-up to America's involvement in the First World War Roosevelt continued to praise the use of boxing as a means of military training and he encouraged the use of professional boxers both as training instructors and as role models for new recruits. John J. 'Black Jack' Pershing, Supreme Commander of the United States Expeditionary Forces, believed that a nation of good boxers had to be a nation of good soldiers. Speaking to an army boxing champion he is quoted as saying, 'this game of yours is what makes the American Army the greatest in the world' (Sammonds, 1990: 50). And, as Sammonds goes on to argue, 'with such praise from military leaders and the endorsement of retiring veterans, the sport gained added prestige and unprecedented public attention in the postwar years'. Moreover, when the war was over, with the carnage of the Western Front etched in the public psyche, the charge that boxing was barbaric seemed less and less tenable. Indeed, by comparison, boxing appeared positively civilised.

Boxing and racism

Despite the boost which the First World War gave to boxing, all was not well with the very heart of the sport. As the twentieth century got under way boxing was struggling to come to terms with a paradox which cut right to the sport's core. Arguably boxing was the essential theatre of activity through which one man's physical mastery over another became manifest. At least in part it was sustained ideologically by notions of social Darwinism, which posited that society was a physical and intellectual meritocracy. Success in the ring, particularly if this led to the heavyweight championship of the world, came to symbolise not only individual achievement, but also racial and national superiority. However, early twentieth-century America was a society with unprecedented levels of racial and ethnic mixing. Wave upon wave of immigrants had been drawn to the United States to swell the pool of labour for this growing industrial giant and the children and grandchildren of freed African-American slaves had left the deep south to seek better lives in the burgeoning cities of the north and mid-west. Racism and related forms of ethnic discrimination were deeply seated and the boom and slump economic cycle characteristic of early capitalism and the shortages of work which often ensued exacerbated tensions among whites, blacks and immigrants (Higham, 1975).

Paradoxically, it was largely as a result of institutionalised forms of racism and ethnic discrimination that blacks and immigrants became anchored at the bottom of American society and, for reasons of economic necessity and subcultural capacity, it was from these social groups that most aspiring boxers were drawn (Weinberg and Arond, 1952). Thus, the best boxers tended not to be indigenous white Americans, but relatively recent immigrants or African-Americans. For a number of years white America conspired to maintain the appearance of physical mastery by introducing a colour bar into the most popular sports. Boxing was no exception.

At this time it was anathema for white America to countenance a black man and a white man in the same ring, particularly if defeat for the white man was a possibility. Despite his demonstrated superiority in defeating all comers between 1907 and 1913, black heavyweight Jack Johnson was hounded out of the sport and eventually out of the country. Ostensibly this was because of his conviction by an all-white jury for crimes of vice, including aiding prostitution, illegal sexual intercourse, sodomy and debauchery. Not only was Johnson supreme in the ring, but also he had earned a reputation as a white ladies' man, which added insult to injury in the eyes of many white Americans.

In order to avoid incarceration Johnson fled to Europe, creating a vacuum for the heavyweight championship and throwing the sport into considerable disarray in the United States. Eventually, he was persuaded to fight the tall, white Texan Jess Willard in Havana, Cuba. The interest in this fight was huge – so much so that it became one of the first contests to be filmed and, even though the distribution of boxing films was illegal in the United States, the film was widely disseminated there through a variety of underground outlets (Sammonds, 1990: 45). Out of condition after his exile and boxing in the open air beneath the relentless mid-afternoon Caribbean sun, Johnson was beaten in the twenty-sixth round. His performance was so lacklustre that many believe the fight to have been fixed. The cause of Johnson's failure notwithstanding, the result stood and once more the world had a white American heavyweight champion. As Sammonds (p. 44) observes:

> Whatever the circumstances most white Americans rejoiced in the return of the heavyweight crown to their race. Willard became an instant hero, one who brought renewed confidence to the physical and moral strength of white America.

Once the title had been recaptured it was possible to reinforce the colour bar and largely because of this it was a white man who wore the heavyweight crown until the 1930s. This is not to deny the undoubted talents of Jack Dempsey, the former hobo who almost single handedly kept boxing in the public eye during the roaring twenties. When he won the title from Jess Willard in 1919, Dempsey assured white America that under no circumstances would he accept challenges from blacks. This greatly endeared Dempsey to the white majority, including those who influenced the legislature. It is not surprising, therefore, that Johnson's demise and the removal of the 'black menace' from boxing's centre stage was rapidly followed by legislation which once and for all legalised boxing in America (Sammonds, 1990: 73).

Professional boxing's golden era

In the short term at least, the appearance of white domination and the sport's legitimacy greatly assisted the development of boxing as a commercial enterprise. Just as a hundred years before in Regency England bare-knuckle prize fighting had experienced its most profitable decade – its 'golden era' – in the 1920s its gloved progeny enjoyed a period of unprecedented commercial success. New York City was established as the sport's capital, and Madison Square Garden, the venue used by P. T. Barnum for his 'Greatest Show on Earth', became boxing's epicentre. Alongside his ability to stage spectacular events, one of Barnum's greatest strengths was his capacity to stimulate the imagination of the paying public in the build-up to one of his wild west shows and circuses. Men like Tex Rickard looked towards Barnum as they developed the role of the boxing promoter. Rickard promoted virtually every heavyweight title contest between 1910 and 1930. According to Sammonds (1990: 67), Rickard made 'boxing promotion an art form' by forging links with the media and through the press and radio exaggerating the appeal of forthcoming contests.

It was Rickard who, in 1921, promoted Jack Dempsey's fight with Georges Carpentier, a journeyman heavyweight from France whose main distinction was the fact that he had been decorated for bravery fighting at the Western Front. Rickard seized upon this and held press conferences during which Carpentier's war record was contrasted with Dempsey's reputation as someone who had dodged the draft. In this way he was able to appeal to those who would support Dempsey because he represented America against France while at the same time appealing to Americans who wanted to see Dempsey the malingerer put in his place by a brave soldier. Rickard skilfully used such emotive issues to increase public interest in what was otherwise an unappealing encounter. As Sammonds (1990: 67) comments:

> In the end, 80,183 fans paid a total of $1,789,238 to see Dempsey, who was never challenged, knock out Carpentier in the fourth round. Millions more listened to a blow-by-blow radio description of the action.

The flamboyant Rickard went on to promote most of Dempsey's remaining championship fights, creating an entrepreneurial style which has characterised boxing promotion ever since. Dempsey was a skilled and charismatic fighter and so long as he was around people like Rickard would always be able to make lots of money. However, boxing is an exacting profession which takes its toll on those who linger too long in the ring. Even fighters with Dempsey's credentials have a limited time at the top and after defeat by Gene Tunney in 1927, in front of more than 100,000 at Chicago's Soldier Field, he began to fade from the boxing scene. In comparison with Dempsey at the height of his powers, Tunney and a long line of other indigenous American 'white hopes' were inferior and proved incapable of

35

capturing the public imagination on the same scale. Without a charismatic champion, boxing, like the rest of America, was facing a slump.

Carnera, Schmeling and the politicisation of the ring

In the absence of worthy white American contenders and with the colour bar still in place, white immigrants and white overseas fighters were looked to. Two such contenders were the German Max Schmeling and the Italian Primo Carnera. Perhaps unwittingly, in their rush to fill their stadia with paying customers, America's boxing promoters helped the propaganda machines of Nazi Germany and Fascist Italy. It is uncertain whether or not either fighter had any political affiliations. It just so happened that their rise and brief occupation of the world heavyweight championship coincided with Adolph Hitler's ascendancy in Germany and Benito Mussolini's dominion in Italy. After the humiliation of the First World War and the draconian terms of the Versailles Treaty, Hitler had resolved to return Germany to the centre stage of world affairs. Just as they were later to use the 1936 Olympic Games as a showcase and symbol of Aryan power, when he captured the heavyweight crown from the American Jack Sharkey in 1930, in the German press Hitler's fledgling Nazi Party attributed Schmeling's success to Germany's purity. As Sammonds observes:

> The seeds of the Hitler youth movement were being sown, and shortly German athletes would march side by side with the fuhrer's storm troopers. Schmeling, willing or not led the way as German athleticism became the metaphor for a fascist perspective of the world. (Sammonds, 1990: 85)

For his part Carnera, the Italian and former circus strongman, was touted as 'Mussolini's emissary in America' (Sammonds, 1990: 101). He was not a great fighter, but his massive size and associations with organised crime in combination served to win him the heavyweight championship from Jack Sharkey in New York in 1933. He returned to Rome to a hero's welcome and, on the eve of Italy's invasion of Abyssinia, was fêted by the Italian dictator as an icon of Italian prowess (Pagnameta, 1995).

Throughout this 'foreign invasion', particularly in the light of the nationalistic propaganda which was associated with the achievements of Schmeling and Carnera, Americans became desperate to recapture boxing's holy grail, so much so that in the absence of a serious white contender the colour bar was relaxed to allow a promising young black heavyweight, Joseph Louis Barrow, to fight his way towards the top of the heavyweight rankings. Joe Louis had a classical boxer's pedigree. He was from a broken home, he moved with his mother from Alabama to Detroit when he was six years old, he dropped out of school when he was eleven and ran in the streets until a friend introduced him to boxing. Unlike the outrageous Jack Johnson, outside the ring Louis was a modest man who did not drink nor seek a glamorous public lifestyle. In this regard he was more acceptable to a white audience whose racism and xenophobia had been blunted by the experiences of the great depression and by watching the unfolding of events in Europe (Sammonds, 1990: 99). Above all else, however, at a time when America was in dire need of a home-made hero, what endeared audiences most towards Louis was his bravery and skill in the ring.

When Louis met Primo Carnera in Yankee Stadium in a non-title fight in 1935 the fight was characterised as Italy versus Abyssinia, with Louis adopting the mantle of Africa. This was not a world title fight because Carnera had already lost his crown to the Jewish-American heavyweight Max Baer, an event which in its own way helped to diminish Nazi claims of Aryan superiority. That Baer then went on to defeat Max Schmeling was an even greater blow to Hitler's anti-Semitic propaganda. Today Jews are more readily associated with the cut and thrust of the commodity markets than with the boxing ring. However, in the first decades of the twentieth century, as they took their turn on the lowest tier of the immigration–assimilation totem pole, in time-honoured fashion, young Jewish ghetto dwellers took their chances in the prize ring. As Sammonds explains:

> Despite traditional values that shunned physicality, by 1928 there were more prominent Jewish boxers than there were boxers from any other single ethnic or racial group. The succession had gone from Irish to Jewish and would pass on to Italians, to blacks and to Latins, a pattern that reflected the acculturation strategies of those ethnic groups located on the lowest rungs of the socio-economic ladder. As each group moved up, it pulled its youth out of prize fighting and pushed them into promising and more meaningful pursuits. (Sammonds, 1990: 92)

When he met Joe Louis, Carnera's inability to box was finally exposed by a master craftsman and after six torturous rounds the giant Italian was knocked senseless. Meanwhile back in Germany Schmeling licked his wounds and prepared his comeback. In 1935 he defeated former champion Steve Hamas, an achievement which confirmed his rehabilitation. Schmeling was embraced by the Führer, who used the boxer's renaissance as a metaphor for the rise of the Third Reich:

> Schmeling set out to win the heavyweight championship of the world as Hitler goose-stepped his way across Europe. Each would use the other to achieve his goals, and each would come perilously close to succeeding. (Sammonds, 1990: 107)

Joe Louis had been steadily climbing his way towards the world crown and the stage was set for a Louis–Schmeling encounter. Although there was some reluctance on the part of the Germans to allow their representative into the ring with a black man, because they believed Louis to be the gateway to a shot at the world title they agreed for their man to meet the 'Brown Bomber' in Yankee

Stadium in June 1936. Apart from some sections of the southern states, the American public, already deeply suspicious of Hitler's intentions in Europe, supported Louis. As the fight approached the American press down-graded Schmeling's record and fighting chances so much that Louis slacked off his training. Schmeling, on the other hand, saw the fight as a 'do or die mission' (Sammonds, 1990: 108) and prepared accordingly. During the bout itself a fitter and sharper Schmeling swarmed over Louis in the early rounds and the brave but battered American was defeated in the twelfth.

In Germany Schmeling was hailed as a hero and his defeat of Louis was used by Nazi propagandists to divert attention away from the success of another black American athlete, Jesse Owens, in the Berlin Olympics the same year. Hitler hosted a party in Schmeling's honour and the fighter duly reciprocated by declaring that his victory had been inspired by the Führer himself (Sammonds, 1990: 109). This would not be the last time that victory in the ring was associated with political superiority. Almost fifty years later in Havana, the Cuban heavyweight Teofilo Stevenson would be eulogised by Fidel Castro and in return the triple Olympic gold medallist would accredit Castro and his version of communism for inspiring his feats as a boxer.

Louis's comeback and the end of the colour bar

Victory over Louis should have earned Schmeling a tilt at the world crown held by another American, James Braddock. However, whether for financial or political reasons, much to the chagrin of Schmeling and his backers, the promotional cartel that controlled heavyweight boxing in the United States managed to avoid the German's challenge. This bought time for Louis, who was able to fight his way back into world championship reckoning after a string of impressive victories over the likes of Jack Sharkey, Al Ettore, Natie Brown and the Welshman Tommy Farr (Andre and Fleischer, 1993: 125–43). In June 1937 Louis fought and beat James Braddock for the heavyweight championship of the world, once and for all breaking the colour bar on boxing in the United States. Apart from some isolated areas in the south, Louis's mastery over Braddock was widely acknowledged and well received by the US public.

This contrasts with the mood in Germany, where Schmeling and his Nazi managers were furious at being excluded from what they viewed as a legitimate title challenge, particularly because as a result of this exclusion a black man now wore the world crown. A rematch between the two men became inevitable. Even though Louis was now world champion, his earlier defeat by Schmeling was a demon which he was desperate to exorcise. With Jesse Owens fresh in his memory Hitler was reluctant to sanction a bout between his man and Louis in case the black man won, providing the world with another opportunity for anti-Aryan propaganda. However, 'after considerable debate, introspection and persuasion by

Schmeling, Hitler himself decided that the potential for glory outweighed the risks' (Sammonds, 1990: 114).

Thus it was that on 22 June 1938, as war clouds were gathering in Europe, Joe Louis took on Max Schmeling in New York City. An enthralled worldwide audience gathered around radios to hear the outcome of the contest. It was impossible not to interpret the fight as a portent of the coming military conflict. Unfortunately the Second World War lasted considerably longer than this fight. Schmeling was knocked out in just over two minutes after receiving a terrible beating from Louis, who was younger, fitter and, unlike for their first encounter, very well prepared. Hitler's worst fears had been realised as the US media celebrated Louis's victory as a triumph of good over evil and as a body blow to Nazism. The *Charlotte Observer* put it thus:

> The Aryan idol, the unconquerable one had been beaten, the bright, shining symbol of race glory had been thumped in the dust. The noise you hear is Goebbels making for the storm cellar. (Sammonds, 1990: 116)

Despite this loss, Schmeling's previous achievements counted for much in Germany, where he was still revered as a hero. As the mobilisation for war continued Schmeling was used by the Nazis as a role model for military training (Pagnameta, 1995). He was enlisted into the paratroops, where he acted as an instructor in the martial arts, and films of Schmeling on active service were used by the Nazi propaganda machine. Similarly, in the United States, just as had happened in the build-up to the First World War, boxers were encouraged to enlist as physical training instructors and also to act as models for wider recruitment. As Sammonds (1990: 123) reports, 'no less than five world champions stood tall among the more than 4,000 boxers in the military'. None stood taller than Joe Louis, who boxed exhibitions at military bases throughout the country, donated purses to veterans' organisations and eventually, in 1942, enlisted and was assigned to 'special services'.

Almost single handedly, Louis had cast the colour bar out of boxing, and after the war the popularity of the sport was unsurpassed. Louis continued his dominance of the heavyweight championship until 1948 when, after his twenty-fifth successful title defence, against Jersey Joe Walcott, he announced his retirement. Later mounting debts forced Louis back into the ring, but he never regained the heavyweight crown, which, after briefly being in the possession of Joe Walcott, was owned by Rocky Marciano until he retired, undefeated in 1956. Marciano remains the only fighter in history to win every single professional fight he took part in and from 1953 until 1956 he successfully defended his title six times, earning an estimated $2,000,000 (Andre and Fleischer, 1993: 151). Furthermore, Marciano did what so many of his fellow professionals failed to do. Once he retired he never returned to the ring. Louis had done so much to remove the colour bar from American boxing and it is ironic that the immediate post-Louis period was dominated by a white boxer. In the wake of Marciano's retirement, however, the heavyweight scene was to be dominated by black Americans.

The exception was Ingemar Johansson of Gothenburg, Sweden, who scored a surprise knock-out victory over Marciano's successor, Floyd Patterson, in New York in 1959. He became an overnight sensation in his home country and even now he is one of Sweden's most respected sportsmen. In this regard it is ironic that in 1970 Sweden became the first non-communist country to ban professional boxing. To date, Johansson is the last white boxer to hold a unified world heavyweight crown. There have been some game white challengers, such as Americans Jerry Cooney and Jerry Quarry, Britons Henry Cooper and Joe Bugner, and the South African Coetzee, but since Johansson lost his rematch with Patterson in 1960, no Caucasian fighters have seriously threatened black supremacy in the heavyweight division.

It may be that black men make better boxers than whites. It is much more likely that the social position of blacks relative to whites in the United States and corresponding societies helps to determine their over-representation in professional boxing. Boxing was and continues to be the product of urban poverty. As the various ethnic groups which comprised the lower substrata of US society became economically mobile and culturally assimilated their youthful representatives began to disappear from the annals of professional boxing. Once people moved out of the ghettos the motivation to box was displaced by aspirations in education and other, less physically demanding, less risky and less negatively stigmatised occupations (Sammonds, 1990: 237). Irish, Jews, and Italians all suffered from institutionalised forms of ethnic discrimination, but their whiteness assisted their eventual integration into the socio-cultural mainstream and their abandonment of the ring. Racism, that is, discrimination based on a person's skin colour, has proven to be a more enduring form of prejudice. By comparison with the upward social mobility experienced by white European immigrants, racism has seriously hampered the efforts of black Americans to break free of the ghetto. The ghetto is the nursery of professional boxing and so long as blacks continue to be over-represented in the ranks of the urban poor so too will they feature predominantly in the ratings of *Ring Magazine*.

Mob rule

Once he regained his title from Johannson in 1960, Floyd Patterson's reign as heavyweight champion was almost as short lived as the Swede's had been. In September 1962 he was flattened in the first round of his world title defence by Charles 'Sonny' Liston. The new world champion was renowned for two things, his huge size and his links with organised crime. Liston was one of twenty-five children. He ran away from Arkansas when he was thirteen and made a living in petty crime in the streets of St Louis. He spent most of his formative years in juvenile detention centres and eventually ended up in the state penitentiary in Jefferson, Missouri, where he was persuaded to take up boxing by a cleric named Father Stevenson. Upon his release from prison, Liston went to work for some noted St Louis racketeers, who took a leading interest in the development of his boxing career. Eventually, Liston's potential attracted the attention of underworld heavyweights Blinky Palermo and Frankie Carbo, who, behind the scenes, exerted massive influence over boxing in America during the 1950s (Sammonds, 1990: 178).

Despite its elevated status as an entertainment spectacle, the roots of boxing necessarily remained in the ghettos of urban America and this rendered the sport vulnerable to exploitation and corruption by those who operated outside the law. In 1919 the Eighteenth Amendment became law in the United States. The unintended consequence of this prohibition of alcohol was the growth of a huge black market economy which in turn fostered the rise of organised crime, whose base was the immigrant communities of cities such as New York and Chicago – the same turf as the boxing subculture. With so much money entering the sport at the top level it was almost inevitable that 'the mob' would get their hands on something which had its origins in their own back yard. As Butler observes of boxing in America before and after the Second World War:

> The disgrace of boxing in America for decades was the acceptance by some politicians that it was inevitable that racketeers and hoodlums would always move in and take over the sport. (Butler, 1986: 15)

During the twenties gangsters were making so much money out of prohibition that it was not financially necessary for them to take control of boxing. However, people like Al Capone, Lucky Luciano and Legs Diamond felt it important to be seen to have associations with a sport which was so popular with the American public in general and which yielded champions who came from social categories over which the mob sought to wield most influence. Even though by now boxing was legal, the roots of the sport remained obscured in the ghetto. The farm systems of other sports, such as basketball and American football, were bound up with schools and universities and as such were relatively open to public scrutiny. Boxers, on the other hand, apart from fight night, existed beyond the public gaze in a shadowy world of back-street gymnasia and under the influence of unaccountable trainers and managers. Under such circumstances it was comparatively easy for mobsters to exert a controlling influence on the direction of a given fighter's career, on the back of which considerable sums of money could be made both legitimately, through successful promotions and deals with media companies, and illegitimately, through the fixing of fights for gambling purposes.

The extent of Mafia involvement in boxing became public in the wake of a series of government investigations for the Antitrust and Monopoly Committee of the US Senate, which began in 1960. It turned out that boxing in the United States in the 1940s and 1950s virtually had been run by a syndicate of gangsters headed by Frankie Carbo and his lieutenant, Blinky Palermo. Carbo's gangster credentials were impressive. In the twenties and thirties he was implicated in a wide range of serious criminal offences, including homicide, and was linked with the notorious gang of assassins known as Murder Incorporated (Sammonds, 1990: 143). After the ending of prohibition, as the Mafia looked to diversify their outlets for racketeering, boxing appeared an attractive prospect. Carbo used Madison Square Garden as a base for his operations, which were carried out by a number of front men, such as the wealthy New York businessman Jim Norris, who gave his promotional activities the appearance of legitimacy. Carbo's activities dominated the upper reaches of boxing in the 1950s:

> He was able to control the movements of several world champions, even though the boxers themselves were not always consulted. He used any methods – bribery, bullying, threats, blackmail – and a few guys who tried to oppose his moving were beaten up. (Sammonds, 1990: 116)

Eventually Carbo and his henchman, Palermo, were convicted for racketeering and extortion by a special court set up by the Attorney General, Robert Kennedy, and even before the finding of the boxing hearings had been made public, both men were serving long prison sentences.

Even though they were behind bars it seemed that the gangsters could still hold influence over boxing. Sonny Liston's affairs were taken over by a business associate of Palermo's who was instrumental in promoting a match between the champion and the young, loud-mouthed, former Olympic gold medallist, Cassius Clay, who hailed from Louisville, Kentucky. In wider boxing circles it was believed that, out-weighed and out-reached, Clay would be no match for Liston. As it turned out Clay defeated Liston in Miami Beach, on 22 February 1964, but under circumstances which aroused considerable suspicion. After an uninspiring opening four rounds, at the start of the fifth Clay had to be pushed into the ring by his trainer, Angelo Dundee, arousing suspicions in the audience that he had been ordered to throw the fight. In fact, resin from Liston's gloves had temporarily blinded the challenger. The focus for the suspicions of the audience that the fight had been fixed shifted dramatically to the champion when at the beginning of the seventh Liston flatly refused to leave his corner. Clay had become champion without having to throw or take a serious punch.

While an official inquiry could find nothing irregular about the circumstances surrounding the fight, it was widely believed that the mobsters who ruled Liston had rigged the outcome of the contest in order to make a killing at the bookmakers' expense. A dramatic shift in the odds just before the contest commenced tends to support this view, as does the presence in the Liston pre-fight camp of Ash Resnick, a notorious Las Vegas gambler. The evidence suggests that Liston had injured his shoulder during training and was not fit to face Clay. By suppressing this information and allowing the fight to go ahead those closest to Liston must have known that he would lose (Sammonds, 1990: 182–3). Liston was granted a rematch the following year, but was knocked out by the champion in the first round. Once more questions were raised about Liston's performance and experts have long since argued whether the punch which put Liston down was powerful enough to incapacitate such a big and strong fighter (Andre and Fleischer, 1993: 161). However, by this time the wider American public were less concerned by the influence of organised crime on professional boxing as they were worried about the new world champion's conversion to Islam and his links with the Black Muslim movement (Sammonds, 1990: 183).

Ali, civil rights and the anti-war movement

Much has been written about the controversial career of Ali (Mailer, 1975; Sammonds, 1990; Hauser, 1991; Plimpton, 1993). It is my intention here to highlight those ingredients which help to inform the unfolding analysis. At a time of unprecedented social unrest over the issue of civil rights, Clay's conversion and his name change to Muhammad Ali worried white America. While Ali's boxing achievements have been compared to those of Joe Louis, outside the ring he more resembled the extrovert Jack Johnson than the modest Brown Bomber. Unlike Johnson, however, Ali used his achievements in the ring as a platform to campaign for civil rights. Of course the colour bar had introduced racial politics into boxing a generation before Ali. However, by reintroducing it into boxing from the canvas up the new champion 'flew in the face of society's rule that athletic heroes must hang their heads in humble appreciation and stay out of politics' (Sammonds, 1990: 197–8).

The extent to which Ali formed his own political opinions or was orchestrated by radical groups such as the Nation of Islam and individuals like Malcolm X and Elijah Muhammad is uncertain. As we have seen, it was by no means unusual for boxers to be exploited for political purposes. But unlike Carnera, Schmeling and Louis, whose careers were welded to the cause of national unity, Ali's achievements in the ring were used to champion the cause of dissident black Americans and impoverished blacks in Africa. Before his fight with George Foreman in Zaire he told a reporter:

> Nobody is ready to know what I am up to. People in America just find it hard to take a fighter seriously. They don't know that I'm using boxing for the sake of getting over certain points you couldn't get over without it. Being a fighter enables me to attain certain ends. I'm not doing this for the glory of fighting, but to change a whole lot of things. (Mailer, 1975: 79)

Joe Louis's stock with the wider American public had rocketed when he enlisted in the army and allowed himself to be used for propaganda purposes.

When in 1967 Ali refused to be drafted during the Vietnam War, on the grounds that he was a conscientious objector, he became the focus for the rage of many Americans, black and white. He was stripped of the world championship and sentenced to five years' imprisonment by a federal court. A series of appeals kept Ali out of prison, during which time the mood in America became more ambivalent towards US involvement in South East Asia. As the numbers of body bags returning from Vietnam increased without any noticeable strategic gains, more and more people began to question the moral and political justifications for the war. Ali became a totem for anti-war protest and as this movement gained ground in middle America it became increasingly difficult to legitimise Ali's federal conviction and his exclusion from the ring.

In 1969 Ali's lawyers successfully filed suit against the NYSAC (New York State Athletic Commission) and his boxing licence was restored. Ali immediately sought to regain the heavyweight crown, which by this time was worn by 'Smokin' Joe Frazier. When the two met on 8 March 1971 in a packed Madison Square Garden, a worldwide audience tuned in on radio and television sets for what was being billed as a confrontation between 'pinko-liberal' and 'patriotic' America. The long, enforced lay-off had taken its toll on Ali's constitution and timing and after fifteen bruising rounds which left both men battered and bleeding the judges awarded the contest to Frazier.

Eventually, in April 1971, after a complex and controversial sequence of Supreme Court hearings, Ali's conviction was quashed, leaving him free to concentrate on his quest to regain his world title (Sammonds, 1990). However, his comeback suffered a second major setback when, after his controversial defeat by Frazier, he had his jaw broken by the relatively unknown Ken Norton, losing on points after twelve rounds. While Ali went into retreat to recover from the physical and mental wounds, the colossal George Foreman began his meteoric rise to the summit of world heavyweight boxing. In contrast to Ali's image of radicalism, Foreman was presented to the public as an authentic, all-American success story. In many ways he was. Like Joe Louis, he came from an impoverished background, ran in the streets as a youngster and, at least as legend has it, was saved from a life of crime by his introduction to boxing. He won a heavyweight gold medal at the Olympic Games in Mexico in 1968. At a time when other triumphant black American athletes, with clenched fists, were using their Olympic success to advertise the cause of domestic black civil rights, after his gold medal performance in Mexico, Foreman paraded around the ring in a US vest clutching a miniature star spangled banner in his right hand. In the media Foreman was presented as the perfect antidote to the likes of Tommy Smith and John Carlos, the black athletes who had given the black power salute on the medal rostrum in Mexico, and, of course, Muhammad Ali. With Foreman's patriotic pedigree, despite Ali's failures against Frazier and Norton, the prospect of a contest between Foreman and the draft dodger and verbose establishment critic had promoters drooling.

Ali and the King

The stage was set for the entrance of Don King. An environment which brought together media money, showmanship, corruption and machiavellian political in-fighting was made for a man like Don King. He made his first fortune from an illegal betting operation known as 'the Numbers' in Cleveland, Ohio, in the 1960s. He served a four-year prison term for killing a Numbers racketeer who had double-crossed him. In virtually any other sphere of commerce this conviction would have barred King from doing business. However, in the unconventional world of professional boxing King, with his outrageous clothes, diamond rings, 'electric' hairstyle and seamless rhetoric was able to make quite an impression.

Don King had two advantages over established, rival promoters such as Bob Arum. In the first place he was black and so long as race relations remained strained in the United States he was able to demonstrate an empathy with black boxers which his white contemporaries could not hope to emulate. Secondly, he had a sense for the great occasion which was matched only by his ability as a propagandist. He first proved this in 1974, when he promoted the championship bout between George Foreman and Ken Norton in Caracas, Venezuela, and in doing so demonstrated that so long as television backing was assured, it was the contest and not the venue which was important. The 'Caracas Caper' turned out to be a pilot for the 'Rumble in the Jungle', the fabled battle when in 1975 Ali reclaimed his world crown from George Foreman in Kinshasa, the capital of the central African country Ziare. Even though the latter event was not a financial success it had captured the imagination of the world and had established King's reputation as a major player in international boxing promotions and in so doing returned Muhammad Ali to the centre stage.

Today, Don King is one of the most powerful figures in the murky world of boxing promotion. There is hardly a major championship boxing match which takes place anywhere without the mark of King's influence. Just as in city gyms all over the world fighters hone skills learned in the streets and harness them to ring craft, so King brought the arts of the street hustler to the business side of boxing. In his study of boxing in the black ghettos of Chicago, Loic Wacquant noticed the proximity of the boxing club to the hustler's terrain. Hustling, he observed, is a way of life in the American ghetto, arguing that because of 'the chronically insufficient level of income received from work or from social assistance, nearly all the residents of the ghetto must, at one point or another, rely on some kind of hustle to get by' (Wacquant, 1994: 5). Of the full-time hustler he goes on to say:

> His trade consists in many instances in unobtrusively inserting himself into social situations, in spinning about him a web of deceitful relations, just so that he may derive some more or less extorted profit from them.

While nobody could describe King as unobtrusive, the remainder of Wacquant's description fits him well. Once, having been accused of trying to influence the decision of a world championship fight, King responded by saying:

> They thought I was trying to change the verdict ... I wasn't. I saw the biggest rematch in the world and I was just trying to put the money in my pocket. I am a living attestation to the American dream. (Jones, 1992: 26)

In 1995, despite significant evidence against him, after a mistrial, King avoided conviction in a federal prosecution on nine counts of fraud, including a bogus insurance claim for a cancelled fight which was never scheduled in the first place – a classic hustler's scam. That he has managed to maintain his pre-eminence despite his criminal record and regular brushes with the FBI and other US government agencies speaks volumes for the current climate within which the business affairs of professional boxing are carried out. As North America's leading sports magazine, *Sports Illustrated*, put it, so long as he stays out of prison:

> King will continue to pull the strings in the fight game, arranging some bouts that shouldn't be made, ignoring others that should, always acting in his self interest. He will continue to play the conflicting roles of promoter, whose profit is optimised by low cost, and manager, whose cut depends on high purse. And he will continue to be the biggest blight on boxing. (McCallum and Kennedy, 1995: 25)

Sometimes a sport gets what it deserves and, arguably, boxing deserves Don King.

The rehabilitation and fall of Muhammad Ali

By the middle of the 1970s the US public's view of Ali began to change as memories of the racial confrontations of the previous decade began to fade and the disastrous involvement of the United States in Vietnam drew to a close. It was also the time of Watergate and President Nixon's impeachment. In an atmosphere of political corruption and perfidy, Ali stood tall as a man who stood by and literally fought for his principles. Don King added the 'Thirilla in Manila' to his retinue of promotions when in 1976 Ali defeated Joe Frazier in the capital of the Philippines in front of a live audience of 28,000 while an estimated 7 million people in 68 countries tuned into satellite telecasts (Andre and Fleischer, 1993: 176). Ali's political rehabilitation seemed to be complete when he was presented with the prestigious Fighter of the Year award by the Boxing Writers' Association and was voted best fighter of all time by a poll of 500 sports columnists (Sammonds, 1990: 226).

Ali's second term as world champion lasted until 1978 when, after a string of victories over the likes of Frazier, Norton, Shavers, Quarry and Bobick, he was matched against the light heavyweight champion of the 1976 Montreal Olympics, Leon Spinks. Ali was expecting an easy win against a man with only seven professional fights under his belt and came to the fight under-prepared. The younger, fitter and more aggressive Spinks won a split decision over Ali. Spinks went on to confirm much that was bad about the social location of boxing. He had been brought up in one of the worst ghettos of St Louis, Missouri, and he was severely lacking in education and social skills. When he became world champion he was manifestly unable to deal with the fame and fortune which came with the title. He was arrested for drug-related offences as news of his wild and violent social life outside the ring overshadowed reports of his prowess in it. As one correspondent writing for the *Philadelphia Inquirer* put it, Spinks was 'an interesting sociological story who never did understand why he couldn't take the ghetto with him' (Sammonds, 1990: 238). He was stripped of the World Boxing Council's version of his crown for refusing to fight Ken Norton, choosing instead a rematch with Ali which he lost on points, thus completing his odyssey from 'the penthouse to the outhouse of the boxing world' (Sammonds, 1990: 238).

Having regained his title for a record third time, in 1979 Ali decided to retire, leaving the heavyweight division in the hands of his talented former sparring partner, Larry Holmes. Then, after more than a year away from the sport, he made the mistake which so many of his fellow professionals before him had made – he came back. Arguably, after bad investments, divorce settlements and the largesse he dispensed to hangers on, one of the highest-paid boxers in history may have needed the money. But what Ali missed most of all was the stage. Despite his many opportunities for public appearances, Ali truly knew himself and reached his public only when he was performing in the ring:

> Despite his self-proclaimed status as 'the Greatest' and 'the Black Kissinger', it is clear that boxing made him what he was and is. He has no skills outside the ring which compare favourably with his once extraordinary boxing dexterity. (Sammonds, 1990: 243)

During his brief comeback, Ali suffered heavy defeats at the hands of Larry Holmes and Trevor Berbeck, which persuaded him to retire once and for all. Unfortunately, the three phases of Ali's career had already taken their toll. The cumulative effect of thousands of punches to the head left Ali punch drunk and, it is widely believed, contributed to him contracting the progressively debilitating Parkinson's syndrome. Unable to walk or speak properly, Ali lost not only the opportunity to express himself in the ring but also the chance to enjoy the fruits of his retirement. Once Ali retired and no credible challengers to Holmes appeared, the profile of heavyweight boxing and boxing in general began to suffer. This situation was exacerbated by the power struggles taking place in the shadows of the ring.

Division and rule in the boxing industry

Until Don King appeared on the scene, the business word of boxing had been dominated by white men. A typical world championship contest would see two black men giving sweat and blood in the ring while a handful of white men fought over the usually considerable profits generated by their boxers' efforts on the canvas. This usually meant a furious scrap over the television rights. By the mid-fifties boxing had become a multibillion dollar industry, and this was not so much due to gate receipts as it was a consequence of the relationship between the sport and television. For instance, even though only a relatively small crowd turned up to witness Ingemar Johannson's victory over Floyd Patterson in Yankee Stadium in 1959, the fight made more than $1 million in closed-circuit telecasts (Andre and Fleischer, 1993: 157). It is estimated that when Ali made his comeback against Joe Frazier promoters made in the region of $20 million, largely through the sale of television rights (Sammonds, 1990: 219). By the end of Ali's era, with the arrival of cable and satellite broadcasting, the money coming into boxing from the media was the sport's life blood, and boxing came to depend television for its survival.

Boxing did not follow the line of administrative growth chosen by other major international sports such as soccer and athletics, which developed a network of democratically accountable national governing bodies which gradually came under the embrace of a single world ruling body such as FIFA or the IAAF. Between them, a handful of boxing promoters and media barons have monopolised professional boxing since the turn of the nineteenth century. Boxing promotion developed a competitive dimension which was a parody of the sport itself. Just as pugilists slugged it out for world domination so too did their paymasters grapple with one another for absolute control of the 'golden goose'. As Butler argues:

> human nature is such that the norm in big business is to grow and grow. Monopoly
> is becoming accepted as inevitable in an age when the tycoons are geared to bigger
> and bigger take-overs. Boxing is no exception. (Butler, 1986: 89)

Monopoly in boxing has its origins in the corridors of the NSC (National Sporting Club), which controlled professional boxing in Britain from 1891 until the end of the first quarter of the twentieth century. The Club revised the Queensberry rules, introduced the famous Lonsdale Belt, and set a monopoly on all title fights by refusing to recognise a championship challenge unless the contest took place in the NSC's headquarters in Covent Garden. Worse still, because Jack Johnson had refused to fulfil an engagement after he had become world champion, the NSC introduced a colour bar which remained in place in British boxing until 1948, long after Joe Louis had established himself as a peerless world champion (Butler, 1986: 93).

As the new century wore on there could be no denying that the balance of power in world boxing had shifted from Britain to the United States. As we have seen, in the 1920s Tex Rickard had made boxing promotion a major business. He also helped to create the conditions for the centralisation of power in professional boxing. During the 1920s boxing in the United States was under the jurisdiction of the NYSAC. Rickard made it his business to seize control of this organisation which, for all intents and purposes, became professional boxing's first world governing body. The NYSAC sanctioned all major fights and throughout Rickard's reign it was virtually impossible for a contender to get a shot at a world title without his cooperation. In a preview of modern developments, in retaliation against the perceived monopoly of Rickard and the NYSAC, a rival organisation, the NBA (National Boxing Association) was formed in America and the European-based IBU (International Boxing Union) and the BBBC (British Boxing Board of Control) asserted their rights to crown champions and nominate challengers (Halling, 1993: 30).

However, Madison Square Garden continued to be the headquarters of international boxing. When Rickard died in 1930, Mike Jacobs took over, using the Twentieth Century Club in New York as his operational base. Jacobs' organisation dominated heavyweight boxing in the United States up to and through the Second World War. Largely on the back of the efforts of Joe Louis, by the end of the war Jacobs had built up a business empire worth an estimated $16 million a year (Halling, 1993: 90). Jacobs suffered a stroke in 1947, leaving the field clear for Jim Norris to form the IBC (International Boxing Club), which dominated the heavyweight scene for most of the 1950s. Unfortunately for boxing, Norris had close associations with mobsters like Frankie Carbo and Blinky Palermo, who, as outlined previously, did a great deal of damage to the sport's reputation. In 1959, after having been found guilty of monopolistic practices, the IBC was ordered to disband by the US Supreme Court, leaving boxing promotion in a chaotic state.

The NBA had been implicated in the corruption of the IBC and was no longer a credible alternative. With business suffering, in 1962 America's boxing entrepreneurs banded together to form the WBA (World Boxing Association), ostensibly to promote the sport internationally, but really constituted to protect the narrower interests of boxing in the United States. The boxing communities in other parts of the world were suspicious of this development and responded with the formation of the WBC (World Boxing Council). With its headquarters in Mexico City and with the backing of the BBBC and the EBU (European Boxing Union), the WBC posed a serious challenge to the authority of the Americans. In 1974 a second crisis was precipitated when, through democratic elections, the United States lost the Presidency of the WBA and a number of other key administrative posts to Latin American delegates, who promptly moved the headquarters of the organisation from New York to Caracas, Venezuela. As Halling reports, this led to the formation of yet another 'world' governing body:

> With both sanctioning bodies beyond the control of the United States, the creation
> of an organisation to promote American fighters was inevitable. The International
> Boxing Federation, another WBA offshoot, formally opened for business in 1983.
> (Halling, 1993)

49

While there was some concern that in the long run this splintering would damage the credibility of professional boxing, there was also a growing realisation that, at least in the short term, it could also be good for business. Internationally, the public seemed to have an insatiable appetite for local heroes and the more world bodies existed the more champions could be crowned to meet this demand. As the President of the IBF (International Boxing Federation), Robert Lee, stated, 'We simply expanded the market place to provide fresh opportunities for young fighters with nowhere to go' (Halling, 1993). He may also have added that the more championship fights there were to promote, the more money boxing entrepreneurs could make. This was the motivation behind the formation of a fourth world governing body, the WBO (World Boxing Organisation), which became yet another progeny of the WBA in 1988.

In Britain the snooker impresario Barry Hearn allied himself with the WBO and used it as a wedge to force his way into boxing promotion, which, hitherto in Britain, had been monopolised by Jack Solomons, Jarvis Astaire, Mickey Duff, Mike Barret and Frank Warren. With at least as many promoters operating across the Atlantic and many others in South Africa, Australia, the Far East and Latin America the marketplace began to look a little crowded. However, the growth in promoters was directly related to the increase in the number of fights there were to promote. The multiplication of governing bodies facilitated expansion at one level while the extension of weight categories allowed for it at another.

By the time the WBO was formed the number of weight categories for fighters had spiralled upwards from the eight which existed in 1960 (heavy; light heavy; middle; welter; light; feather; bantam; fly) to a staggering seventeen (cruiser; super-middle; light-middle; light-welter; junior-light; light-feather; light-bantam; light-fly; straw). Today, this means that at any given moment there may be up to sixty-eight world boxing champions. Once more, not only does this proliferation in weight categories increase opportunities for aspiring professional boxers, but it also multiplies significantly the numbers of world-ranked boxing promotions. For instance, as Halling (1993) has calculated, in 1958 across all weights there were just ten world championship contests in contrast to 1991 when there were 124.

This situation suits the ruling bodies, which get a percentage of the gross purses of fighters whose contests they sanction, and of course the promoters who, in an exemplary manner, are demonstrating the seemingly endless ability of capitalism to create new markets and exploit existing markets more efficiently. How long the consumer will be prepared to tolerate this situation remains to be seen. In 1992 the former heavyweight champion Evander Holyfield called for government intervention into boxing to ensure a single, fair and unified ranking system. William Roth, a Republican senator, took up his challenge and sponsored the Boxing Corporation Act, which proposed to replace the existing 'four-ring circus' with a professional boxing corporation headed by a commissioner appointed by the President of the United States. However, with assistance from international organisations, to date the professional boxing lobby has resisted such reform (Cornwell, 1992: 23).

Exploitation

So long as the clamour for local heroes is sustained and the armchair viewing audience continues to tune in, media companies will be happy to invest in boxing. Likewise, so long as there are enough people prepared to set foot in the ring to fulfil the promotions of the various governing bodies it is unlikely that there will be any hurried rationalisation. It is impossible to get accurate information on the number of active professional boxers in the world today, but we can make some educated guesses. In order to gain eligibility for a world title fight, a boxer has to be ranked in the top ten by at least one of the four world governing bodies. This means that potentially there are 680 contenders; even if we conservatively assume that for each contender there are 100 fighters with realistic aspirations to gain entry to the world's top ten, this means that there are more than an estimated 68,000 active professionals, all of whom regularly risk their physical and mental wellbeing in the ring.[1] Without this pool of willing labour the boxing industry would collapse. What do they get in return for their labours?

Like any other form of capitalist enterprise, professional boxing is dependent on exploiting the labour of its workers for the generation of profit. As with all professional sports, however, boxing differs from the production of other commodities inasmuch as the work is incorporated into the performance which is eventually sold on the night of the big fight. It would be a mistake to believe that boxers are paid only for what they do in the ring. Even though few boxers are paid a wage, relying instead on a percentage of the purses for which they fight, each performance is built upon weeks of hard road work, gym training, fasting and related abstinences. Any money which they receive from a boxing match must cover them for the time spent in preparation and recuperation, and the rewards in boxing are very, very uneven.

Today professional boxers figure among the highest-paid athletes in the world. However, only world-ranked contenders at the very peak of their careers are offered over $1 million a purse, and for every one of them there are thousands taking fights at the base of the pyramid for three-figure sums. Furthermore, even at the upper reaches of the sport, by the time managers, trainers, agents, match makers and the tax people have taken their cut, a fighter's earnings are usually seriously depleted. Many of the world champions featured in this chapter finished their lives physically broken and financially impoverished. A century ago, Yankee Sullivan is estimated to have made $1 million in the ring, but within ten years of his loss to Jim Corbett he was 100 pounds heavier and bankrupt (Mitchel, 1992: 34). After winning and losing the world heavyweight title, Primo Carnera finished up in a Brooklyn hospital, partially paralysed and broke. The great Joe Louis was peerless in the ring, but had no financial acumen and he was severely exploited by those who ran his career. As Butler observes:

[1] The physical risks associated with boxing will be discussed more fully in the concluding chapter.

51

His fists grossed $4.5 million. Yet in retirement and after an enforced comeback he owed nearly $2 million in unpaid tax which he believed had been settled from purses.... Louis finished his days a pathetic man, living with financial help from gamblers in Las Vegas. (Butler, 1986: 121)

Sammonds has calculated that in 1932 New York boxing clubs dispensed nearly $1.5 million to prize fighters, but points out that at that time there were 945 registered professional boxers in New York, meaning that their average earnings that year was in the region of $1,500 per man – a sum not far from the poverty line. He goes on to point out that the reality was often worse than this calculation might suggest, as the top 100 boxers shared $1 million, leaving $500,000 to be fought over by the remaining 845, which, even if it had been evenly distributed, meant a yearly per capita income of less than $600. Quoting from Weinberg and Arond's (1952) classic study, Sammonds reported that out of 127 boxers active between 1938 and 1951 only 8 (7 per cent) made it as contenders. From a related piece of research he discovered that from a nationwide survey of professional boxers in the United States only 600 made enough to make ends meet and only sixty became relatively well off headline fighters (Sammonds, 1990: 237).

Today, while the sums available at the top continue to soar, there is little to suggest that the sport is any less exploitative of its journeymen as it was fifty years ago or any easier on its fallen heroes. At the bottom end of the market boxers continue to step through the ropes for less than $200 per fight, while at the top end a couple of defeats can mean the end of a way of life and enforced retirement, for which the contemporary professional boxer is as ill prepared as his predecessors were.

In this regard boxing's cycle of exploitation is indeed vicious. It recruits the children of the urban poor – those whose life chances and educational opportunities and achievements are minimal. It nurtures them within the confines of the boxing subculture and builds in them a sense of identity which has little meaning outside the ring. It makes them dependent on boxing not just as a source of income, but also as a touchstone of personal pride and self-respect. It equips them with few skills other than ring craft. Their inability to manage their financial affairs is usually matched only by a dearth of interpersonal skills, evidenced by the difficulty most boxers and former boxers experience in forming meaningful relationships outside the confines of their occupational subculture. If they are successful, their glory is fleeting and, during their short time at the top, they are often surrounded by unscrupulous managers, greedy promoters and other hangers on who are a constant drain on their income.

For all these reasons, professional boxers are not like old soldiers. Rather than fading away too many of them come back to the ring long after their best fighting days are behind them. With the notable exception of Rocky Marciano, it is hard to think of a big-name ex-boxer who has retired and who has not made a comeback. It is also hard to think of one who did so successfully and with dignity. Joe Louis,

Sugar Ray Robinson, Joe Frazier and Muhammad Ali are but a few examples of fighters who at the peaks of their careers covered themselves in glory before allowing themselves to be humiliated on the comeback trail. While there are usually financial reasons for these second comings, it would be a gross oversimplification to view them exclusively in monetary terms. Because the role of 'boxer' comes to be absolutely central to a fighter's sense of who he is and the ring the main stage for his character display, once he is deprived of this platform he may experience levels of dissonance which, in the absence of other life interests and occupations, can be alleviated only by a return to the canvas. Promoters are usually happy to facilitate the comeback trail, particularly if it involves former big-name fighters. But boxing is not like other branches of show business. A singer like Frank Sinatra can make a dozen comebacks without seriously damaging his health. His timing may be off and he may be weaker, but, unlike in boxing, these failings will not increase the likelihood of him sustaining brain damage should he return to the public stage.

In the United States organisations such as the Veteran Boxers' Association have been set up to help alleviate some of the misery experienced by former pro-fessionals (Sammonds, 1990: 244). To date the fragmentation of the administration of boxing has worked against the introduction of multilateral systems dedicated to promoting the welfare of current and former prize fighters. This came a step closer in 1993 with the formation in Britain of the PBA (Professional Boxers' Association). Under the stewardship of ex-world featherweight champion Barry McGuigan, the PBA is committed to establishing educational and vocationally relevant training programmes, setting up pension schemes and working with the medical authorities to make boxing a safer sport. However, the PBA's highest priority is helping young professionals form sensible contractual relationships with managers and promoters.

According to Simon Block, the assistant general secretary to the BBBC, within Britain the relationship between managers and promoters is a complex one. Officially they are considered two categories of persons and they are licensed as such. This tacitly recognises that the manager's job is to look after the best interests of his fighters while the promoter's main interest is the successful production of an event for profit. Clearly, the two functions are not always compatible. For this reason the courts have ruled that a conflict of interest can exist in the juxtaposition of the two roles and that no single person should be both manager and promoter. However, the Office of Fair Trading has ruled counter to this, stating that preventing people being both managers and promoters is acting 'in restraint of trade'. The BBBC has responded to this confusion by including in the contracts through which they license both managers and promoters a clause which is designed to protect the interest of fighters should they find themselves fighting on the bill of an event promoted by their manager. This appears to be very important in the British boxing scene as, despite the ideals of the BBBC, the reality is that almost all top promoters, such as Frank Warren, Mickey Duff and Barry

Hearn, are also managers who regularly use fighters from their own stables to fight on the cards of the shows which they themselves are promoting.

Problems arise if for whatever reason a fighter is not ready for a particular fight in which his manager cum promoter has a vested interest. For instance, when Barry McGuigan lost his world title to Steve Cruz in the desert heat of Las Vegas in 1986 he claimed that he was not ready to fight and that he did so only on the insistence of his manager, Barney Eastwood, who had a stake in the overall promotion.[2] It is highly likely that experiences such as this motivated McGuigan to take a leading role in the establishment of a boxers' union. It is too early to judge whether the PBA will have a significant impact on the way boxing is run locally or globally. At least in the short term it is likely that the majority of professional boxers will continue to be exploited.

And yet, despite the physical risks associated with boxing and the sport's undeniable history of gross exploitation it continues to be an attractive prospect for thousands of young men with nowhere else to go. From drawing rooms in suburbia and in the debating chambers of universities boxing may have the appearance of an activity belonging to a bygone and more barbaric age. Scrutinised from the vantage point of inner-city streets, however, boxing looks like a rare intervention on behalf of order and civility. As a young, relatively unknown professional from a gym in London's East End put it:

> I ask myself, if I wasn't doing this, what else would I be doing? There is nothing for
> me in this area. Without it I'd be nowhere. The only thing around here is thieving.
> All my mates are on drugs. I'm almost the opposite. I get a real buzz out of being fit.
> It's nice to get up early and go for a run. (MacKinnon and White, 1995: 2)

Indeed, what would he be doing? Under prevailing conditions of urban poverty, with all of its problems boxing can still be perceived as a liberating experience. It does keep youngsters off mean streets and teach them a particular code of honour, including self-respect and respect for one's opponent. However, the ghetto experience needs to be kept in the forefront of a fighter's consciousness if he is to be successful in the ring. The ghetto, with all of its vices and temptations, must be kept within touching distance of the occupational subculture of the boxer, which is why so many boxers self-destruct once they make the big time. This is the paradox which is at the heart of boxing and which is exploited so well by those whose own wealth depends upon the efforts of others who would rather take their chances in the ring than in the streets.

In the 1980s world heavyweight boxing was once again lit up by a boy from a New York ghetto, Mike Tyson. More attention is paid to Iron Mike's career in the concluding chapter. At this stage, suffice it to say that just like so many before him, Tyson seemed incapable of understanding that, if he was to stay at the top, the

---

[2] In 1992 McGuigan lost a libel case over this allegation to Eastwood.

ghetto experience was a force which he could unleash only in the ring for a specified number of three-minute intervals. Until he met James 'Buster' Douglas in Tokyo in 1990, Iron Mike had destroyed everything put before him in the ring. Unfortunately, he also destroyed almost everything he touched outside boxing, especially women. In February 1992, he was convicted of raping a black beauty queen from the state of Rhode Island by an Indiana court and sent to prison for six years. The question to be answered is to what extent was Tyson's success in the ring dependent upon his social inadequacies outside it and, crucially, did the boxing subculture within which he was carefully nurtured maintain these character failings precisely because they made Tyson a better fighter?

Conclusion

In ancient Rome slaves had fought as gladiators to save their own lives and in the hope of winning their freedom. In the pre-industrial towns and cities of Regency England, prize fighters emerged from urban poverty traps to fight for financial security and self-respect. A hundred years later across the Atlantic, from the slums of Boston to the shanties of New Orleans, immigrants slugged it out with working-class Americans for ethnic pride and personal reward. As the twentieth century progressed, throughout the developing world, pugilism's more sophisticated offspring, boxing, emerged as a product of a more complex, but nonetheless deprived, inner-city landscape. As the following case studies reveal, however, just as in the past pugilism had been a noble art to those who practised and patronised it, boxing, for those who are engaged in it today, means so much more than a flight from poverty.

3

Hartford, USA: the exploitation
of disadvantage

While the causal dynamics within the nexus of economic, class, ethnic and racial structures which frame amateur and professional boxing in the United States are exceedingly complex, it has been suggested that there is a tendency for them to overlap around the experiences of young males within settings of urban poverty (Hare, 1971). However, observing that there are long-standing relationships between urban poverty, youth culture and boxing does not, of itself, enable us to understand the nature of these relationships. From the back pages of the newspapers or from the television screen in the lounge, we are able to understand little in terms of the experiences, feelings and motivations of young men who live in the inner city, living through both poverty and boxing. We are not certain why and how male youth and urban poverty appear to have an unbroken bond with the prize ring. By and large, we have left interpretative explanations to the cliche mongers of Hollywood: the 'hungry fighter', the ragged youth who walks off the city streets and into a boxing club with anger in his eyes, fire in his heart and dynamite in both fists and proceeds to bludgeon his way to a world title and its attendant riches.

As with most myths, there is a grain of truth which underpins this characterisation, but the full reality of why people get involved, and stay involved, in boxing is far more complex. Unlike the farm systems of many other professional sports, which tend to be embedded in the school system and a range of other visible and accountable institutions, the world of professional boxing is subterranean, located in pockets of urban poverty and largely unexposed to the public gaze. What follows attempts to demystify the occupational socialisation of the boxer and reveal how, rather than being a strategy for escaping from urban deprivation, learning to box, in complex ways, is a means of coping with life in the ghetto.

For more than a century the United States has been the centre of the boxing universe and at the core of that centre has been the American ghetto. The ghetto is a concept implying both material and less visible, social-structural qualities. It is a physical description of a certain type of urban habitat: a boundaried area of inner-city slumland characterised by decaying buildings, overcrowded and substandard dwellings, ill-kept streets and alleyways and a general profile of confined dilapidation. Ghetto also indicates a certain relationship with the wider society. It is a term which bespeaks institutional factors such as race, poverty, social class and powerlessness, which knot together and deposit within hidden inner-city boundaries the most underprivileged and discriminated against segments of a given social order. Finally, ghetto is also a descriptor of how people live through the shared experience of urban poverty: the things people who live in the ghetto do to get by; the language they use; the work they do; the music they make and listen to; the way they dress and walk; the food they eat; the drugs they deal and take; the crimes they commit; the games they play; and all of the other practices and products which grow out of living in poverty in the shadow of affluence. In sum, ghetto characterises a way of life that emerges as people in the inner-city confront and live through multiple structures of disadvantage. This chapter looks in detail at the relationship between the American ghetto and the farm system which has produced most of the twentieth century's greatest fighters. The bulk of the field work for this chapter was done in the early 1980s when the United States was experiencing the first phase of Reaganomics and ratios of relative affluence to deprivation were increasing.

The setting

From the distant hills, looking down and across the flood plain of the river valley, Hartford rises out of the evergreens like a small version of Manhattan. Glass and concrete, sky-scraping office blocks cluster around the centre creating a giant stockade within which the city's corporate business commuters ply their daily trades. The broader picture of cutting-edge affluence is deceptive. Below the horizon, in the shadows of the houses of corporate finance and partly hidden beneath the elevated network of highways which bring the commuters to and from work, there is a wasteland of urban decomposition and social subsistence.

Here the run-down old and flimsily built new form an abrasive architectural alliance punctuated by derelict building sites and garbage-strewn tracts of open ground. An occasional dilapidated eighteenth-century town house, long since converted into small apartments, hints at the inner city's prouder colonial heritage. More common are the solid brownstone terraces and corner houses built for prosperous single families towards the end of the last century, but now haphazardly redeveloped as a warren of low-calibre rented accommodation for the city's poor. But this area of decayed residential grandeur is insufficient to meet their demand. In its hinterland, squeezed between a stratum of half-empty factories and warehouses, and the green belt which separates the city from the suburbs, there is a purpose-built network of low-income housing projects, into which the poorest of the city's poor are drawn. Every American city has a ghetto, and this is Hartford's.

The Charter Oak housing project is as bad as it gets. It was constructed shortly after World War Two as temporary housing for returning service veterans and their families. In keeping with its military heritage, the layout of the streets is grid-like and, in their original condition, the buildings would not have been out of place in any American army camp. An internment camp impression is reinforced by an eight-foot-high steel wire fence which contains the south and west sides of the project while the northern perimeter is marked by the steel and concrete undercarriage of the inter-state highway carrying traffic to points between New York City and Montreal. The aspect of quarantine is barely relieved at the east end of the estate as it opens out on to Flatbush Avenue, a busy, four-lane, cross-town arterial which divides Charter Oak from a no-man's-land of warehouses, railway sidings and the commercial centre of the city beyond.

Forty years of neglect and intensive occupation by the city's poorest families have gradually and seriously undermined the project's original purpose as a temporary reservation for returning military heroes. The buildings are all in a state of chronic disrepair, held together it seems only by the creative and profane murals of graffiti which adorn the outer walls of most houses and apartments. Crumbling brickwork, broken and boarded up windows, leaking roofs, poor drainage and rising damp are features of most dwellings. The narrow streets, uneven and pock-marked with craters, are strewn with a synthetic tumbleweed of waste paper and household garbage. Along the sidewalks, on the threadbare grass verges and in virtually any open space, are scattered a wide variety of used and abused cars, many of which, long since, have been abandoned and picked clean: the cast-off transport of a bygone era of ultra-cheap gasoline.

In Charter Oak unemployment is high, with up to two-thirds of the adult residents out of work. Those who have jobs tend to be part of an itinerant, minimum-wage labour force which makes the short journey down town to service the menial needs of those working in Hartford's thriving nine-to-five commercial sector. People with better jobs or better prospects simply do not come to or linger long in the likes of Charter Oak. As the welfare officer responsible for this area put it:

> This place and places like this are the bottom line. Nobody chooses to live here. You only live here when you have nowhere else to go. At least I don't think many people live here by choice. They may tolerate it, but given half a chance most of them would be away tomorrow. But very few get that chance. Those that do just up and leave.

Many of the families in the project are single parent and the local economy tends to boom and slump with the bi-weekly cycle of welfare payments and food stamps. Most of the money goes on rent or is directed towards the few heavily fortified and over-priced food markets and package stores (off-sales) which stand like trading posts on the fringes of Charter Oak. Surrounded by a tall wire fence and patrolled by a pair of lean and threatening German shepherd dogs, Giorgio's general store is a typical ghetto business. It thrives on an inversion which has taken the shopping out of the cities into suburban malls, leaving behind the poor and needy, along with a handful of resilient entrepreneurs to prey on their captive custom.

The overwhelming majority of people who live in Charter Oak are either African-American or Hispanic. Out of approximately 800 households less than fifty are white. Consequently, as well as being economically and environmentally deprived, the residents of Charter Oak are oppressed by broader structures of discrimination which, in the United States, determine a correlation between poverty and skin colour. This racial dimension compounds the other layers of social disadvantage making Charter Oak one of a multitude of repositories for America's under-class: a stagnating community of predominantly non-white unemployed and under-employed and their dependants, struggling to survive day to day.

Charter Oak is not the sort of community where people spend warm summer evenings sitting and gossiping on porches and doorsteps. It is not a safe place to hang out, particularly at night. Frequently a muffled silence is pierced by the wail of a siren as a police cruiser sweeps through the project. Deprivation, frustration and boredom combine to fuel an always threatening and often violent street life. Hartford's Police Department considers Charter Oak to be the worst neighbourhood for violent crime in the city. Drug-related gang warfare is endemic and the murder rate in this quadrant is as high as anywhere in the United States. Perpetrators and their victims are overwhelmingly young, African-American or Hispanic males.

Alternatives to the deadly pastime of running in the streets are few and far between, and what is on offer may seem tame by comparison. In the heart of the project stands an oblong block-house, somewhat larger than any of the warren of dwellings which surround it. This is the Charter Oak community centre and, like its neighbouring buildings, it is heavily daubed with multicoloured graffiti and in a poor state of repair. Most of the windows are either bricked or boarded up and the rest are screened with heavy, wire-mesh grills. Large sections of cement and plaster on the outer walls have crumbled away, leaving the building with a mottled and camouflaged appearance. This is not the place for community singing, amateur dramatics, bridge or other forms of family recreation, and the city's housing development executive has given up trying to impose a formal timetable of rational community use.

In the daytime, when the heavy steel door which guards the entrance to the hall remains barred, local youngsters use the exterior of the building for a variety of improvised sporting activities. The broad and flat rear of the centre looks on to an open square, making an ideal backdrop for a number of improvised ball games. The meshed window grills, together with the drain pipes, make the north face of the building a tricky climb, and the concrete canopy which overhangs the main door is an excellent highboard from which to execute acrobatic leaps into the tangle of shrubs and bushes below. If this becomes too exhausting, there are always the folk murals to add to and, as the daylight begins to fade, the sheltered doorway becomes a favourite gathering area for talking, horse play, listening to music and shouting comments to anyone who happens by.

In the early evening, a troubled caretaker pushes and curses his way through the crowded porch and unlocks the steel door. The inside of the community centre is little better than its exterior. With broken doors and window frames, flaking paint work and crumbling plaster, the whole place is badly in need of renovation. A large hall, complete with stage and gallery, dominates the centre. Originally intended for public meetings and other forms of community entertainment, the seating has been removed to make way for the spontaneous local drama acted out in the chaotic game of basketball, which is the main event of each evening. There is no obvious structure to the game: no referees; no official teams; no formal scoring system; no out of bounds; no stoppages for fouls; and no time keeping. It appears to be every man for himself as players join and leave the game as they please and attack baskets at either end of the hall. A pass is rare and most of the time the ball is carried end to end through dazzling displays of dribbling, to arrive in or near the basket after an acrobatic lay-up or shot from an improbable angle and distance.

The atmosphere is thick and scented with a mix of cigarette smoke, reefer, alcohol and the more pungent odour of the poorly maintained washrooms. Around the edges of the game, on the stage and in the hallways, young men and women hang out, half watching the play, teasing and joking with each other and calling out to the players as they go hurtling by.

The conversations are necessarily loud, shouted above the pandemonium of the basketball game and competing with a confusion of rhythm blasting out from the large portable tape recorders spread throughout the company. In a parallel social world, gangs of younger boys and girls dash in and out of the rubble-strewn rooms which open into the main hall, demonstrating their own spontaneous athleticism as they weave in and out of the basketball game, shrieking at one another and adding their own shrill commentary to the general discord.

The boxing club

Beneath the unrestrained youth culture surrounding the basketball game there is a more formally organised drama taking place. Each evening, in a basement room directly below the main hall, the members of the MBC (Memorial Boxing Club) gather to share in a different sort of ritual. Anybody wishing to enter the club has first, as we have seen, to thread a path through the throngs gathered in the entrance to the community centre and turn across the crowded lobby before descending a short flight of stairs into the darkness below. At the foot of the stairs there is a reinforced wooden and steel door which is barred from within, and it takes a sustained drumming to coincide with a lull in the activity taking place inside before the bolts are drawn and the visitor is invited into a different world.

The club consists of a single, rectangular room, no larger than 30 feet by 35 feet. Immediately in front of the door, like a muted belfry, hang three large, worn, sail-cloth punch-bags: heavy, heavier and heaviest. Flush to the near-side wall, and sited ominously next to a set of scales, stands a small, electrically powered Turkish bath. It is hard to imagine the need for such a device since the ceiling of the gymnasium is slung with the central heating pipes for the rooms above. Owing to a defective thermostat, they carry a volume of boiling water twenty-four hours a day, throughout the seasons, ensuring that the whole room heats up like one big sweat box. When it rains, a steady flow of sluggish grey water drains in from the streets above and gradually evaporates in the unnatural heat of the basement, exaggerating the sweated body heat of the boxers and making the atmosphere in the gym fetid and steamy.

One half of the club is dominated by an undersized boxing ring with loosely hanging ropes and worn canvas, long since rendered threadbare by ten years of dancing feet and falling bodies. Surrounding the ring is a series of rough wooden benches; on these and on the hooks above are draped a mixture of sports gear, street clothes and the general bric-a-brac of the boxer's trade: gleaming red and black boxing gloves; high-waisted shorts; flashy robes; protective headgear and defensive equipment for the waistline and groin; a selection of mouth-guards; multicoloured boxing vests; jump-ropes; hand wraps; and several pairs of boxing boots. Every inch of wall space is covered with a colourful array of photographs, posters, magazine features and yellowing newsprint, blending to herald the past and present achievements of the club's own heroes and the feats of boxing's legendary champions.

The most important figure in the club, its manager and patron, J. 'Mack' Murphy, leans on a broom in the centre of the gymnasium, taking a break from a vigorous spell of sweeping which has left the bottoms of his $350 business suit speckled with mud and dust. In opposite corners of the ring, two ebony-skinned youths wearing gloves and protective headgear move slowly from tiptoe to tiptoe, loosening and flexing their muscles and gulping in precious draughts of the warm and clammy air. One or two others lean across the ropes to give advice, tie a loose glove, offer a drink and generally act as seconds. Throughout the rest of the room, skinny boys, athletically developed teenagers and powerfully built young men sit on the benches or rest against the walls, likewise breathing heavily in competition for the scarce oxygen.

Apart from the fidgeting of the youths in the ring, the scene is relaxed and sedentary until the red second hand of the large clock on the wall sweeps around to twelve and, in the baritone voice and brisk manner of a Boston bar tender, Mack bellows, 'Time!'. The gymnasium erupts into life. The boxers in the ring gingerly leave their respective corners to begin an ever-diminishing circular dance around the faded canvas. As they draw close, there is a sudden change of tempo and direction as one or other of them darts inside and both fighters momentarily become engulfed in a blur of jabs, hooks, crosses and upper-cuts, before breaking away to recommence orbiting soft-shoe. The sporadic slaps and thuds of leather against flesh blend into the steadier beat of more measured energy and aggression being unleashed outside the ring: muffled combinations hammered into the heavy bags; the metronome rhythm of jump-ropes slapping off the concrete floor and the jarring rat-tat-tat-tat of the speed bag. Meanwhile, several young fighters manage to exhaust themselves without equipment, boxing shadows or stabbing and snorting at their own image reflected in a full-length mirror which dominates one wall. In the remaining space, other club members balance on mildewed matting and execute an exhausting series of callisthenics: sit-ups; push-ups; sit-ups; squat-thrusts; sit-ups; toe-touching; and inevitably back to the stomach-hardening sit-ups.

Even the manager takes some aggressive sweeps with his broom, guiding a dark trickle of dust mixed with the evening rain water towards a small drain in the middle of the floor. At the same time he provides his audience, real or imaginary, with a loud and abrasive running commentary, shouting advice and insults to the fighters in the ring and encouragement and abuse to the characters working throughout the gymnasium. The whole performance builds to a frenzied physical climax and deafening crescendo as the second hand sweeps towards twelve for the third time and, without looking up, Mack interrupts his own diatribe once more to call, 'Time!', bringing the scene to a gasping halt.

The athletes in the ring, the young men boxing their own shadows, the powerful men hammering the heavy bags, the manager in the $350 business suit and the physical structure of the basement gymnasium are at the core of an occupational subculture: a social milieu which connects the impoverished streets of Charter Oak and the leisure practices of its inhabitants at the MBC to the multimillion dollar atmosphere of the sports entertainment industry and Madison Square Garden. The roots of this process and the bedrock of the subculture are to be found in the everyday practice of boys and young men growing up in and around the streets of Charter Oak.

The farm system: street life

The story of the MBC begins in the maze of houses, apartments and streets which hem in the Charter Oak community centre. It is here that the overwhelming majority of boxers who use the club live or originate from, and it is through their early experiences in this modern ghetto that most of the current members developed an appetite for boxing and were drawn into its subculture. Most of the club members first became actively involved with boxing during or before early adolescence, between the ages of ten and fourteen. Asked why they became involved, they provide no single, simple reason. There is a complex range of motivations, some complementary, others less so, which encouraged and continue to encourage their association with the sport.

From more searching inquiries, it became clear that the boxing subculture is grounded in the social relations which emerge as child's play becomes embroiled within the aggressive, male-dominated and brutally athletic youth culture of the housing project and the surrounding neighbourhood. To a greater or lesser extent, all sports can be thought of as relatively formal extensions of activities made up and encountered within play. Playing is something which children do naturally, as a facet of growing into an unknown physical and social environment. Through play, the child learns concepts of time, space, things and people, and develops the social and physical skills to move among them. Among other things, children learn to run and jump, to catch and throw and engage in rough and tumble. They also begin to learn the appropriate social skills to accompany a nascent athleticism.

However, while the impulse to play might be a universal one, the style and product of the process of play vary according to the cultural surroundings within which the child grows up. Play begins within touching distance of the youngster, but gradually develops out of reach and, in many respects, out of control, to include the objects, people and sentiments which comprise an expanding social and physical environment. In this way, the child's urge to play is progressively harnessed to a pattern of social practice already established in the home and in the streets and school yards of the local community. Whereas in upper- and middle-class communities children are kept within the adult-patrolled sanctuary between home and school, often until they are teenagers, in a community such as Charter Oak at a relatively early age children do their playing and socialising in and around the local streets. In terms of physical capacities, attitudes and motivations, it is at this point that the foundations of the boxing subculture are laid.

Ask the young boys of Charter Oak what they do when they are not at home or at school and they will tell you that they 'hang out' or 'mess around', doing nothing in particular. Watching them, eavesdropping on their conversations and consulting with adults who live in the neighbourhood confirms Corrigan's (1979) observations: that when unsupervised working-class kids get together in and around the city streets to 'do nothing', they actually become involved in a wide range of energetic activities. Messing around in Charter Oak includes a range of standard and improvised sports and games, particularly versions of basketball. It also involves skateboarding, commando-style assaults up the walls and across the rooftops of local buildings, break-neck gang chases and skirmishes around the project, individual and gang fighting, disruptive forays into the city's main shopping area and a variety of petty illegal and antisocial activities which often result in real games of cops and robbers with the local police.

The kids of Charter Oak do not need to attend gym classes or go to summer sports camps to develop the athletic ability and temperament suited to boxing. Many of the delinquent activities of inner-city juveniles are aggressively athletic and contain an element of risk. As has been argued elsewhere (Sugden and Yiannakis, 1982), while antisocial, within the context of urban deprivation, such activities can also be thought of as local improvisations, inspired by a more generally displayed youthful need for mastery, competence, challenge and adventure. This is the core of messing about for the youngsters of the project and, through a prolonged involvement in the local street scene, they grow to be physically assertive and to be quick on their feet. They learn to have hands as quick as their wits: attributes of some importance in an environment within which youngsters learn at a tender age that the weakest go to the wall.

Among the retinue of activities involved in messing around is an established pattern of street fighting. Much of this begins as semi-playful rough and tumble, but as kids get older it develops into more serious and exacting trials of strength and courage. There is nothing exceptional about this. It has been observed that at a certain stage in their social development, boys everywhere seem to settle disputes and build reputations around competitive demonstrations of physical prowess (Tiger, 1971). Veblen (1953) referred to this feature of boyhood as 'the predacious interval', a passing phase of growing up which occurs between the protective custody of the home and the regulatory institutions of adulthood, wherein less abrasive and more socially acceptable strategies for settling disputes and earning status are made available. While a potential for fighting has been observed to be common to all boys, as Lefkowitz *et al.* (1977) argue, whether or not they do fight and how long the predacious interval lasts are culturally, rather than biologically, determined.

In the ghetto, where boys spend a considerable amount of time hanging around the streets, social conditions ensure that the 'predacious interval' begins early and lasts long, until the early teens, when patterns of individual fighting begin to merge with a more sinister, and potentially more deadly, network of gang affiliations. This atmosphere of 'might is right' guides certain individuals to the boxing club, but not all for the same reasons. As would be expected, some youngsters get involved because they are good at fighting and have a proven record of 'good hands'. For them the boxing club is viewed as a place where they can extend skills and reputations already established in the streets and spotlight otherwise deviant skills for more formal approval.

For others who lack weight, strength or natural fighting ability, the MBC is viewed as a place where they can learn to take care of themselves. Charter Oak affords rough justice to those who cannot or will not fight. The pecking order of the streets is generally indifferent to relative factors of size, weight, skill or experience, and the toughest kid on the block is generally the biggest kid on the block. The boxing club turns out to be a good bet for adolescents who have learned the importance of being physically assertive but invariably lose out in a meritocracy where brute strength counts for everything. In the first place, regular work-outs at the gym improve their overall chances of survival, if not victory, should they be caught up in a brawl at school or in the streets. Secondly, and of greater significance in the long term, these youths find that within the boxing subculture they are given the chance to earn respect, using the aggressive currency of the streets, but within a neutral structure which, as much as possible, equalises inherited physical differences and takes account of different levels of skill and experience.

Even some of the hardest cases in the neighbourhood are attracted by the MBC's neutrality. Charter Oak is notorious for its youth gangs and their violent conflicts. Boys who live on the estate are expected to show allegiance to one or other of these local street gangs and participate in confrontations with rival organisations. As they grow older, the stakes are raised and their chances of getting seriously hurt increase as fist-fights give way to skirmishes with knives and, occasionally, guns. Those wishing to opt out of this potentially deadly factionalism face a major problem inasmuch as the activities of the gangs are focal to the process through which young men are supposed to display their masculinity and earn respect in the local, male-dominated youth scene. The MBC offers a solution to this dilemma by concentrating on aggressive skills which are broadly similar to the cut and thrust of adolescent street life, but practising them in a controlled and relatively safe environment. Moreover, because boxing is a sport with a traditional following in the inner city, particularly among blacks and Hispanics, the prestige which youths can earn within the boxing subculture tends to travel with them outside the club. Carried outside on the backs of jackets and on the sides of kit bags, the symbols of the boxing club act as a neutral colour and give the carrier a kind of informal immunity, while at the same time enabling him to hold his head high. Learning how to fight in the streets, and developing strategies of avoiding fighting in the streets, emerge as powerful complementary motivations for embracing the boxing subculture.

While learning how to cope physically with a cycle of confrontation and challenge, the young men of Charter Oak pick up a streetwise repertoire of attitudes and sentiments: a stoic, male code of honour and courage; a simmering 'machismo', requiring cool-headedness and resilience in the face of danger. These values, activated by a streak of machiavellian opportunism, invest social encounters with an atmosphere of ruthless self-preservation and a sense of timing whereby 'to get in first' becomes the rule of thumb. As one fighter remarked, in order to get through the day in the ghetto, a youth has to be 'tough-tough', that is, to be cool and calculating and able to stand up for himself. When translated into the ring, toughness and coolness blend to provide the foundations of 'a fighting heart', a quality much valued in a business built around the spectacle of giving and taking punishment.

The push of inner-city youth culture in the development of a boxing subculture is augmented by the sport's traditional affinity with the urban poor. As Edwards (1981) argues, sport in general takes on an enlarged significance in the ghetto. An overarching ideology, or sports creed, penetrates areas like Charter Oak, stressing the all-American virtues of sport and its capacity to serve as an escalator to wealth and status for those who are effectively barred from other avenues of social mobility. Because only a tiny minority of the multitudes who try can ever make a decent living from professional sport, Edwards views this promise as false and damaging to the general development of black communities in America. This view is endorsed by Brown (1978), who views the massive commitment to sport by minorities as an indication of oppression and a buttress to racism, rather than a sign of integration or equality.

From the perspective of a young man growing up in a pocket of urban poverty such as Charter Oak, the image of the black or Hispanic professional sport superstar is undoubtedly a powerful one. Other careers and educational opportunities tend not to be available. Even if they were, in a largely unsupervised adolescent world, given a choice between training to be a professional athlete or preparing for a career in law or teaching, the vast majority of teenagers would opt for sport. Also, because the farm system of professional boxing is not tied up with survival in the education system, unlike American football, basketball and, to a certain extent, baseball, it is held in special regard by the children of the inner cities, who traditionally underachieve at school.

The farm system: the manager

It would be mistaken to conclude from the evidence presented so far that all inner-city areas like Charter Oak spontaneously produce professional boxers. Not all pockets of urban poverty produce and sustain boxing subcultures. They provide the raw materials, delivered in quantities of muscle, blood and the streetwise attributes outlined above. But, by themselves, the urban poor do not have the resources to organise and finance the farm system for the production of professional fighters. This is generally done from the outside, by people who, at least in part, view the deprivations of the people of the ghetto and their special relationship to sport as an opportunity for developing and marketing athletic talent. The MBC is no exception and, as a material and ideological presence, it is not an initiative of the residents of Charter Oak.

The club was established by Mack, who continues to be its leading patron and general manager. He is a successful criminal lawyer, with expensive offices in the heart of Hartford. While he likes to refer to his humble, Irish-émigré heritage, Mack is third generation and from solidly upper-middle-class stock. His motives for being involved in boxing revolve around two sets of values, which seem to be ethically incompatible, but which have been operationally welded together to form the guiding philosophy of the club: missionary amateurism and commercial professionalism.

In the first instance, his exposure in the home and at school to middle-class values on sport, in concert with his own experiences as a boxer as a young man, have instilled in Mack a firm belief in the character-building qualities of the ring. This has been reinforced through an ongoing involvement with law enforcement, wherein he is professionally associated with some of the more serious social problems arising out of urban decay. Sport is traditionally valued by a variety of public agencies as a deterrent to juvenile crime and as a vehicle for the rehabilitation of young offenders. Keeping 'at-risk' youths off the streets and resocialising those who have fallen by the wayside are features of a welfare ethic which has been central to inner-city sports provision for more than a century (Clarke and Critcher, 1985). This ethic is central to the boxing subculture and is personified by Mack, who is an active member of the PAL (Police Athletic League), an organisation dedicated to the provision of sport for kids in the inner city. Several of Mack's best young fighters have been in trouble with the law and a few were actually recruited by him as they passed through the city's criminal justice system (one such recruit, a former armed robber, who was starting out when this research was being carried out, went on to win the WBO light-heavyweight championship of the world).

While the PAL provided some of the equipment which helped Mack set up the MBC, most of the moral and financial support for the club has been his own. Mack suggests that he selected Charter Oak as the site for his club because of its poverty and high rates of juvenile crime. He claims that the MBC tempts youngsters away from the trouble-filled streets, keeps them on the straight and narrow and, for a gifted few, offers them opportunity for fame and fortune.

Despite the caring tone, it is this last aspect, the production of professional fighters, which in practice emerges as the most powerful driving force behind the MBC. Mack might well have had a certain amount of concern for the youth of Hartford's urban poor when he went prospecting for a home for his boxing club. But when he settled on Charter Oak, there can be little doubt that he was mostly influenced by its potential in terms of yielding street-hardened recruits for training for the prize ring. The MBC is an amateur club, but at the same time and in the same space it is a professional stable. The vast majority of the forty or more youngsters who come regularly to the gym understand it not as a temple of muscular Christianity, but as a meeting place where they can get a good work-out, exchange information about the local street scene, box a little, improve their standing in the neighbourhood and rub shoulders with the professional fighters in whose footsteps they may tread. While this might be a slowly dawning aspiration for most of the new members, as they take their first steps through the doors of the basement, whether they realise it or not, Mack views each and every one of them as a potential professional.

Indeed, while all of the newcomers to the club are aware of its professional dimension, initially at least most of them are more concerned with non-occupational issues such as having a good time, staying in shape, winning junior and amateur titles and travelling to tournaments. One of the more significant features of the boxing subculture is the way in which the young fighters' original, avocational definitions of the situation are gradually and subtly remodelled around commercial objectives which are clearly professional. This is achieved through the structure of the club in tandem with the instrumental interventions of the manager, who guides the boxers through three levels of participation: junior, amateur and professional.

The farm system: the juniors

The most numerous attendees are the juniors, the bottom tier and foundation of the pyramid-like boxing subculture. The youngest age at which a person can be officially registered as a boxer is twelve years. In practice, however, nobody checks birth certificates and, so long as a boy looks big enough and tough enough to handle himself in the ring, he is allowed into the gym to train. Thus, the age range of the juniors who frequent the MBC is between ten and sixteen, the point at which a boxer must either become an amateur or give up the sport. In the beginning the commitment of most of the juniors to boxing is open ended and a matter of individual choice, coming and going as they please and putting in as much or as little effort as they see fit. This intermittent pattern of participation is a trial period, during which time the youngsters test their own ideas, aspirations and capacities against the established procedures of the club.

Once inside the gym, they become involved in a straightforward pattern of training, which all of the fighters share. It begins with a period of warm-ups involving stretching exercises, callisthenics and light work-outs with jump-ropes and the punch-bags. The warm-up period is followed by sessions of gloved sparring in the ring. Once the sparring is over, the boxers commence a second, but more intense circuit of training outside the ring. The whole sequence of warm-ups, sparring and circuit training is paced at three-minute intervals, with a minute rest in between, imitating the rhythm of rounds and breaks in a professional boxing match.

While each cohort of fighters experiences the same pattern of training, more or less, simultaneously and in the same space, the quality of the experience is different. For the juniors, the routine is not very vigorous. They do not have to spend much time getting fit for the ring, but tend to rely on the natural fitness of youth to carry them through. A junior boxing match is fast and furious, but it is also very short (a maximum of three two-minute rounds) and while there are many punches thrown, few tend to have the weight to do much damage or sap much strength. The juniors spend most of their time in the club acquiring the boxer's style: learning how to look, feel, think and sound like a boxer. They receive little formal tuition from the manager and, for the most part, the youngsters learn to be boxers by playing at being boxers. They hang around the gym, taking in the performances of the older fighters and doing their best to copy them. Any coaching that they do receive tends to come informally from their more established peers or from older fighters. Sometimes, one or other of the club's professionals may take time out of his own schedule to correct a stance or offer a word of advice to a newcomer.

This is an important and unique feature of the boxing subculture in the United States. All professional sports have some kind of farm system, formal or otherwise, through which athletes of professional potential are recruited, trained and tested and from which an elite is selected for the upper levels of the sports entertainment industry. In most cases, such a farm system is structured so that the stages of occupational socialisation are contained within relatively independent organisations. For instance, the stages of the farm systems of American football and basketball are contained within the structure of interscholastic and intercollegiate sports as well as training programmes built beneath the professional leagues.

In the MBC, junior boxers learn their trade alongside and under the same roof as their amateur and professional mentors. Boys of twelve and younger come to the gym and find themselves involved, shoulder to thigh, in an unbroken pattern of training with boxers of local, national and international repute. They undress alongside one another on the same rough wooden benches, share the same clothes hooks, use the same equipment, drink out of the same water bottles and dance to the tune of the same manager. There can be little doubt that learning the role of the boxer while actually performing and training under the gaze of experienced amateurs and professionals is a most powerful mechanism of anticipatory socialisation.

Mack simply fine-tunes this process. He provides the facilities and the incentives, recruits the performers and, from a distance, stage manages the interactions between them. He observes the youngsters as they spar and monitors their progress in local tournaments, such as the Junior Olympics and the Silver Mittens, events which themselves appear as microcosms of the big time.

The New England Silver Mittens take place each year in Lowell Boys' Club in the old mill town of Lowell, Massachusetts. The preliminaries take place on three consecutive Friday evenings and are followed a week later by the finals, which are spread over the weekend. Lowell is about eighty miles east of Hartford and Mack uses a large station wagon to transport his young team back and forth. Most of the junior fighters are packed in the back while alongside Mack sit a couple of the more experienced amateur boxers who will help him in the dressing room and at ring-side. For some of the novices the trip to the Silver Mittens is the first time they have strayed far from the apron of Hartford. They look, wide eyed, as the New England countryside flashes by and listen enthralled as Mack, beneath the brim of his cowboy hat and between puffs of his cigar, embarks on an equally rolling and colourful commentary, regaling his captive audience with tales of the latest heroics and scandals of the boxing world.

As Mack's station wagon pulls up outside the boys' club the other fighters are beginning to arrive in teams and with supporting casts of trainers, managers, seconds and general hangers-on. Inside, out of the chill November night air, the young fighters mingle, sizing up possible opponents and renewing acquaintances with boys they have fought at previous championships. Those who have been reasonably successful as novices tend to reappear the following year with the beginnings of a pedigree established. Each time they come back they do so as more polished performers after another year of training and appearances in local competitions. In any given weight class many of the better fighters will have boxed against each other up to half a dozen times during their junior careers. Those who are not successful or who are not willing to dedicate themselves to the increasing discipline demanded of more experienced juniors are gradually eased out and, as the years go by, the best and most dedicated juniors emerge at events such as the Mittens.

In this way, the informal pecking order established in the home gym is incorporated into a more comprehensive and open system of regional and national competition through which the most gifted young boxers can emerge and be publicly acclaimed. Above and beyond any short-term value that competitions such as this may have for junior boxing, this annual shake down of young talent has vital long-term significance to individual boxing clubs and to the farm system of professional boxing in general. 'Marvellous' Marvin Hagler, who went on to dominate middleweight boxing in the late 1970s and early 1980s, first came to public attention when he won a junior title at the New England Silver Mittens, as did the jewel in the crown of the MBC, world welterweight champion Marlon Starling. Thus, whether they have teams entered or not, most of the region's boxing managers make a point of attending the Silver Mittens to gauge who are the likely candidates for professional stardom in future years.

However, this pre-professional cattle market has little immediate effect on individual fighters, who are in Lowell for the fun and challenge of boxing for junior titles. They may express vague desires to 'be like' Marlon Starling, Sugar Ray Leonard or Roberto Duran, but at this stage in their careers this does not amount to a crystallised vocational objective to be professional fighters. While people like Mack may view things differently, the juniors are not at the Silver Mittens because they see this as an important phase in a professional apprenticeship. Miguel is a professional who boxed at the Mittens several times, but at the time he did not calculate this as part of his professional training:

> I guess the Mittens were important. I won my first title there and I guess you could say that I learned what it was like to be a boxer there. But I didn't think of that then. I didn't think of the pros. I just took boxing as a sport to do, to enjoy, to keep in shape with, you know. I kept going to the fights and winning trophies and it was good. I didn't think of the pros until I was nineteen.

Likewise, Marlon Starling explains the subliminal nature of this level of pre-professional training:

> Yeh, the Mittens and all that junior stuff was important. It's all experience you need if your gonna' be a contender. You gotta' see it, you gotta' go through it. Not just to win, but to go through it, to get the feel of it. I can say that the years I boxed as a junior gave me a big advantage as an amateur against guys who were just startin' out. I can see that now, but then, y'know, I was just goin' through it and enjoyin' myself. Like when I started boxing I was just interested in making a name for myself at the Silver Mittens. I never used to think about professional boxing, I was too young. I was just going there to win titles and trophies and that was enough. I never had no

idea about turning pro. It was fun. It was great being around all those people, seeing your name in the programme and you got to travel. Nobody thought about the pros then.

The same could not be said of the assembled managers. In Starling's case, Mack spotted him at the Mittens when he was boxing out of another gym in Hartford and persuaded him when he turned amateur to move to the MBC. At this particular tournament there is great excitement among the managers when a previously unknown, powerfully built fourteen-year-old, recently moved from Washington DC to Boston, turns on the style and wins his bout impressively. Who does he fight for? What is his past record? What are the chances of him moving stables? While the different stable managers may be covetous of each other's best fighters, most intense interest centres upon those promising young fighters who box out of youth clubs or church-related associations which do not have a professional dimension. These youngsters are generally considered to be legitimate targets for recruitment into organisations which also have professional boxers.

However, it would be mistaken to view these processes as wholly conspiratorial and instrumentally exploitative. Mack and the other managers with professional interests are not involved in a secret operation to manipulate certain youngsters towards professional careers behind the backs of the guardians of the game's amateur ethos. There is no need, since for the most part the structure and processes which sustain junior and amateur boxing automatically facilitate the needs of the prize ring.

There are no locker rooms in the boys' club, just an empty hall adjacent to and above the hall where the fights will take place. Each team claims its own space and makes it as private as possible by erecting barriers of fold-away chairs. Eventually a doctor shows up and after setting up a makeshift office in a small equipment room, he invites each boxer in for a brisk once-over: eyes, pulse, blood pressure and breathing. Once declared fit they strip to their underwear and join the line for the weigh-in which, with the white officials and mainly black boxers, is evocative of the preparations which were made for slave auctions in antebellum America.

Ten minutes before the first bout is scheduled to start, Mack finishes taping the hands of a ninety-pound novice, 'Cookie', and ties on a huge pair of shiny red leather boxing gloves, crowning him with head-gear to match. As he bandages his hands Mack gives each fighter a forecast of how well the bout is going to go:

> You're fighting a dummy, kid. Look at him, he's scared out of his pants! All you gotta' do is remember what we learned in the gym. Jab it out, keep movin' and pace yourself. Cut down the size of the ring, get him in the corner and finish him off. Let's go!

Eyes wide, peering from within his head-guard, Cookie is led by Mack down the stairs and into the auditorium. An almost all-male crowd of all ages shout their favours as the two young gladiators move towards the flood-lit ring. This is a full-sized canvas square, raised six feet off the ground, with an apron draped with red, white and blue sashes beneath the stars and spangles of Old Glory, which hangs proudly from the rafters. It is a scene deserving better than the muffled version of the national anthem which strains out over an ancient and crackling loudspeaker system.

'In the blue corner, from the Memorial Boxing Club, Hartford...'. After the introductions both contestants stand nervously in opposite corners, listening to the last-minute instructions from their respective mentors. There is a split second of silence as the crowd holds its collective breath until the sharp peel of the bell breaks the spell, and to the roar of the crowd the two fighters rush to meet in the centre of the ring. The loneliest moment at any level of boxing. The seconds are out and it is just you against him. For most of the novice bouts the skills and techniques painstakingly practised in the home gym are forgotten in a first round of toe-to-toe school-yard aggression. During the first break Mack tells his exhausted fighter to cool down and to use the whole ring to stay away from the unpredictable attacks of his opponent, who he says will burn himself out before he can do any damage. 'Keep working the jab, keep working the jab' is the advice of Troy, one of the amateur boxers who is helping Mack to work the corner. Cookie jabs and moves his way through the second round, tiring his opponent, and at the next bell Mack tells him to double up his jabs and follow with straight and hooked right hands. This strategy works and mid-way through the third and final round the referee steps in to stop Cookie dishing out any further punishment. High on his first victory, the 'champ' is escorted out of the ring and back to the dressing room by his seconds and an entourage of young admirers. Cookie will be back. In his wake follows the crestfallen, thirteen-year-old loser, accompanied by nobody except his glowering manager. It is unlikely that he will return to the scene of his humiliation.

As the evening gives way to night the bouts involve older, heavier and more experienced fighters. Some will have met before in this and other junior championships and the best will have developed distinguishing and quasi-professional styles and postures. Hubert, Mack's top junior, is announced into the ring to loud applause as last year's 120 lb champion. He is very well built for a fifteen-year-old, having grown out of the gangliness of early adolescence. His boxing gear fits him tightly, adding to his powerful frame's menacing definition. He gives the audience a series of short, stylish bows and begins to dance and skip close to his corner, throwing an occasional flurry of shadow punches while listening carefully to the final words of advice being shouted to him by Mack and Troy above the din. This is the last of Hubert's three years at the Mittens and he wants to bow out having won a title each year. He already has a psychological edge over his opponent, whom he defeated in the Junior Olympics two years previously. He knows his style and with Mack's advice and some helpful mimic sparring with some of the MBC's amateurs, Hubert has been well prepared for this contest.

At the bell Hubert taps his gloves together, puts up his guard and with measured strides advances cautiously towards the centre of the ring. He checks his advance slightly out of range of his opponent and the two begin a familiar circular dance around the canvas, each trying to cut down the other's space and open up room for an assault. One, seeing or imagining a gap in the other's defence, lunges forward and the two begin to drive back and forth, punching and counter-punching diagonally across the ring. The aggressive stalemate continues until mid-way through the second round when Hubert gets inside his opponent and stuns him with a short right uppercut, forcing him to slump against the ropes where he is immediately assailed with a blinding series of right and left hooks and crosses. The referee moves in and helps to disentangle Hubert's victim from the ropes before giving him a standing eight count. After checking his eyes and rubbing his gloves on his chest he allows the fight to continue. Sensing victory, Hubert is on his opponent instantly with vicious combinations of head and body shots, causing the crowd to rise to their feet to cheer and complain as the referee once more steps in, this time to stop the fight.

Age will preclude Hubert from taking part in next year's Mittens. All being well he will make his debut appearance in the New England Golden Gloves. However, Hubert is at that crossroads stage between street life and the boxing club. A few weeks after his victory in Lowell he is shot in the leg in a gang- and drug-related incident in Charter Oak. Despite his prodigious talent the signs are that Hubert's days in the ring could be numbered.

It is almost midnight when Mack's station wagon is finally repacked with people and equipment ready for the journey back to Hartford. This year's Mittens has been very successful for the MBC and on the final night they are taking away four individual titles, the team award, and the best fighter in the tournament trophy (Hubert). All the fighters will have learned from their experiences, even those who did not win titles, and Mack will have learned lessons about his novices and the rate of development of his more experienced juniors. Most of those who are eligible are keen to come back and try again next year, a commitment reaffirmed at the victory banquet of burgers, fries and ice cream at the highway service station on the road back to the empty streets of Charter Oak.

Mission accomplished, Mack turns his station wagon around and drives twenty-five miles outside the city to his twenty-acre ranch-style home. He has seen enough to know that the Charter Oak gym will continue to produce champions for a few years yet. The diffusion of attitudes and motivations which occurs through the role playing which accompanies the pattern of competition described above, in concert with the status given to winners within the boxing subculture and in the immediate community, ensures that when the most gifted juniors reach the age of sixteen, the vast majority of them accept the invitation of Mack, the gatekeeper, and register as amateurs.

The farm system: the amateurs

From the short-term perspectives of the fighters, amateur boxing is taken seriously and can be considered as a sport in its own right. But, as a critical feature of the subculture, in the long run, this level of performance provides the dynamic link between the fun-filled, itinerant and piecemeal pattern of junior boxing and the no-nonsense occupational world of the professional fighter. Unlike the juniors, who become involved in a reasonably homogeneous pattern of participation, the social organisation of amateur boxing is itself informally broken down around three integrated categories of ability and expectation, negotiated between the boxers and their manager.

First, in keeping with the ethic of moral and social development, which is the official rationale of the club, there is a small group of boxers who, in terms of their own motivations and ambitions and in terms of the manager's view of them, are pure amateurs. They maintain an involvement in the sport for a range of mostly recreational reasons, including health and fitness, friendship and 'having something to do' in their spare time. Through their amateurish approach to training and performance and general lack of ability, they exclude themselves from consideration as professionals and are happy to stay on the periphery of the main activities of the club.

Vic and Dave are pure amateurs. Vic is a six-foot two-inch white heavyweight with the head of a bulldog, supported by a massive neck and sloping shoulders. (Vic's eyes lit up the first night that I came to the gym – because of my size he assumed that Mack had brought me down to spar with him. I had every intention of being a fully fledged participant observer and 'doing a bit' when I first went into the club. However, once I saw Vic and realised what was on his mind I reached for the broom and water bottle, rationalising that the role of part-time janitor/corner man would be sufficient for my research purposes.) Vic lives in a small town about twenty miles away and commutes to the MBC each evening after work at an engineering plant. He is also doing a part-time degree, courtesy of the 'GI Bill' – legislation which provides free higher education for ex-service personnel. It was while in the army that Vic became hooked on boxing, and it is his dedication to the sport which seems to keep him going now that he is a civilian:

> In the services I seemed to spend most of my time boxing or training for boxing. That was the best part of it I guess. After I got out I had to find something to do to keep me in shape and discipline myself. So I found out where the nearest good gym was and started comin' down. It's hard to keep it up and work as well, but if I didn't have boxing I don't know what the hell I would do!

Mack is happy enough to have the likes of Vic about the place because through his diligence and application he sets a good example for the younger local kids. Also, once in a while Mack needs a heavyweight sparring partner for one of a small number of visiting heavyweight professionals who occasionally use the MBC.

Similarly, Dave is a wiry and hawkish, white welterweight who is tolerated in the club not for his fighting prowess but because he is a walking advertisement for Mack's beneficence. Dave made his initial contact with boxing through Mack, who acted as his attorney when he passed through the Hartford courts on a drugs-related offence. At that time Dave was experiencing a series of social and personal problems and Mack suggested that getting involved in boxing might help him to straighten things out. At twenty-nine Dave has few illusions about his future as a boxer, but is more than content to work out at the gym and help with the general maintenance of the place. Dave's rationale for involvement in boxing could have been scripted by Mack himself:

> I guess I just needed something to do, you know, something to belong to, something to aim for. Mack and the rest of the guys are really good to me, they made me feel right at home. It's tough to start a sport for the first time at twenty-nine, especially this one. When I was at school I was always in trouble and I never got to play other sports. The closest I came to athletics was running away from street fights and the cops. So now I think that boxing's something I can understand, challenge myself, you know, just to see if I can do something, even when the odds are against it.

If only for ideological reasons, amateur boxers such as Vic and Dave are important within the subculture. Without the likes of them those who speak for the sport at the professional level would struggle to sustain the welfare-driven and rehabilitative arguments which are so often used to defend boxing against those who seek to have the sport banned. However, in the MBC Vic and Dave are marginal to the practical processes through which raw recruits are turned into professional contenders. On the other hand, most of the rest of the amateurs, whether they realise it or not, are part of this framework of occupational socialisation.

This cohort of fighters starts out as potential professionals by subscribing to a structure of training and competition which, if they are good enough, will, in time, edge them towards a career in the ring. A few will begin as amateurs with clear aspirations to become professionals, but most carry forward an ill-defined interest, picked up as juniors and balanced against the increasing demands and challenges of adolescence as it is experienced in and around the streets of Charter Oak. Not all of this second category of apprentices make the grade. Whether they do or not is a feature of their physical abilities, personal motivations and ambitions as they are worked out within the more demanding routines of the subculture. A minority opt out of their own accord. Some are forced out by changes in their personal circumstances. Many others are 'cut' by the manager or informally 'cooled out' by their peers and a small number are encouraged steadily to increase their commitment to become professional understudies.

Because of the low quality of life and lack of opportunities in Charter Oak, the vast majority of boxers who are good enough to be allowed to progress towards professionalism are only too happy to do so. Occasionally, however, an odd contender, like Tony, slips through Mack's net. Tony first came to the MBC when he was twelve years old and from that day until the moment he got a decent paying job, he was one of the best prospects to come through the club's ranks. Tony does not fight competitively any more, but he drops by the gym once in a while for a work-out and a little friendly sparring. Although he is a pound or two over his fighting weight, he still boxes with style. While Mack wishes him well, he is also mournful about what might have been:

> Tony was one of the best fighters I worked with. He came down here as a scrawny kid, but by the time he was sixteen he was the best fighter at his weight in the state, and that includes the pros! He could have gone a long way, but he doesn't need it any more. Moved out of the project three years ago, went to a white high school and now he keeps himself busy in a bank counting other people's money and taking home a steady pay cheque. Once they see the steady money and the life it brings they lose their appetite for this game. Don't get me wrong, it's good to see the kid do well and if I were in his shoes I would do the same. But Tony was a kid who really could have made it.

Here Mack betrays the limits of his welfare-driven motivations by recognising that in succeeding with Tony as a person he loses him as a boxer. Other fighters like Leroy are pulled away from boxing for a number of complex reasons, which involve both the increasing commitment demanded by senior amateur boxing and the lure of other occupations and pastimes. Tyrone has to his credit a whole series of regional amateur titles and has featured in two national finals. It is likely that Mack will urge him to turn professional in a year or two, but Tyrone has some misgivings about this:

> But man it's hard y'know. When you get this far in the nationals it's like being a pro. You got no time for yourself, training all day and every day. Mack says that he might let me turn pro if I do okay, but I don't know man, there's no foolin' with that shit. You gotta' give it everything, to be totally into stayin' in shape. No women, nothin'. You gotta' stay clear of trouble or you're not gonna' make it. It's okay if you make it, but what if you don't, then what are you gonna' do? That's why I'm goin' back to school, but it's a lot of pressure with the fight comin' up, it's hard for me to get any studying done and I don't know if I can make it. Makes me tense, y'know, inside it makes me tense.

It is at this point in the boxer's development that Mack has to work hardest to ensure that a carefully nurtured talent such as Tyrone looks forward to full-fledged professionalism and commits himself to the ranks of the gym's elite amateur fighters, the apprentice professionals. From the manager's perspective, the main purpose of supporting amateur boxing is the development of this third, elite cohort of professional understudies. These are the fighters who have a proven physical capacity to make it as professionals and who, through their participation within the subculture, have begun to adopt this role as a central feature of their identities. Troy and Luis are two outstanding young amateurs who are on the threshold of professional careers. They both started boxing at the MBC the same year and after winning most of the junior titles on offer they moved into the amateurs together and have continued to impress at prestigious regional and national tournaments.

Troy, Luis and Tyrone are involved in a different training regime to most of the other amateurs. Mack pushes them harder, expecting them to be at the gym each evening and questioning them when they are absent. He involves them constantly in the pre-fight itineraries of the club's professionals: using them in the gym as sparring partners; taking them to his country farm as part of the team for final preparations; taking them on the road to big professional 'shows'; putting them up in fancy hotels with the professionals; and using them as ring-side helpers when the fights are in progress. Occasionally he will send one or other of them to a different stable in a different city, on loan to do some role-play sparring with other professionals, some of them world-ranked contenders. In short, this elite group are kept as close as possible to the professional experience, from which vantage point they can anticipate and prepare for their own professional careers.

Mack's strategy involves offering the fighting style, training, discipline and ethos of the professionals for the consumption of his elite amateur fighters. In this regard Mack creates and manages an environment within which, for the chosen few, the transition between amateur and professional seems as straightforward and reasonable as was the move from the juniors to the amateurs. This project is made considerably easier by the presence of successful professional role models in the club. As Troy explains:

> When I got to fifteen it just seemed natural to box as an amateur. Both me and Luis had boxed as juniors, but a lot of the other guys quit after the Junior Olympics and the Mittens were over. I guess they liked messin' around too much. When I became an amateur I could see all those important titles that people were gettin' and I wanted to be up there too. Then I saw Marlon turning pro and getting all those deals and, well, I just wanted it more. I know it's hard to be a pro, but I think it's worth it when you make it.

Mack clearly expects more of Troy and his colleagues. He pushes them harder in training than the other amateurs and pays more attention to points of style and technique. In the meantime, he ensures that his professional understudies maintain a serious challenge in the national network of amateur boxing championships, such as the Golden Gloves. These operate as clearing houses for talent in much the same way as the junior tournaments, but on a grander scale. Fighters can build up an impressive record through these competitions which stands them in good stead when they turn professional. If a boxer gets to a national final, win or lose, such an encounter provides him with valuable experience of the nature of the competition to come, while at the same time giving Mack the opportunity to assess an understudy's performance under professional-like conditions.

Yet another damp, cold night in a depressed Massachusetts mill town. This time it is Holyoak Boys' Club which offers a venue for the New England Golden Gloves, an event which is almost a carbon copy of Lowell's Silver Mittens. The Golden Gloves stand alongside the national championships of the USABF (United States Amateur Boxing Federation) as the most important structure for progress as an amateur boxer. Each regional competition affords opportunities for local achievement while at the same time feeding into a broader network of eliminators for national amateur titles for each weight division. In turn, success at a national amateur level leads to international representation, all of which can have a considerable bearing on the starting point of a given fighter's professional career. No matter what a fighter's reputation might be within the boxing fraternity, he still has to establish his ranking through achieving success at every level and stage of the Golden Gloves/USABF competitive structure. This can lead to tensions between officials and managers who operate at different ends of the amateur–professional boxing continuum.

In New England the administrative hierarchy of amateur boxing is dominated by a group of die-hard traditionalists who cherish the amateur ideal and try to diminish the influence of those who view amateur boxing as a series of stepping stones towards the prize ring. Bill Mendoza is the regional representative for the AAU (Amateur Athletic Union) and he is a fierce defender of the amateur's style:

> When I boxed as an amateur you had to be tough. You were in there for three hard rounds and for nine minutes you didn't stop throwing punches. No fancy footin' around like the kids are taught today, but real boxing: goin' at it toe to toe till one of you was knocked down or the final bell finished it.

However, the New England Golden Gloves is too important a stage in the development of the region's apprentice professionals to allow Bill's ethos to go unchallenged. Mack worries that a lack of appreciation for professional boxing style by referees and judges might disadvantage his fighters, spoiling their progress towards national and international success. One of Mack's rival professional/amateur stable managers, Johnny Dukes, states the general position:

> We just want to make sure there are no foul ups. That the draw's fair and that the referees and judges know their jobs. I don't want my fighters getting hurt or losing fights because these bums don't know what they're doin'. Some of these guys [the administrators etc.] think the whole tournament's put on for their benefit. Well let's get it straight, a mistake here could cost us a place or two in the national finals and that's what this nonsense is all about.

The tensions between amateurism and professionalism which lurk beneath the surface of boxing at this level are brought to the fore in contrasting ways through the experiences of two of Mack's elite fighters at this particular tournament. Luis returns to the ring as last year's Golden Gloves champion at 119 lb and gets a warm reception from the knowledgeable crowd who remember him from previous contests. Tonight he is boxing a weight heavier, at 125 lb. His opponent was a regional novice champion last year, but is making his first appearance at this level of amateur boxing. At the first bell Luis springs from his corner and for three minutes proceeds to take his opponent apart, weaving and dancing around the ring, making his hapless victim dizzy with the speed and precision of his range of punches. While in theory both fighters qualify to be in the same ring, in practice the fight is a mismatch. In the interval Mack warns Luis against 'show-boating' and tells him to finish the fight in the next round. Luis obliges by stunning his adversary with a straight left and two short, hooked rights in the first minute. He bravely staggers back to his feet, but not before his corner has dispatched the towel into the ring.

Shortly afterwards the loser's trainer, a policeman who does voluntary work at an inner-city youth club, complains to Mack that Luis's performance was too professional. Mack is sympathetic, but argues that it is the structure of the sport rather than his approach to it that is at fault:

> These guys come to me after their kid has lost complaining that it was not a fair fight. What do they expect me to do, train my fighters to lose? They say Luis should be a pro! That's a joke, he's too young to be a pro. What do they think he's doin' fightin' in this joint?

He also argues that because of the attitude of senior administrators like Bill Mendoza, the professional style of his star pupils does not always prevail:

> I've lost count of the number of times I've seen my kids robbed in tournaments like this and I won't be surprised if it happens here. Either the officials aren't up to it or they're not looking for it. I've seen a kid come out and throw hay-makers for three rounds without laying a glove on my boy. He moves well, rolls away from the punches and jabs it out and those fools think that he's gettin' hit! Last year Michael Bell jabbed this kid's face to a pulp in the Nationals, but he got splashed with the other guy's blood and the damn fool of a referee though Michael was cut, stopped the fight and gave it to the other kid with his nose spread all over his face!

This turns out to be a prophetic complaint when Troy, a fighter ranked in the top ten amateurs in his weight class in the country by *Ring Magazine*, is out-pointed by a relatively unknown local fighter who is short on skill, but high on aggression. Throughout the contest Troy's nimble feet and Ali-like reflexes enable him to avoid the vast majority of his opponent's punches and for every blow that comes close to him, Troy flicks three or four lightening jabs into his adversary's reddening, swelling face. In the final round the local boy keeps steamrollering forward, taking three shots for every one landed on Troy, who continues to box on the retreat displaying excellent defence and counter-punching. Nevertheless, the judges award the fight to the local boy for 'showing more aggression'.

Troy and his manager are both outraged and saddened by this verdict, but not especially surprised. Mack would rather Troy lost (or was robbed) fighting well, than revert to brawling tactics which might win him regional titles, but which will get him nowhere in the higher echelons of the sport. At the same time, when a gifted amateur is old enough to turn professional, but is undecided whether or not to go for more amateur titles, one 'robbery' too many can sometimes hasten the start of his professional career. Marlon Starling recalls the decision which caused him to turn professional:

> I finally decided to turn pro in 1979. I had won the Western Mass. Golden Gloves and I went to the New England championships in Holyoak. In the final I met the local hero, Robby Simms, Marvin Hagler's half-brother. Hagler even climbed into the ring to stand in his kid brother's corner. Well, I whipped that son of a bitch, but I should have knocked him cold 'cause the judges gave it to Simms. The crowd knew, they booed him and gave me a standing ovation. But I was sick of gettin' robbed and instead of goin' through it all again the next year, Mack suggested that I turned pro and I did.

Six months after Holyoak Troy was once more the victim of a dubious decision at a national qualification tournament in Albany, New York. By this time Troy had passed his eighteenth birthday and was eligible to turn professional and when Mack offered him the chance he took little persuading:

> I got so sick of being robbed I was so mad that I was gonna' quit boxing altogether. But then I figured that I had put too much into it to quit now, especially with Marlon makin' it. Mack came up with this deal and I don't know where else I'm gonna get that kind of money at my age, so now I'm a pro!

The farm system: the professionals

The world of professional boxing is the most critical dimension of the boxing subculture, being both its product and its progenitor. Within the MBC there are two relatively simple criteria which qualify a person for entry into the professionals. To begin with, a boxer must have demonstrated through his record as an amateur that he has the dedication and the blend of skills and attitudes to enable him to survive and perhaps thrive in the prize ring. Unless there is a chance of selection for the Olympic team, the most visible showcase of pre-professional achievement, amateur boxers with exceptional talent are generally encouraged to turn professional at eighteen – as soon as they are old enough. The remaining pool of apprentices, however, having established their pedigree, must wait for a space to become available on the local professional circuit before they are offered a contract.

It is not in the long-term interests of a boxing manager to graduate too many professionals if there is not enough work around in the local boxing scene. If they are not getting enough fights they may lose their edge and interest or be forced to seek other ways of making money, ending up weakening the calibre of local boxing and depressing demand even further. Mack, and stable managers like him, are the gatekeepers in this network of recruitment. From the ranks of the eager amateurs who operate out of his gym, Mack decides who turns professional and when. It is also through his agency that boxers are assigned to one of a number of informal status groups shortly after embarking on their professional careers.

In the MBC, all of the fighters who turn professional believe they have a chance of 'going all the way' and making the big time. However, as their careers progress and their potential, or lack of it, is realised, they find themselves allocated to one of several informal categories. First, there are the local boys: fighters who rapidly reach a ceiling in their progress, but show sufficient ability and 'heart', measured in terms of staying power and aggression, to please the crowds in a network of small-time promotions, or on the under-card of a more prestigious event. Most of these fighters retire after a few years in the lower reaches of the sport, but a few box on until they lose what edge they had and finish up being knocked to the bottom of the professional boxing heap to join the flotsam and jetsam of the boxing subculture in the 'meat market': has-beens, stumble-bums and never-has-beens, who have been plucked straight off the street or hurried through inglorious amateur careers, all for a handful of cash, to make up the time and numbers at the wrong end of a fight card in some small-time promotion.

To end up in the meat market is the professional boxer's dread. Miguel is twenty-one and has been fighting professionally for just under two years. He is a steady performer without being a world beater. Miguel recognises these limitations and is determined not to fall victim of the 'meat movers' – unscrupulous managers who put the under-qualified and the has-beens into mismatches simply to take their share of the purse:

> I saw this manager just give up on one of his fighters. He'd won about five fights, but then he started to lose and his coach just said, 'That's it, from now on you're gonna' start payin' for yourself,' just like he was feedin' him to the dogs. He said he would match him with anybody so long as the price was right. If I think I'm losin' my edge I'm gonna quit right there, find a job, maybe play a little baseball. There's no way that I'm gonna' end up being beaten silly like some old punch-bag.

While Mack does not encourage his fighters to continue their careers after they have experienced a string of defeats, he constantly invokes the image of the meat trade as a means of inspiring extra effort from those more successful boxers who are showing signs of slacking. These are the third group of professionals, a small group of likely-lads, fighters who have had their 'shot', or who are in the process of having it, and, to a greater or lesser degree, are maintaining a level of performance in the mainstream of professional boxing: the structure of events which leads directly into the national and international rankings and ultimately, for those who continue to be successful, to the role of contender. Most of these fighters graduate directly from the elite group of amateur understudies and continue to receive special attention from the manager, who carefully monitors their progress in training and matches and moves them gingerly through an introductory series of professional contests. The aim is to accumulate a respectable tally of wins against losses in the local scene. This gives Mack the currency to bid for the matches he wants outside the state and enables him gradually to move his best professionals towards the threshold of an international ranking. If he achieves this, and produces a contender, purses counted in hundreds of dollars are rapidly displaced by those measured in tens and hundreds of thousands of dollars.

This is perhaps the most perilous stage of the fledgling professional boxer's career. He must continue to win bouts to boost his ranking and he must take on increasingly difficult opponents to gain credibility on the big-money professional circuit. One or two losses at this stage can be devastating in terms of his professional future. Marcus came to the MBC from Johnny Duke's gym because he thought Mack would handle him better once he turned professional. To begin with things worked out well as Mack matched and moved him with care as he produced the goods in the ring. Marcus won seven local bouts and two more prestigious contests, taking his professional record to nine wins and zero losses before events outside the ring began to catch up with him. He had a series of violent domestic problems involving his common-law wife which attracted police attention. Mack was able to use his influence with the legal authorities to keep his boxer out of court, but Marcus's training suffered and this was reflected in the ring. He lost three out of his next five fights, the last one badly in front of a big crowd in Hartford's civic centre. Unfortunately for Marcus, a fourteen–three record does not get him close to the big-money contenders. Mack has begun to recognise Marcus's failings:

> Marcus could have been a good fighter. I'm not sayin' he would have been a champion, but he could have made a decent living. But he hasn't got the dedication or discipline of Marlon or even Troy. He wants it bad alright, but he thinks it comes easy. Well it doesn't. If he wants to get anywhere he's gonna' have to spend a lot more time down here [in the gym] and a lot less time foolin' around.

Marcus recognises that if he continues to slacken off he will be finished as a fighter. However, in talking about his last fight he clearly betrays the pressure he feels in dedicating himself to his profession:

> I should have took him out in the third when I had a chance; I wasn't ready to go ten rounds. Man, that's a long time in the ring. You gotta' be in great shape for that, you gotta' train for weeks and weeks, all day, every day. You gotta' spar a hundred rounds for every one that you're gonna' box. But man, sometimes it gets like a prison down here [in the gym]. It gets to me. Y'know, once you come in it's like you're locked away, but you gotta' do it if you want to make it.

Hartford, USA

The farm system: the contender

Before you can be a champion you have to be a contender. (Robert Lypsyte, 1967)

In contrast to Marcus's fortunes, while this research was in progress, Marlon, who also boxed as a youngster at Johnny Duke's gym before joining Mack at the MBC, broke away from the pack of local professionals to become a world-ranked contender in the welterweight division. A boxer gets to be a contender through a combination of ability, record and reputation. Unlike the portrayals of the ring in Hollywood hokum, the ability to challenge for world professional honours requires a solid foundation and needs to be nurtured and styled in the home gymnasium through thousands of rounds of sparring and hundreds of amateur and junior contests. Before Marlon ever got near a professional fight his natural attributes of speed, agility and power had been carefully honed into a formidable boxing talent in Duke's and Mack's gyms and in boys' clubs throughout New England.

Boxing ability alone, however, is not a sufficient guarantee that a fighter will rise from the pack to be a contender. As Marcus's case illustrates, the accumulation of a record of many wins and no or few losses is vitally important if a fighter is to make his way into the big time. It is relatively easy for a stylish but inexperienced boxer to be picked off by a less talented professional with more experience, or an old campaigner who is on the way down. In this regard the skill of Mack in matching and moving Marlon on his way to a contender's shot is fundamental, and throughout the early stages of Marlon's career Mack accepted fights only against opponents whom he thought his fighter stood a very good chance of defeating. He avoided contests with seasoned professionals, fighters with an awkward or unusual style and boxers with a big punch. He also arranged all of Marlon's early fights at local venues, to ensure the presence of large and partisan crowds. In addition, Mack worked very hard with the media to convince them that Marlon was a genuine prospect and to reinforce the emergent view of the 'Magic Man' (Marlon's fighting name) as a local hero who was capable of going all of the way.

However, for those who aim to go all the way, there comes a time when they have to take on the big boys. Floyd Mayweather had been a contender who two years previously had gone ten rounds with Sugar Ray Leonard. Problems with drugs had set him back, but his pedigree made him a good public relations opponent for Marlon, who defeated him in the sixth round in front of a packed house in Hartford's civic centre. This victory took his record to sixteen–zero, but more importantly caught the attention of the promoters and match makers of the traditional home and heartbeat of professional boxing: Madison Square Garden.

Almost as long as there has been professional boxing in the United States, 'the Garden' has been its showcase. An unknown boxer can win the fight of his life in Dayton, Houston or Hartford without having much impact on the wider boxing fraternity, but if he gets a spot on the main event at the Garden he is on the threshold of joining the big time. In this regard Madison Square Garden is to boxers what Broadway is to actors and, symbolically, it casts a long shadow which easily reaches to the doors of the MBC in Charter Oak, Hartford.

At this stage in his career Marlon is not a big enough draw to win top billing in the main auditorium, but he is considered well known enough to top the bill in the Felt Forum, the Garden's smaller hall, which is a regular boxing venue and which still carries the prestigious name of the Garden. In addition Mack has worked out a closed–circuit television contract which will boost the purse to $50,000 and give his star even greater exposure. Marlon's opponent is to be Johnny Resto, a Puerto Rican fighter with a respectable record who fights out of New York. Resto is an ideal opponent inasmuch as he is not reckoned to have a knock-out punch and his stooped, advancing, inside style is tailor made for someone like Marlon with a raking jab, long reach and big punch.

Once the deal is signed Mack has three weeks and two days to prepare his fighter for a chance to box his way into the world's top ten. Back in Charter Oak the local grapevine has already accumulated an impressive dossier on Marlon's opponent. His boxing style, his strengths and weaknesses, his state of fitness and his private life are all subjects for speculation designed to boost Marlon's expectations:

> This dude Resto, I hear he ain't fought nobody except a bunch of stiffs. I saw him fight in the Gloves about five years ago and he didn't look like nothin'. He's only fought once this year and he won't be sharp, won't be in good shape. He don't like to train, spends all his time chasin' pussy and gettin' high.

Mack is much more cautious in his assessment of Resto. Overconfidence can be as much of a hindrance as excessive apprehensiveness in a fighter, and Mack measures his commentaries according to his judgement of Marlon's mood, which gets decidedly edgy as the big fight draws near. He is running five miles in boots every morning and, after a light breakfast, he reports to the gym along with Marcus, Troy, Luis, Tyrone and the manager for two hours' training and sparring. Marlon spars wearing ankle weights and faces a fresh opponent every two rounds. As the days pass by his aggression in the ring increases and his sparring partners take quite a pounding. The action is a mixture of spontaneity and role play. Through films and advice from friends in the know in the New York boxing fraternity, Mack has analysed Resto's style. He gives each sparring partner a series of simple instructions which require them to imitate aspects of Resto's style.

After a warm-down, Marlon's weight is checked before he and the rest of the team head home for a light lunch. Mack drops him off at his apartment, where he takes a shower before settling down to watch television, listen to music or watch a videotape of himself or some other boxer in action. Marlon lived in Hartford's ghetto until his professional earnings enabled him to follow Mack's advice and rent a small apartment about five miles away. Mack may want Marlon's heart and mind in the ghetto, but he recognises that he is physically safer living away from it. In the early afternoon Marlon usually goes bowling with a few club mates before heading back to the MBC at about four o'clock for another training session, which is a more intensive version of the morning's routine, featuring a batch of fresh sparring partners.

During the second week of training preparations are bomb-shelled when Resto pulls out of the contest with a sprained wrist. This represents a major crisis for Marlon and his team, who have been training with a single opponent in mind: Resto. But once a promotion at this level has been arranged, the tickets printed and the television contracts set up, the promoters will do almost anything to ensure that the show goes on, and they usually come up with a substitute fighter. This is dangerous because Mack loses his grip on the match-making process and has less say over the nature of the opponent whom his fighter will be facing. In this case, Resto is replaced by Miguel Hernandez, another experienced Hispanic fighting out of New York. Unlike Resto, Hernandez is tall, with a long reach and fights from the outside. Even more distressing for Marlon's camp is the fact that Hernandez is reputed to carry a big punch.

Ten days before the fight Mack moves the training camp to his farm outside the city where he has a gym, complete with ring, set up inside a barn. The training camp in the countryside has a long tradition in boxing. No doubt the fresh air, healthy food and solitude help the final training sessions. However, these country retreats have as much to do with preventing boxers getting up to mischief in the city as they are about their physiological preparation. In the long term the ghetto and the consciousness it engenders may be the best reference point for the cultivation of boxing talent, but in the few days before an important fight, outside the ring, it is also the place where the greatest threats to a fighter's wellbeing can be found.

The fight is scheduled for Friday night and on Wednesday evening a small group of well-wishers have gathered outside the Charter Oak gym to see off Marlon and his entourage as they leave for New York City. Troy and Luis are travelling to keep Marlon company and to help Mack in the corner. The party is booked into the Waverly, a modest hotel within a short walk of Madison Square Garden. Mack has the adjoining room to Marlon who, if he should choose, can look out of his window and see his name in lights on the electronic billboard outside the Garden.

The weigh-in takes place the morning before the fight. It could be the Mittens or the Gloves except that there are fewer fighters and more officials. The familiar auction-room atmosphere is evoked as the two black boxers strip down to their underwear and step on to the scales under the appraising eyes of a mainly white, male audience. Back at the hotel, in the quiet of his room, as the time for the fight draws inexorably nearer, Mack is getting increasingly nervous:

There's a chance he could lose tonight, just a chance, but this guy Hernandez can punch and if Marlon gets tagged it could be all over. Then where would we be? It wouldn't be the end of the world, we could probably come back after just one loss, but I don't know what losing would do to his head. He thinks he could make a living outside of the ring. He's a smart kid and maybe he could, but he's got to realise that he's on the verge of something special, we all are. If he loses tonight I'm afraid he might do something crazy like pack it in altogether, then we'd be in a real mess. It's not only me, there's a lot of other people who have invested money in this kid's future.

The main event is scheduled for ten o'clock and in the early evening Marlon and his team make the short journey along Pennsylvania Avenue and into the Garden. Backstage in his dressing room, with taped hands and half-closed eyes Marlon lies on a small mattress listening to music which drowns out the hubbub generated by the under-card. By this time the buses loaded with supporters from Hartford have arrived and Mack stands at the dressing room door repelling the throngs of well-wishers who have come to support their local hero. Three men in suits are ushered in. These are part of the syndicate who have invested in Marlon's professional career and they are granted special access. They waste a few words of encouragement on Marlon, who seems to be oblivious to their presence.

In the fifth round of the last bout of the under-card, an otherwise competent middleweight from up-state New York steps on to a right hook and is felled to the canvas. In the wings Marlon skips and dances, throwing jabs, crosses and hooks into hand-pads held by Troy as Mack gives him his final instructions. As if mocking my attempt to expose the Hollywood myth, the theme from Rocky explodes out over the Forum's hi-fi system, cueing Marlon's entrance. Gloves on his manager's shoulders and with Troy and Luis (and me) in his wake, Marlon begins a slow jog towards the flood-lit ring. It is as if half of Hartford is there to greet him as the crowd catches sight of Marlon and ripples of applause give way to an explosion of partisan enthusiasm. The cheering reaches a crescendo as Marlon steps between the ropes and dances around the ring, saluting his supporters. There is a second wave of cheering as he slips out of his robe to reveal a white T-shirt with 'Magic Man' printed on the back and a red heart on the front supported by the pledge, 'I love New York'. A simple but nonetheless clever public relations stunt arranged by Mack to woo the uncommitted local fight fans.

There is more cheering as Hernandez and his party make their way towards the ring and step into the spotlights. Hernandez coils himself between the ropes before springing into the ring to begin his ritual war dance. The tension is palpable and an inadvertent brush of the shoulders between the two boxers almost results in the fight starting early. They can literally kill one another once the bell rings, but any blows aimed before that could result in one or both fighters being disqualified. The crowd roar in anticipation they are pulled apart and led to their respective corners. Weeks, if not years, of preparation have come down to this for Marlon. A win tonight and he will be a seventeen–zero contender. A loss and he will remain a sixteen–one journeyman fighter. Suddenly his stool is taken from beneath him,

Mack and the other seconds step out of the ring, and Marlon is all alone. His own fate and perhaps that of Mack and the other hopefuls in the Charter Oak gym rests upon how he performs in the next half hour or so. The bell tolls and he steps out to meet Hernandez.

For a welterweight, Hernandez is an unusually tall fighter and for the first few rounds Marlon has been instructed to get inside his long reach and work Hernandez's extensive diaphragm. Ever mindful of his competitor's cocked right hand, Marlon dances away, provoking speculative jabs which he ducks under before delivering a rapid series of punches to Hernandez's guts and ribs before darting away to safety. This pattern continues until the sixth round, by which time Hernandez has hardly laid a meaningful glove on Marlon who, following his corner's instructions, begins to vary his attack from the body to the wilting New Yorker's head. In trying to use more of his forearms to protect his aching stomach, Hernandez leaves his head unguarded and he begins to pay the price as Marlon flicks two jabs in his face followed by a stinging right cross to the temple.

Hernandez survives the seventh round, but in the eighth the crowd rise to their feet in expectation as Marlon backs Hernandez into his own corner and hits him with two vicious hooks in the ribs, causing him to stagger and drop his guard. With controlled ruthlessness, Marlon is on him in an instant, whipping measured left and right hands into his head and face. Only the corner post and ropes prevent Hernandez hitting the canvas before the referee dives in to save the forlorn and defeated fighter from taking further punishment. The crowd bellow their approval as Marlon wheels away throwing his arms triumphantly in the air. Mack rushes from his corner and hoists his protégé high in the air like a long sought after trophy. At last he has a contender.[1]

The short-term pay-offs of becoming a contender are made obvious to a fighter by the size of his next purse. However, it is the long-term and indirect rewards which are even more significant. To begin with, he gets automatic national and international exposure through the media. If he wins, his reputation is boosted globally, enabling him to be moved closer to a shot at the world title and its attendant glories and riches. The better his record against fellow contenders, the higher he is ranked and the more power his manager has in terms of arranging his next contests: whom they are against; where and when they are fought; and the size and relative share of the prize money. In this manner, the further he goes, the further he is likely to go and, even if he does not 'go all the way', if he is carefully matched, he can linger long enough in the top rankings to make for a relatively comfortable retirement.

The production of a contender is also a major milestone for the home club. There is a bandwagon effect which travels in the wake of a contender's success and changes the status and practices of the club within which he learned his trade. The

---

[1] Starling went on to become WBA world welterweight champion, defeating Olympic gold medallist Mark Breland in 1987. By this time Starling had severed his relationship with Mack.

spotlight shining on a contender illuminates the other up-and-coming professionals, increasing the demand for their services and indirectly improving their chances of making a go of it themselves in the mainstream. Secondly, his success will increase the number and range of opportunities for all the local professionals by attracting bigger promotions to the region. This gives Mack the space to allow more of his pool of professional apprentices to pass through the gate into the local professional circuit. Also, having a contender in and around the gym electrifies the atmosphere and inspires the younger members of the club. At the same time, it improves the club's standing in the neighbourhood and swells the crowds of youngsters begging admittance at the doorway. All of which, alongside his share of the profits, serves to improve the goodwill of Mack's business.

In this way, the long-term stability and development of the boxing subculture is both conditioned by its roots in the ghetto and guided by the achievements of its elite professionals. Through the husbandry of the manager, the club is set up to produce world-class fighters. The various stages of the subcultural career are essential experiences in the passage of a contender and once he makes the big time, it is that subculture which, more than anything else, keeps his consciousness anchored in the streets of the ghetto, sharpens his edge and fuels an appetite for the ring. In return, as his career progresses, so too does the fame and fortune of the stable within which he learns and refines his trade.

Thus, the determining is likewise determined as the formative layers of experience which produce professional boxing are themselves contained within, and changed by, structures generated by the specific needs of the professional circuit. The essentially exploitative nature of this process is disguised from the boxers themselves by the rhetoric of amateurism, social welfare and the gradual manner through which they are encouraged to grow into the occupational role of the boxer. The has-been professional fighter is the ultimate expression of this deception: a person who has developed a self-concept and an accompanying repertoire of skills, attitudes and desires which are unsuitable for any other trade apart from the one which he can no longer safely perform.

4

Belfast, Northern Ireland: fighting for the Holy Family

More than a decade after I had completed the research upon which the preceding chapter was based, I went once more into the field to learn what I could about the boxing subculture, this time in Belfast. This work was carried out two years before republican and loyalist paramilitaries declared a ceasefire in Northern Ireland. At that time the boxing club which features in this chapter was located in a neighbourhood at the front line of sectarian confrontation and violence.

Sunday, 26 September 1992, and it is business as usual in the New Lodge, north Belfast. As smartly dressed family groups make their way to mass at the Holy Family Catholic church half a mile away on the Limestone Road, a number of young men head in the opposite direction to the Holy Family Boxing Club at the centre of the estate. As they walk to the gym the boxers ignore the camouflaged and heavily armed soldiers who scamper through entries and squat behind garden walls before sweeping their way back to the fortified barracks at the edge of the estate.

Mid-morning and the boxing club is occupied mainly by boys from the immediate neighbourhood. Posturing beneath the gaze of local boxing heroes, whose photographs and posters occupy all available wall space, the young pugilists playfully jab and stab at the heavy bags slung from the rafters of the attic gymnasium. By noon most of the youngsters have drifted away as the gym becomes filled with older and more serious fighters, who change into an assortment of training gear before wrapping and tying each other's hands with sweat-stained bandages. To the accompaniment of loud music bellowing from a ghetto blaster, the boxers dance, skip and shadow box through a variety of fitness and skills routines. In the meantime, the club coaches and a handful of hangers-on sit in the corner of the room, eying proceedings and taking an occasional break from boxing gossip to shout encouragement or friendly abuse at one or other of the sweating fighters.

The New Lodge is one of Belfast's most renowned nationalist enclaves and this is reflected in the Irish republican flags, slogans and murals which adorn many of the buildings surrounding the boxing club. Nevertheless, while almost all of the younger boys who attend the gym are local Catholics, more than half of the senior boxers are Protestants from loyalist parts of the city. Likewise, the people who run the club come from both communities. The highlight of the training session comes shortly after 1.30 p.m., when all present gather around the apron of the ring to watch John, a local Catholic, spar with Neil, a Protestant from a loyalist estate on the outskirts of the city. Neil, with a longer reach and a raking jab, inflicts a bloody nose on John who, displaying superior inside work, knocks the wind out of his opponent with a series of bruising blows to the ribcage. At the end of the contest the two young men embrace and trade congratulations for each other's contribution to a good bout of boxing. By 2.30 p.m. the training session is over. Freshly showered and changed the boxers leave the club and go their separate ways as the coaches and the club secretary head to a local pub for a Sunday lunchtime pint.

Meanwhile, no more than 150 yards away from the club, eighteen-year-old Gerrard is watching television when masked men wielding sledge hammers smash their way into his North Queen Street home. Despite the desperate pleading of his mother the gunmen, who are members of the loyalist UVF (Ulster Volunteer Force), shoot Gerrard dead, making him the 594th fatal victim of sectarian-related violence in this part of Belfast since 1969. North Belfast has borne more suffering than any other part of Northern Ireland and it has also produced some of the region's best amateur and professional boxers. How is it that a neighbourhood which can cultivate a boxing club dependent both upon the discipline and control of aggression and upon the mutual respect of fighters from different religious and cultural traditions, can also sustain a subculture of boundless violence which preys upon community division and sectarian hatred? Are the two forms of conflict in any way related?

The social roots of boxing in Belfast

Boxing has its origins in maritime and commercial centres such as London, Bristol and Dublin. A knowledge of and ability in bare-knuckled pugilism was a staple element of the occupational subculture of rough and ready British and Irish seafarers, who helped to spread an interest in the sport throughout the British Isles and the developing world. Swelled by the streams of the surrounding mountains, the River Lagan empties into Belfast Lough, at the end of which lies the port of Belfast, which for centuries has vied with Dublin as Ireland's largest sea port. More than commodities have been imported into Ireland through ports such as Dublin and Belfast. For generations the ways of life of other countries, including their distinctive sporting preferences, have been carried across the seas by sailors, merchants and various classes of immigrant workers. Organised boxing in one form or another has been taking place in Belfast for at least 200 years. During the first quarter of the nineteenth century, at a time when British favourites such as Tom Crib and Tom Molineaux fought bare-knuckle before large crowds in fields and boxing booths in and around London, Ulster people would gather at Chapel Fields and Points Fields on the outskirts of Belfast to wager on fighting animals and cheer on local pugilists. Since that time boxing has been integral to the city's sporting heritage.

In addition to its seafaring heritage, Belfast has long been a garrison town. There is a mistaken perception, in some circles, that the British army have been in Northern Ireland only since the current episode of political violence began in 1969. Like any region of the United Kingdom, Northern Ireland has recruited and been the base for several local regiments, such as the Irish Rangers, the Royal Irish Rifles and the Enniskillen Fusiliers. Unlike other areas, however, the long history of civil unrest and civil war in Ulster has meant that the British army has maintained a stronger presence in the Province than elsewhere. For more than 300 years boxing has been an important part of physical training and recreational life in the services, and the army has produced more than its share of amateur boxing champions. There is evidence to suggest that the British army helped to lay the foundations for organised amateur boxing in Belfast. Before the onset of the 'troubles', Belfast-based regiments would open their recreational facilities for community use as well as taking part in a full range of local sporting competitions, including boxing. Regimental boxing matches and contests between regimental teams and local boxing clubs were a regular feature of the city's sporting calendar before the late 1960s. Likewise, before partition in 1921, the RIC (Royal Irish Constabulary) played a significant role in the development of the sport in Belfast. After partition this role was enthusiastically embraced by the RUC (Royal Ulster Constabulary), which, until the onset of the troubles in 1969, was a leading force in Ulster boxing, both within the ring and in the administration of the sport.

The Catholic Church also played an important part in the growth and development of boxing in Belfast, and through uniformed youth organisations such as the Scouts and the Boys' Brigade, Protestant churches have shown a considerable commitment to youth sports, although they have been more reluctant than their Catholic counterparts to include boxing as an appropriate activity. Thus, while the principles of muscular Christianity are ecumenical, in Northern Ireland only the Catholic Church to any significant extent has embraced boxing as an acceptable avenue for the physical expression of spiritual devotion to God. Sustained by this ideal and a belief that idle hands make work for the devil, in an attempt to instil physical and spiritual discipline while at the same time turn boys and young men away from the ill-discipline and vice of the streets, parish priests have been instrumental in setting up a number boxing clubs throughout the Province. In some cases boxing clubs are housed within church premises, and even where there is no direct association between church and ring it is quite common for boxing clubs in Catholic neighbourhoods to take on the names of their respective parish churches. Boxing clubs in Protestant districts, on the other hand, are usually associated with works, factories or secular youth clubs and are often set up by local ex-boxers who combine an interest in their former sport with a concern for the welfare of youngsters in their local communities. To a certain extent the different attitude of the two churches to the sport explains why most boxers in Northern Ireland are Catholic. However, it is when religious differences overlap with class factors that a clearer picture emerges.

Social class is recognised as being one of the most important influences on sports preference and participation. A necessary precondition for boxing to take root and thrive is the existence of a sizeable and largely impoverished working class. Alongside trade and commerce, in the second half of the nineteenth century, Belfast built a significant industrial infrastructure around textiles, ship building and engineering. The rapid and accelerated increase in the city's population which occurred during the nineteenth century centred on a burgeoning working class. The population of Belfast at the turn of the eighteenth century was 20,000 and it doubled approximately every twenty-five years during the nineteenth century, reaching 80,000 by 1850 and almost 200,000 by the beginning of the twentieth century, levelling off at roughly 300,000 in the 1950s. Wages among the workers in Northern Ireland are lower than in other regions of the United Kingdom and rates of unemployment are usually significantly higher. A combination of low rates of pay and high rates of unemployment has led to the emergence of a large lower-working-class population which, because of institutionalised forms of discrimination, traditionally has been Catholic dominated. The fact that there is a higher proportion of poor working-class Catholics than Protestants in Belfast helps to explain why the city produces more Catholic than Protestant fighters.

There is clearly a relationship between the lower working class and boxing which requires detailed investigation. At this point suffice it to note that the boxing subculture is sustained by a mixture of aggressive masculinity generated by lower-working-class communities, the capacity of boxing to provide a positively sanctioned channel for this trait, and the impression that the sport can offer temporary or even permanent sanctuary from urban poverty and related social problems. In Northern Ireland to this general equation we have to add the impact of two decades of political conflict, terrorism and community division.

Even though participation in boxing is in general decline throughout Britain and Ireland, the rate of that decline seems to be less pronounced in Belfast. Currently, there are more than thirty amateur boxing clubs in central and suburban Belfast which are registered with the Ulster Provincial Council and which box under the auspices of the IABA (Irish Amateur Boxing Association). While the density of boxing clubs per capita may be greater in Belfast than in other cities, religious affiliation notwithstanding, the socio-economic context of boxing here is the same as can be found in towns such as London, Dublin, Liverpool and, in some measure, New York and Detroit. That context is the ghetto. The trend towards the compartmentalisation of poverty which is so noticeable in modern British cities is exaggerated in Belfast, where twenty years of community violence have accelerated Belfast's inner-city ghettoisation into an orange and green patchwork of neighbourhood stockades. Following the contours of the city's sectarian geography, almost all of Belfast's boxing clubs are located either in traditional inner-city neighbourhoods such as Shankill, Short Strand, Divis, Dock and Sandy Row, or within dislocated, low-income housing estates such as Andersonstown, Ballymurphy, Turf Lodge, Rathcoole and Monkstown. Each of these neighbourhoods can be categorised either as Catholic/nationalist or Protestant/loyalist.

In certain ways the demography of sport in Belfast follows a general UK pattern, according to which working-class sport and recreation tend to be located within clearly identifiable communities. However, unlike cities elsewhere in the UK, in Belfast community-centred sport and recreation can help to promote sectarianism by providing an emotive and highly symbolic sphere of exclusive affiliation and identification (in other cities, of course, different forms of ethnocentrism may be promoted by community recreation). Understandably, after more than twenty years of serious political and social violence, people do not feel safe venturing too far away from home and familiar faces when attempting to enjoy their free time. While in themselves the leisure pursuits of Belfast's working class are not sectarian, because favoured pastimes such as social drinking, gambling and visiting friends and relatives take place locally and exclusively in the company of those of the same religious persuasion, leisure tends to promote polarisation between the city's two cultural traditions. It is a case of lack of familiarity exaggerating contempt. Likewise, certain sports clubs, most notably in soccer, become clearly associated with a particular neighbourhood and a given religious label, and this can often lead to conflict, particularly between supporters of Protestant and Catholic teams when they compete against one another. Apart from direct affiliation to a particular church or involvement in political organisations, sports preference and support are the most powerful indicators of who you are and what you stand for in Northern Ireland (Sugden and Bairner, 1993: 18–22).

At one level, boxing in Belfast follows this pattern, but in important ways the sport has been able to resist sectarian stereotyping. Of the thirty or so clubs in Belfast more than two-thirds are in nationalist neighbourhoods, catering for fighters who are predominantly Catholic. The same dynamic operates in favour of Protestants for clubs in unionist districts. There is nothing surprising or sinister about this observation. In the case of boxing, it is the city's demography which is sectarian rather than elements within the sport itself. The same could not be said of, for instance, rugby union or Gaelic games, which have been demonstrated to have deep-seated links with different notions of national identity (Sugden and Bairner, 1993: 23–67). It is only to be expected that when youngsters first take up the sport they elect or are directed to train at the club nearest to home. However, teams of boxers and their supporters travel to and from each other's clubs and arenas, free from the fear of molestation, to be warmly received and well treated, even though these venues are likely to be in the hearts of the most vehemently nationalist or loyalist neighbourhoods in the whole of Northern Ireland.

For instance, in the early 1970s, during the height of the troubles, while many other community-based sports such as basketball and youth football went into decline because people were not prepared to travel outside their immediate areas, amateur boxing managed to continue. Fighters from the nationalist Falls district regularly went to box at a venue on the Shankill Road, even though it was within a social club run by Protestant paramilitaries. Moreover, once boxers get older and become totally dedicated to their sport they will change clubs if they believe they will get better coaching elsewhere, even if this means relocating to a gym in a district which is dominated by the other religious tradition. In the case of the club which is the main focus of this research, the clientele is actually mixed, with young boxers from areas with radically different political reputations training and fighting side by side each night of the week, supervised by trainers and coaches from both sides of the sectarian divide.

Apart from religious/sectarian influences, one other factor which distinguishes boxing in Belfast from that in most other regions of the UK is that here the vast majority of fighters are white. This is a direct consequence of the fact that immigrants make up only a very small percentage of Northern Ireland's population. It is the Province's long-term economic problems in tandem with a reputation for political violence that has rendered it unattractive for immigrants. Thus, whereas in Britain the poorest of the inner-city poor are a mixture of whites and a range of ethnic minorities, in Northern Ireland the worst off are virtually exclusively white. It is from this section of society that the majority of Belfast's boxers are drawn. Occasionally it is possible to witness small groups of black and Hispanic boxers undertaking training runs along the shores of Belfast Lough. However, invariably these fighters will not be from Northern Ireland, being rather overseas fighters brought into the Province to train in and box for Northern Ireland's only remaining professional stable.

While the overwhelming majority of people who participate in boxing or occupy a role within the boxing subculture in Belfast are working-class males, this excludes the tiny number of influential entrepreneurs such as 'B J' Barney Eastwood, the scrap-metal and bookmaking magnate, who operates at the upper level of the professional fight game. The role played by the boxing entrepreneurs is a complex one and is not the subject of this investigation. Nevertheless, it is important to note the mutually dependent relationship between amateur and professional boxing, with the former being the farm system for the latter. People like Eastwood animate this relationship by providing the opportunity for good local amateurs to turn professional. Unlike the situation in the United States detailed in the previous chapter, within the United Kingdom and Ireland it is against Boxing Board of Control rules for amateurs and professionals to be part of the same club set-up. While there are no amateurs in Eastwood's stable, he keeps a sharp eye on the better local amateurs, hoping to get the best of the best, such as Barry McGuigan and Dave 'Boy' McAuley, to turn professional and join his organisation. While the relationship between amateur and professional boxing in Northern Ireland is not formally as close as it is in the United States, informally, through personal relationships between the likes of Eastwood and the managers of the city's most successful amateur clubs, the two levels are intimately linked. Undoubtedly, the presence of a relatively successful professional boxing stable in Belfast generates interest in boxing at all levels and greatly assists recruitment into the junior and amateur ranks in clubs throughout the city.

Murder mile, north Belfast

During the darkest days of the troubles in the mid-1970s, when indiscriminate bombing was a significant weapon in the terrorists' arsenal, the centre of Belfast was as dangerous a place as anywhere in the world. As the troubles progressed, however, agreement was established between the rival factions in terms of their targeting of the city centre. This resulted in a diminution of blasts, a greater emphasis on strategic targets and, above all, longer and more reliable warnings from the paramilitaries to the security forces as to where and when explosions would occur. In the 1990s the centre of Belfast is a haven of relative safety for pedestrians and shoppers who mingle there, comforted by the religious anonymity of one of the few areas of the city not claimed by one side or the other.

The same cannot be said of those neighbourhoods which immediately surround the city's commercial and business districts. Travel north out of the city along Great Victoria Street and within a mile or so you will pass the bottom of the Shankill Road. Continue to skirt Divis and Unity Flats, cross the Crumlin Road and approach the confluence of North Queen Street, Duncairn Gardens and the Limestone, Cliftonville and Antrim Roads. This is north Belfast, a district where Protestant and Catholic communities adjoin each other and where sectarian murders are commonplace. The area is known locally as murder mile, and it is here that the 'Shankill Butchers' carried out most of their atrocities in the 1970s.

It is often mistakenly assumed that serious sectarian confrontation in Northern Ireland is a relatively recent phenomenon. For almost as long as records have been kept Protestants and Catholics have fought bitterly over land, jobs and political power in Ulster. From its first recorded mention, north Belfast has been a killing ground. During the nineteenth century, Belfast boomed as a sea port and manufacturing centre. This encouraged the migration of a famine-ravaged and largely Catholic population from the countryside to the outskirts of the city, where they competed for jobs and homes with an established and largely Protestant workforce. Sectarian rivalry was given a sharper edge by the political vicissitudes which accompanied the struggles for Irish independence and the partition of Ireland in the first quarter of this century. North Belfast was engulfed by violence, the level of which was unprecedented, even by today's standards. The establishment of a divided Ireland and the end of the civil war which followed that settlement led to a long if uneasy truce. However, the collective memory is long and sectarian conflict is never far from the surface in north Belfast.

The emergence of the civil rights movement in the late 1960s and the reaction which it provoked from loyalists rekindled the smouldering, undeclared war between the Protestants and Catholics of north Belfast. Trouble exploded, leading to a significant reorganisation of the population. People in the north of the city left their homes in large numbers. They went to their Catholic and Protestant encampment ghettos. And in the mixed areas on the fringes they died violently, often for no better reason than for being in the wrong place at the wrong time. For over twenty-five years they have faced each other from their respective territories, which are well defined and often ferociously defended.

While the troubles did not obliterate north Belfast's community structure, they have radically changed its nature. The 1991 census reveals that Belfast is now more polarised than ever before. Of the city's fifty-one electoral wards, the population of thirty-five comprises 90 per cent of one religion or the other. Apart from two professional and middle-class neighbourhoods in the suburbs which are broadly integrated, the remaining 'mixed' wards are in fact sharply divided into Protestant and Catholic enclaves, which in some cases are physically separated by structures resembling the Berlin Wall. In north Belfast Catholics have consolidated their position in areas such as Ardoyne, Cliftonville, the lower Antrim Road and the New Lodge, while Protestant families who had lived in these areas moved into the loyalist strongholds of Ballysillan, Shankill, Shore Road and Tigers Bay or went even further afield to Newtownabbey, North Down or Lisburn.

Duncairn Gardens is the boundary between the New Lodge and Tigers Bay, an area which is as Protestant and loyalist as the New Lodge is Catholic and nationalist. The two communities are separated by large corrugated iron fences, euphemistically known as the peace line, which are high enough to preclude exchanges of petrol bombs, but still sufficiently permeable enough to allow the coming and going of rival terrorists. This is the epicentre of the urban front line of Northern Ireland's political crisis. It is estimated that within a two-mile radius of Duncairn Gardens more than one-fifth of the deaths associated with the past twenty years of political violence in Northern Ireland have occurred. People have been slaughtered as willing participants in a triangular guerilla war among republican and loyalist terrorists and the security forces, or have been innocent civilian victims of that war.

The New Lodge is an urban village which is physically bounded by busy roads, economically defined by poverty and culturally enclosed by community division and sectarian suspicion. It consists of approximately one square mile of low-income housing, half of which consists of old-fashioned terraced streets, the remainder being a post-1960, breeze-block, high-rise estate built on land formerly occupied by an army camp. The housing estate covers land which would hold about ten football pitches. Approximately 100 people have been killed in or close to the estate since 1969 – ten per football pitch. The neighbourhood is bisected by the New Lodge Road, which is the most murderous street in Northern Ireland. Twenty-five people have lost their lives in terrorist-related incidents on this 150-metre stretch of asphalt. In the six months when the field work for this research was carried out twelve people were killed in the immediate area as a direct result of political violence.

There is hardly a family living in the New Lodge which has not been directly affected by the troubles. A husband in prison, a son knee-capped, a boyfriend maimed in a bomb blast, a daughter widowed, an uncle murdered and such like are all familiar experiences for the people who live in north Belfast. While the indirect impact of this liturgy of political violence on the whole neighbourhood is impossible to measure, it is easy to sense the atmosphere of a community under siege. Shared suffering, fear of a common enemy and mutual feelings of persecution are powerful stimuli for communal bonding, giving the neighbourhood a strong collective identity.

The Holy Family

Getting into the New Lodge can be a hair-raising experience. On this particular night the streets are tense and have been since Peter McBride, an eighteen-year-old youth with no known terrorist connections, was shot dead in Upper Meadow Street by soldiers of the Scots Guards the previous weekend. The night before, just around the corner, in a Catholic section of the Crumlin Road, in a random sectarian attack a loyalist gang had shot through the door and windows of a Catholic household, seriously injuring an adult and a schoolgirl. Several streets have been sealed off by the RUC in anticipation of another night of confrontation and violence. Visitors to the New Lodge have to negotiate the police/army roadblock outside the heavily fortified barracks on North Queen Street. Travelling along a rubble-strewn road, through the gloom and drizzle, the smouldering wreck of a delivery van and groups of youths hanging around on the street corners can be seen. A combined army and RUC foot patrol, dressed and armed for battle, makes its way gingerly along one side of the street supported by two grey, armour-plated Land Rovers while somewhere in or above the low cloud throbs the motors and blades of an army helicopter.

In the New Lodge itself the green, white and gold tricolour of the Irish Republic flutters from the top of several blocks of flats, while on top of another is the brooding presence of an army observation post. The slogans of Irish Republican factions (PIRA, Provisional Irish Republican Army; INLA, Irish National Liberation Association; and IPLO, Irish People's Liberation Organisation) provide the themes for a competition of graffiti and murals which are festooned on walls and gables throughout the estate. A huge image of dead hunger-striker Bobby Sands glares out over the New Lodge Road. Groups of young children scamper in and out of the narrow passages which separate utilitarian terraces of 1960s maisonettes while their older brothers and sisters engage in horseplay in the shelter of the multistories apparently mindless of yet another army foot patrol dodging from doorway to doorway in their midst. Younger children are allowed to chat to the soldiers and even take sweets from them, but the older boys and girls know better and ignore them either through personal choice or for fear of being branded as collaborators.

In the heart of the estate stands a small chapel-like structure which has long since been converted into a youth and community centre. In fact the building used to be the recreation hall for the British army's Victoria Barracks, which occupied most of the land upon which the New Lodge estate now stands. The 'reky', as the building is locally known, houses North Queen Street community centre, which is funded by Belfast City Council's Community Services Department. Locked double doors, reinforced with steel plate, keep out a small group of children and teenagers who have gathered impatiently on the steps waiting for the centre to open. During the day it serves as an unemployment advice/drop-in centre and is the venue for meetings of a wide variety of neighbourhood organisations. In the evening the main body of the 'reky' is taken over by local children's and youth groups for five-a-side football, band practice, teen discos and general recreation. When the youth worker arrives and finally opens the doors most of the youngsters flood into the main hall, eager to get on with a game of football before the centre's more formal timetable overtakes them. However, a handful of quieter and earnest-looking boys slip upstairs and head towards the attic.

The attic is not part of the community centre. It is sublet by the Council to the Holy Family, one of Northern Ireland's most successful amateur boxing clubs. The Holy Family has been one of the city's most productive gyms for more than fifty years. It has been a second home to hundreds of young amateur fighters, many of whom have won Ulster and national titles at boys', youth, intermediate and senior levels. The club has provided a steady stream of talent for Northern Ireland boxing teams in successive Commonwealth Games and several Holy Family fighters have represented Ireland in the Olympic Games. The attic gym has also produced a small number of moderately successful professional boxers. On any given evening the club is packed with boys, youths and men undertaking the universal and time-honoured rituals and rhythms of the boxing club. Not surprisingly, most of the young boys come from the immediate catchment area, most of them living in the New Lodge itself. However, many of the older fighters who attend come from further afield and not necessarily from Catholic neighbourhoods. Some come from areas in east Belfast, the Shankill Road, Rathcoole estate and Monkstown: all Protestant and aggressively loyalist communities.

The apprentice boys

This particular evening, relative to the scenes unfolding in the streets and the hall downstairs, the boxing club is an oasis of order and social restraint. The youngest boxers, the novices and youths, normally are permitted to train only three evenings per week, between 6 and 7.30 p.m. and early on Sunday morning. Officially, IABA rules do not permit youngsters below the age of ten to box competitively. However, the age of the novices and youths who attend this gym ranges from about eight to sixteen. The club operates an open-door policy and boys are allowed to attend regularly or spasmodically so long as they take part in the training routines and refrain from messing around inside the gym. Any form of kit is tolerated, but the boys are discouraged from wearing football jerseys which suggest a particular sectarian identification. Thus, while Manchester United, Liverpool and Leeds are well represented, the colours of Glasgow Rangers, Glasgow Celtic, Linfield and Cliftonville are conspicuous by their absence. Some of the smallest in attendance are younger brothers or cousins of more established fighters. Otherwise there is little to distinguish most of these young fighters from those who use the downstairs hall for indoor football. They are all products of a social environment within which having scant regard for authority, being cocksure and reckless are valued attributes in a rough-and-tumble, dog-eat-dog daily routine. Fighting and talking about fighting rival playing and talking about football as a main peer-group concern. Outside of the Holy Family the only fighting which the boys experience has little in common with the disciplines of the ring. As one youngster explains, the kind of skills they learn at the boxing club are of little use to them in the scraps they get into around the streets of the New Lodge:

> Boxing's not much good to you in the street. You don't only just punch when you're fighting in the street. There's kicking, biting, pulling hair, scraming [scratching] and poking eyes. Boxing doesn't count much.

Thus, these boys do not come to the boxing club to learn a form of self-defence to keep them safe on the streets. Neither are they attracted to boxing because it gives them an excuse to extend their participation in the culture of violence which exists in the streets outside the club. Compared with the routine of street crime, gang fighting and sectarian attacks endemic to north Belfast, the Holy Family is a relative haven from violence. Nevertheless, the broader context of urban deprivation and the menace of violence is important insomuch as it frames the consciousness of those who attend the Holy Family. They may not be able to box the first time they visit the club, but the lads from the New Lodge possess some of the values, appetites and abilities which are at the root of the serious boxer's make-up: physical agility, aggression, fearlessness, and self-confidence. In the school playground, in their homes and in the streets they are used to giving and taking physical punishment and this experience hardens them. So long as the apprehension of hitting and the fear of being hit can be overcome, boxing can be considered great fun. In this regard, the younger members of the Holy Family have a considerable advantage over children of their own age growing up in more salubrious areas of Belfast. However, this not to suggest that most of them will develop into serious boxers.

Boxing may be stylised by the Holy Family's managers and trainers as an important diversion from the dangers of the streets, but there is a limit to their interpretation of the sport as mission. The abiding rationale for the club is the recruitment and development of good boxers who will win fights and championships in the name of the Holy Family. If in the process this helps a few youngsters stay out of trouble then this is a welcome bonus. It is generally accepted that few of the novices who pass through the door will develop into career boxers, most dropping out before they reach sixteen, the age at which boys begin to turn into men. It is then that the aspiring boxer begins to experience greater demands on his time and energy. For a minority of fourteen- to sixteen-year-olds there are the increasing pressures associated with school as threshold examinations approach. For a few others the need and opportunity to earn a living outside school hours or after leaving school undermine their commitment to the Holy Family. However, for all the youngsters who attend the club a wider range of leisure/pleasure activities become available as they progress through their adolescence.

During the transitional period between boyhood and manhood boxing becomes a harder sport, physically and mentally, as the ascetic demands of the ring come into conflict with the prevailing hedonistic values of inner-city youth. The values which sustained the rough-and-tumble street life which led them to the ring as children are no longer appropriate to support the endeavours of the serious fighter. Junior and senior amateurs have to train much harder than youth and novice boxers. For most of the latter, boxing is a fun thing to do in between school, home, football, discos and the streets. While the serious fighter may still enjoy his chosen sport, it is no longer fun. The energy and exuberance of childhood are not of themselves sufficient to sustain a serious adolescent fighter. The principles of pleasure which motivated him as a child have to be renegotiated in the unfamiliar terms of stoicism and deferred gratification. He has to develop and hone his maturing muscles, work on his stamina, expand his cardiovascular endurance, watch his weight, develop fast hands and learn to give and take hard punches to the body and head. Regular road running, diet, self-denial, self-control and much longer nightly work-outs in the gym are essential features of the serious boxer's discipline. It is at this time, when boxing begins to really hurt inside and outside the ring, that most youngsters quit.

Morris (known by his nickname of Bongo) and Hugh, the trainers responsible for the novice and youth boxers, have a realistic view of the material with which they have to work. There are many other activities taking place outside the club which are attractive to these youngsters, particularly when they enter their early teenage years, and boxing must take its place among them. In terms of sport, while most of the boys said that they liked boxing, almost all of them admitted that they preferred football, adding that for them boxing was something which they did 'for something to do' in between football matches and discos. Teen discos and 'raves' in the neighbourhood throughout the week provide further distractions from the all-male company and more rigorous physical disciplines of the boxing club. The onset of puberty and the discovery of girls as objects of desire can have contradictory effects on the career of a young boxer. Thirteen-year-old Pat's attendance at the club began to drop off once he began dating a twelve-year-old girl from Short Strand. Nevertheless, Morris rejects the traditional taboo associated with girlfriends and wives in the boxing subculture, believing that in an environment like the New Lodge having a steady girl, even at such a young age, can help to keep local youngsters out of trouble by distancing them from the streets and the influence of the pack.

While both Morris and Hugh can reconcile themselves to the inevitable teenage drop-out due to girls, discos and football, they are less sanguine when it comes to the sport's other big recreational competitors: drinking, drugs, running in the streets and political association. In certain respects the New Lodge is not unlike inner-city, low-income housing estates throughout the United Kingdom. Juvenile misbehaviour follows a familiar pattern and includes such things as alcohol abuse, car theft, joy riding, petty theft, vandalism, gang fighting, sexual promiscuity, solvent abuse and some drug taking and drug dealing. However, unlike cities outside Northern Ireland, this pattern of misbehaviour overlaps with sectarian conflict and political violence and the security measures which are taken to contain them. This gives Morris greater incentive to work with the club's younger members:

> There's a lot of bad things go on in Belfast, in all areas, Catholic and Protestant. If the kids stay at the club, come training three or four times a week, they're not getting into trouble with the police, getting involved in mischief, or falling into the wrong hands.

There are many 'wrong hands' to fall into in north Belfast. Running in the streets in the New Lodge is a particularly dangerous business and can be lethal. Those who spend their nights hanging around the estate inevitably come into regular contact with the police and the army and quite often get 'lifted' (arrested) for a variety of mainly petty offences. Persistent offenders will end up in court and some of them will be sent to reform schools. The presence of the security forces in the streets of the New Lodge is both a threat and a challenge to some local youngsters who enjoy the thrill of the chase. Once in a while, however, juvenile misbehaviour can be defined by the security forces as something associated with terrorism, leading to their use of excessive force which, as in the case of Peter McBride, can be deadly. Some others, particularly those who steal cars, get involved in drugs or generally become neighbourhood nuisances, fall foul of the paramilitaries, whose justice can be summary. Beating, tarring and feathering and knee capping (having the knee cap shot off through the back of the knee) are frequently used to dissuade (usually) young males from engaging in those activities which the paramilitaries, particularly the PIRA, deem antisocial. Repeating offenders have been exiled from their home communities and, in the most extreme cases, executed.

The standard of secondary education in Northern Ireland is generally considered to be high. However, this view is based upon regional GCSE, 'O' and 'A' level results produced largely through the Province's network of grammar schools. Such evidence masks the educational underachievement of thousands of youngsters from districts like the New Lodge who leave secondary schools with few or no qualifications. There is a familiar anti-school ethos among the lads of the New Lodge, who have little or no respect for education or the authority of their teachers. Most attend school reluctantly and some 'beak off' (play truant) regularly. Almost all leave at the first opportunity at the end of their fifth year. While many of these youngsters are athletically talented, their rejection of school and associated activities bars them from participating in school sports competitions, particularly in their favourite sport of soccer. Thus they are reduced to playing pick-up games in the street or taking part in the semi-organised games facilitated in the community centre by local youth leaders. School is an imposed discipline, but because boxing is a direct product of their own environment they are more disposed to accept the discipline of the ring and the authority of people such as Morris and Hugh.

Once they leave school these young men enter a job market where there is very little work anyway. In fact, the estimated level of youth unemployment in the New Lodge is in excess of 75 per cent. At a time when other young people may be looking forward to the income, independence and status which comes with a steady occupational career or life as a student, many teenagers from this area face a hand-to-mouth future of social security payments, job creation schemes, participation in the black market economy and long periods of idleness. For some, in the absence conventional careers and other socially approved alternatives, the boxing club provides an important venue for expressing physical and mental agility. It may also afford legitimate opportunities for experiencing personal fulfilment and for the construction of a positive self-image and status which are recognised both within and outside the New Lodge.

Recognising the high turnover of novice and youth boxers, the club coaches do not spend too much time working with all the youngest members. However, they keep a watchful eye on an odd one or two who attend regularly, who have a modicum of ability and who are dedicated trainers. If this level of interest and participation is sustained, then these youngsters will receive more attention from Morris and Hugh. Two fourteen-year-olds, Declan and Thomas, have shown enough to indicate that they may have the qualities to develop into serious boxers and have been singled out for special treatment. They receive more coaching and, if they choose, they are allowed to stay behind after 7 p.m., when the seniors begin their training. Both boys are selected to represent the Holy Family in one-off contests at other boxing clubs or on the bottom end of the bill of one of the one-night fight 'shows' which are held regularly at a local bar. Also, the coaches take more interest in their lives outside the gym, finding out about and getting to know their families and generally keeping appraised of what Declan and Thomas get up to around the estate. Any rumours of misbehaviour leads to sometimes gentle, otherwise harsh public admonishments in the gym. This is tacit recognition of the fact that while these two contenders may have one foot each in the boxing ring, their other feet are still firmly rooted in the rough-and-ready street culture of the New Lodge.

Thomas and Declan are fairly typical of their peers. The boys are near neighbours, living two doors apart in a small alley within a maze of small prefabricated housing units in the heart of the New Lodge. Thomas has four brothers and two sisters. His next eldest brother, Paul, works at a meat packers in town on a YTP (Youth Training Programme) scheme and is paid £29 per week. Apart from the wages, the biggest drawback of Paul's job is the fact that he has to walk 300 yards to get a bus to and from work. Paul's father tried to dissuade him from taking the job because he was afraid that he might be attacked and murdered by Protestants on the way home. Tom's eldest brother, Michael, works in a bar on the Antrim Road. He too is fearful of his walk home late at night and, with the memory of the Shankill Butchers clearly on his mind, he is ready to sprint at the sight of cars, particularly taxis, driving slowly. Tom's parents, Paul and Margaret, are in their late thirties and are both long-term unemployed, although occasionally they do some part-time work. Margaret sometimes works behind the counter in the local sweetshop. She served Peter McBride just five minutes before he was shot dead by the army. Margaret's cousin was active in the IRA and he kept a loaded gun at home. One of his sons found it and accidentally shot his two-year-old brother. Before they were married, Margaret and her fiance were arrested and held for three days by the security forces as suspect bombers because they were walking through an area when a bomb went off. Since then neither parent feels comfortable travelling too far away from the New Lodge. They have little affection for the security forces and are fearful of the paramilitaries. They see their own children as being sandwiched between the two and worry about their future. Margaret believes the fact that she has four sons means that her family is particularly vulnerable. She remembers the height of the Shankill Butchers' terror and is thankful that then her boys were young enough to keep in the house. Now that they 'are up' and old enough to roam the streets, it is different:

> It used to be that you worried more about daughters – getting pregnant! Now it's more worrying having sons. You can't keep them in and if you hear shots they could be caught in the cross-fire, they could be murdered by Protestant paras [paramilitaries], they could get involved with some organisation.

Despite such fears, Margaret is content to stay in the New Lodge, the community where she has always lived, near to her mother and her sisters, one of whom returned from living in Scotland because she missed her extended family and the community life of home. Like most boxers' mothers, Margaret is worried that Thomas might get hurt in the ring. However, like her husband, she is happy that

Thomas shows an interest in boxing, believing that the more time he spends with the Holy Family the less time he has to find trouble in the streets with his side-kick, Declan.

Declan also comes from a large family. He has two elder brothers and three younger sisters. These children are products of one of Northern Ireland's rare mixed working-class marriages. Mary, Declan's mother, is Catholic and is originally from the New Lodge area. She works long hours in the kitchens of a local hospital. Declan's father is unemployed. He is a Protestant who moved into the New Lodge when he married Mary. Mixed marriages are not generally tolerated in Protestant neighbourhoods and it is unlikely that the family would have been allowed to settle in east Belfast, where Declan's father's extended family reside. He does not feel threatened in the New Lodge, but he worries about being targeted by paramilitaries from neighbouring Protestant districts. For the same reasons, he rarely visits his relatives in east Belfast for fear of being attacked. Declan, who has been brought up as a Catholic, is resentful that he is not allowed to visit any of his relatives on his father's side, particularly his grandmother, who lives less than three miles away, but his parents are afraid that he too would be victimised if he was caught outside his own territory. As Declan's mother explains:

> Right enough, Declan's never seen his grandparents, but I'm afraid to take him to see them. They live in a predominantly Protestant district. It's not that they'd not make us welcome, it's just that we are both Catholics and some cowboy might pick on us, do us harm. It's fear more than anything that stops us going.

Mary and her husband find Declan a difficult boy to control. Like Tom's parents, they worry about what he gets up to on the streets, but they feel unable to influence his behaviour either inside or outside the home or at school. Declan's mother confesses to feelings of powerlessness to control forces which shape her children's destiny, particularly that of her three sons in the streets of north Belfast:

> When they go out I sit and watch the clock wondering if they are where they said they were going. I try to get them in early, but they're big boys now and they don't like to come home early. I like to get them in with the door closed and I believe they're safe then. Declan's only fourteen and I think because he's young he's safe, just about. But the other two are sixteen and eighteen and I really worry about them, where they are and who they're with. I worry that someone would harm them, shoot them or something.

Neither Tom nor Declan are high achievers at their school, St Patrick's, which has a reputation of being one of Belfast's toughest Catholic secondary schools. The overwhelming majority of schools in Northern Ireland are either Catholic or Protestant. As the crow flies, St Pat's is about a mile away from Tom and Declan's street. However, because the shortest walking route would take them through Protestant Tigers Bay, they have to take a long detour up on to the Antrim Road to catch a bus to school. As with the schools themselves, the school buses are segregated. The journey to school presents many opportunities for displays of sectarian hatred between Catholic boys going to St Pat's and their Protestant counterparts going to Castle High, 200 yards away.

In an effort to improve cross-community relations, 'education for mutual understanding' has been introduced as a compulsory subject within Northern Ireland's secondary school curriculum. Under its rubric boys from St Pat's exchange visits and go on trips with their counterparts from Castle High. But such experiments seem to do little to dampen the ardour of the likes of Tom and Declan when they encounter Castle pupils outside school time. As the 'fenians' taunt the 'orangies' and vice versa it is obvious that ancient hatreds are affected little by tampering with a small proportion of the school curriculum. Sometimes the symbolic conflict becomes triangular when parties of 'toffs' going to the nearby Belfast Royal Academy grammar school are encountered at the junction of the Antrim and Cliftonville Roads. Like most of the boys who attend the gym, Thomas and Declan espouse a distinctively anti-school philosophy. Declan is particularly hateful of St Pat's and seems to spend much of his time suspended from school for a variety of offences, including being disruptive in class, fighting and vandalism. Neither boy is invited to take part in inter-scholastic sports and, because of their anti-school demeanour, they both spend most of their time banned from PE and games.

Both boys are well versed in the street lore of sectarian conflict. They are able to talk knowledgeably about the various factions of nationalist paramilitaries and the disputes between them. They can also speak with informed enthusiasm about the range of weapons used by the Provos (the PIRA) and describe the consequences of falling foul of their draconian code of conduct. It is uncertain whether or not they have participated in antisocial activities, but both boys can talk about the thrills of stealing cars and joy riding and they are equally well informed on the rituals and anatomical details associated with knee-capping, the price paid by joy riders who are caught.

These youngsters spend almost all of their free time within the New Lodge estate, the physical and symbolic boundaries of which they know intimately. In the streets of north Belfast it is critically important to know the limits of your own territory and the start of your enemy's. This learning process is helped by the flags, murals, slogans and painted kerb stones which mark most of the neighbourhood's significant boundaries. As Thomas explains:

> If I saw an area with a Union Jack flag flying or red, white and blue on the pavements I wouldn't go near it, because I'd know it was Protestant territory. When you see green, white and gold, you know you're safe.

They dare not play in local parks in case they are set upon by 'orangies' from neighbouring Tigers Bay. Indeed, avoiding being captured and beaten or worse by the 'orangies' from Tigers Bay is a major preoccupation of the lads from the New Lodge. Despite the fact that the groups of teenagers who roam around the streets of Tigers Bay look identical to those who hang around the New Lodge, there is a cherished belief that a Catholic would soon be found out if he wandered across Duncairn Gardens. According to Declan:

> First thing is your name. If you were Catholic and you went over there you'd have to pretend to be called John or Paul or Billy. Some of us have names like Padraig and Declan so you really know we're Catholics. Then it's the way we say the letter 'h' too. Protestants say 'aitch' and Catholics say 'hatch', so they'd just get us to say the alphabet and when we got up to 'hatch', they'd know that we're Catholics and do us.

Once in a while the boys escape from their territory and make an expedition up Cave Hill, the ominous black mountain which rises up above north Belfast. The wilderness, greenery and fresh air of Cave Hill contrasts sharply with the grey concrete and grime of the New Lodge less than fifteen minutes away. As Declan puts it, pointing to the smoking city below, 'it's good to get away from all that down there ... all the hassle you're getting'. On Cave Hill Tom and Declan's street wisdom and battle hardness seem to fade as they chase one another across fields, explore caves and climb trees with boyish innocence and enthusiasm. Sometimes they climb over the back wall of Belfast Zoo which sprawls over one side of Cave Hill to take a free peek at the exotic animals. But even in this wilderness the signs of the troubled metropolis are ever present in the form of burnt-out cars in the distance and sectarian slogans which are carved into trees and painted on slabs of rock.

Back in the New Lodge, the coaches at the Holy Family realise that they are engaged in a tug of war with the likes of Tom and Declan. Until the stage is reached that 'boxer' becomes one of the most important dimensions of the boys' developing sense of who they are, there is a danger that one or many of the counter-attractions of the neighbourhood may pull either or both of them away from the Holy Family. The interest and support of the family appears to be a key factor in determining which youngsters come to the gym in the first place and which ones stay on to develop as boxers. Thomas has a highly supportive family in contrast to Declan whose family take less interest in his exploits either in or out of the ring. Thus, despite Declan's superior raw talent, it is likely that it will be Thomas rather than he who develops as a boxer.

In the case of fifteen-year-old Connor, the Holy Family has almost won the tug of war and he is on the threshold of becoming a serious boxer. His grandfather was a boxer and Connor was introduced to the club when he was ten by his uncle, Bobby, a former boxer and professional boxing coach who still hangs around the gym. The encouragement and support of one's family, particularly one which has a history of boxing, is critical to the process through which the role of serious boxer is assumed. Connor attends the gym every night that it is open and takes his training very seriously. While many of his friends rate football over boxing, Connor has become single-mindedly devoted to the disciplines of the ring, eschewing all of the potentially self-destructive aspects of life in the New Lodge and at least tolerating the demands of school. He laughs as he describes boxing as 'fun – it keeps me off the streets and out of trouble!'. But behind Connor's parody of the official boxing/social-worker line is the truth that he has made a deliberate choice to stick with boxing, not simply because it is a good sport, but also because it offers him immunity from the social and political malaise which exists outside the Holy Family. The coaches have recognised Connor's ability and his dedication and give him extra tuition. Connor also acts as a junior coach to the youngest members of the club. He acts as Bongo's assistant and it is usually Connor who organises and conducts the warm-up and cool-down sessions at the beginning and end of each evening training session in the gym. There is a distance between Connor and his peers in the gym and while he remains friends with the likes of Thomas and Declan to some extent, this distance is maintained outside the boxing club. Confirming his status as an apprentice serious boxer, Connor has reached the stage when he is included on the under-card of up and coming boxing 'shows' in local hotels and at venues further afield.

Serious boxers

After 7 p.m., with the exception of a handful of apprentices like Connor, most of the younger boys clear out of the gym to make room for the older boxers. These are mainly young men who have adopted boxing as a central element in their lives and who take the sport very seriously. Gerry Storey, the manager of the Holy Family, arrives slightly late after picking up a couple of fighters from Protestant neighbourhoods and having been delayed by army/RUC security checks. During the troubles random security checks were a fact of life in Belfast and their intensity varied with the level of terrorist activity. Security is particularly rigorous during this particular phase. It is rumoured that the security forces have lost track of a 2,000 lb bomb which the IRA is moving around Belfast, waiting for an appropriate time, place and target for detonation.

Gerry, a thick-set man in his fifties, has been involved in the Holy Family for more than forty years. As a young man he was an accomplished amateur who won Irish titles and boxed for Ireland on several occasions in the late 1940s and early 1950s. Both his sons followed in his footsteps at the Holy Family to become good amateur fighters. While Martin gave up the ring in his early twenties, his brother, Sam Storey, turned professional and he currently fights for Barney Eastwood. This earns him a place of honour on the Holy Family's wall of fame, where his photograph and record of achievement in the ring are prominently displayed alongside those of Barry McGuigan, Paul Douglas and other local legends such as Hugh Russell. Hugh, who won an Olympic medal and had a respectable, if short, career as a professional before taking up a career in sports photography, helps Bongo work with the junior fighters and is a very important role model for them.

It is largely Storey's reputation as a coach which has enabled the club to attract so many boxers from other parts of the city, including Protestants. This reputation travels with him outside boxing circles, where he is a well known and well respected figure in the toughest nationalist and loyalist neighbourhoods, where he has an apparent immunity from the paramilitaries. One evening in the early 1970s, when the Holy Family used to be housed in a building on the New Lodge Road, Gerry arrived to open the club in the middle of a gun battle which was raging between the army and the Provos. As Gerry's well known car pulled up outside the boxing club, much to the wonderment of the security forces the Provos ceased firing until Storey had let himself into the club, at which point the gun fight recommenced.

In certain respects Gerry Storey is the Holy Family. He has been running the club since the early 1960s and has witnessed the growth and development of several generations of amateur and professional fighters. While Gerry loves the boxing for its intrinsic qualities he also believes passionately in the character-building value of the sport, viewing it as an important alternative to many of the less legitimate diversions on offer to young men in places like north Belfast. In order for the Holy Family to survive it is essential that the club is protected from the divisive social and political influences which dominate in the surrounding neighbourhood. Storey is the guardian of the club's apolitical status and its sectarian neutrality:

> We've got simple rules and basic discipline, the same as when the club was set up in 1948. No swearing and no political talk. You leave the political talk outside the door. When you come in here your business is boxing. We don't care what colour you are, what religion you are or anything like that so long as you come to train and box. Hopefully, when they grow up they remember these things.

Gerry has been coach to the Irish national boxing team in the Olympics and to the Northern Ireland team in the Commonwealth Games. In addition to Storey's reputation as a coach, one of the Holy Family's greatest attractions, particularly for boxers from other districts, is that the club organises regular overseas tours. Storey feels that local boys who are fortunate to be selected to box in these and other international tournaments have their social and cultural horizons broadened to the extent that it affects the way they view life once they return home:

> Obviously, if they're not involved in boxing, they're not out of their own areas, out of their own districts, not getting an opportunity to get about and meet different people. They might think that other people have two heads. It's different for the boxers who get out and meet these people. They find out the way we live and our fellahs find out the way others live. They realise that we're not that different.

While the boys and novices who come to the Holy Family are nearly all from the New Lodge or other neighbouring Catholic estates, the intermediate and senior boxers come from all over Belfast. This includes many Protestants from loyalist neighbourhoods. On this particular evening there is a good cross-section of the club's serious membership in attendance.

John is currently a first-year student in economics at Queen's University Belfast. He comes from a family of amateur boxers and he began learning to box as soon as he could walk. He is proud to talk of his first boxing trophy, which he won as a four-year-old and which sits among hundreds of others in a cabinet in the living room of the family home, a small terraced house between the Antrim Road and the Limestone Road. John lives about half a mile away from the club, close to the Holy Family Church where, on Sundays and holy days, he serves mass as an altar boy. On his way to the gym, in order to avoid walking through loyalist Tigers Bay, he has to take an indirect route which means walking an extra mile or so. He has the same sectarian geography in his mind when he plans his daily training runs. In addition to worrying about hills, crowded pavements and traffic, John is keenly aware of which streets he should not run along for fear of sectarian attacks. Along with a small group of fellow boxers he once made the mistake of running along Duncairn Gardens which separates Tigers Bay from the New Lodge. They were forced to quicken their pace considerably when attacked by stone-throwing youths:

> When you go for a run anything can happen, therefore you sort of plan your route and you try to cover all uncertainties, all things unforeseen and unexpected.

John can avoid harassment from loyalists by not running through their territory, but he cannot help being reminded that his own neighbourhood continues to exist on the brink of civil war. As he runs down the New Lodge Road towards the boxing club John passes the spot where his uncle was killed in an incident which is known locally as the New Lodge massacre. It began when loyalist gunmen from a passing car shot and killed two Catholic civilians standing outside a pub on the New Lodge Road. The sound of gunfire attracted the attention of the British army who, perhaps believing that they were under attack from the IRA, opened fire on individuals whom they saw in the street. The firing brought John's uncle out of his New Lodge home and he was shot dead by an army sniper as he went to attend to the two men who had been shot in the earlier incident. A total of six civilians were killed that day on the New Lodge. John does not blame the soldiers as individuals but resents the fact that his neighbourhood continues to be more or less occupied twenty-four hours a day by the British army. Like most other people who have grown up through the troubles, however, he has learned to ignore the sights and sounds of the occupation:

> When you're running down to the boxing club you usually see the troops and army on the streets, but I don't really notice them. They're like part of the houses, part of the bricks and walls, they're there so often. You get conditioned to see them every time you go and when you see something so many times you don't take any notice of it.

John's education and his religious devotion set him apart from most other boxers in the club. A matrix which balances the routine, order and discipline of the Holy Family against the chaos, disorder and anarchy of the New Lodge does not work for the likes of John. Outside of boxing he leads a disciplined and orderly life at the centre of which is his family. He is reflective on the social conditions which frame his daily experience. John understands concepts such as the poverty trap, long-term unemployment and urban deprivation but he is nonetheless contemptuous of 'the hoods', those who hang around the streets, and he believes that such idleness is a waste of talent and breeds discontent and uncontrolled violence of a kind considerably more malevolent than that meted out in the ring. This he believes is true of modern cities the world over. Even the kind of community division which requires him to live under conditions bordering on apartheid he believes to be a global condition rather than a local aberration:

> It isn't just special to Belfast. In New York the Irish have their area, the Jews their area, the blacks theirs and in each individual area there is a way of life worth respecting and if these people want to keep to the confines of a particular area, then that's fair enough.

Some boxers view their sport as an avenue which may one day take them away from their social roots, but for John, the university student, active membership of the Holy Family allows him to keep one foot firmly grounded in the street culture of north Belfast. He seems to need boxing as a means of keeping in touch with the more elemental aspects of his own nature, which he also seeks to control. He loves boxing as a sport because it provides him with the opportunity to express his physical, mental and emotional powers within an acceptable social framework. While his intellectual powers are developed and judged in the lecture theatres and examination halls of Queen's University, the boxing ring for John is a proving ground upon which his physicality and courage can be tested, and, as he puts it:

> Whatever way you come out of the ring you are a winner, because it takes a lot of courage to get in there in the first place.

Some Protestant fighters will make their own way to the club, but others, particularly the younger ones who do not have their own transport, will be ferried in and out of the New Lodge. Colin and Stephen travel every night from distant neighbourhoods to train at the Holy Family. Both developed an appetite for the sport in a gym in Protestant east Belfast, in one of the city's most insular loyalist communities, and both are absolutely dedicated to the disciplines of the ring. Colin is a quiet young man who keeps to himself while in the gym. In the ring he is a terrier who is respected by the rest of the fighters, but he is yet to win any major titles which is why, despite its location in a nationalist area, he transferred to the Holy Family. His friend, Stephen, has a boxing pedigree straight out of

Hollywood. During the day he punishes his mind emptying bins and sweeping streets in affluent Bangor, County Down, while at night he punishes his body with the Holy Family, surrounded by the poverty of Belfast's New Lodge. He is worried by the location of the club but his appetite for risking his life in the ring overcomes his fear of risking his life out of it. The east Belfast club could only develop his skill so far and he knew that he would get better coaching, more matches and more opportunities for travel if he joined the Holy Family. Unlike John the university student, Stephen lives for boxing and boxing only. It is the only thing which has any meaning in his life and the only activity which gives him any sense of self-respect. His ambition is to turn professional and make a career out of the ring, and he is prepared to sacrifice almost anything in pursuit of this goal.

Similarly, Neil and James journey from New Mossley, a loyalist estate on the outskirts of the city, to fight for the Holy Family. Both boxers learned their trade in a small social club regularly frequented by loyalist paramilitaries, but like with Stephen and Colin, they realised that in order to get better-quality coaching they would have to move to another club and followed Gerry Storey's reputation to the Holy Family. Neil is one of the club's rising stars. He is Irish amateur senior champion at his weight and in October 1992, boxing on a very high-class card, he won a bronze medal for Ireland at the world amateur boxing championships in Montreal. Neil is a regular member of the Irish national team and he spends a considerable amount of time training in Dublin under the instruction of coach Nicholas Hernandez-Cruz, who is seconded by the Cubans to the Irish team.

Neil's experiences through boxing set him apart from his neighbourhood friends and acquaintances, most of whom rarely venture too far away from the insular comfort of their housing estate. The house next door to Neil's is festooned with symbols of loyalism and a large Union Jack flutters from the gable across the street. Neil's approach to his daily training run is similar to that of John's except for the fact that in charting his route he tends to stick to the streets which display the symbols and colours of loyalism. Also, significantly, because he comes from and runs in a predominantly loyalist area, he rarely encounters the security forces:

> I live in a mainly Protestant area on the outskirts of Belfast. You never see the security forces here. You only see them in Belfast. There's no need for them here. When I'm training there could be a few problems if I ran into a Catholic area where nobody knew me. I feel safer running in the country or where there are Protestant murals and the kerbs are painted red, white and blue. I know then there'll be no problems.

Neil trains regularly and hard at the club, but he has reservations about going there by himself. None of his Protestant friends from New Mossley would dream of going near a place like the New Lodge. He tends to rely on one or other of the coaches to pick him up and escort him to and from the boxing club. Sometimes, if things are particularly hot on the political front, Neil stays away from the Holy

Family. However, his burning desire to become a successful professional boxer usually outweighs the fears associated with training in a nationalist neighbourhood:

> Sometimes, when things are really bad down there, I'm a bit worried and sometimes my dad tells me not to go, but I'm always on my guard and nothing has ever happened to me. I want to give myself the best shot in boxing with the best coaches and the best facilities and if that means going into an area like the New Lodge, then so be it.

Both the Irish champion and his friend James claim to be less worried about training with the Holy Family than about the attitudes of local political hard-liners who are not involved in boxing but object to Protestants having associations with any organisation with Catholic and Irish connotations. Even then, they are less worried for themselves than for their parents, close relatives and friends.

Neil's main ambitions are directed towards the 1994 Commonwealth Games in Victoria, Canada, and the 1996 Olympics in Atlanta.[1] In terms of the former he will be boxing for Northern Ireland and can do so unambiguously. However, in the Olympics, Neil will be boxing for Ireland. Reflecting the complexities of political and national identity for people from Northern Ireland, athletes from Northern Ireland can elect to play either for Great Britain or for Ireland in certain sports in senior competitions in which both national entities are represented, such as the Olympics. In boxing such a choice is not available to Neil who must, if he wishes to perform at the highest level, fight for Ireland, and this causes a degree of dissonance for a young working-class Protestant who has been brought up to see himself first and foremost as British. However, because of his total dedication to the sport, Neil must set aside his personal views on national/political affiliation. Nevertheless, he still worries about the consequences for him and his family should he be filmed wearing an Irish vest, under the Irish flag and standing for the Irish national anthem.

In this regard, Neil is mindful of the experiences of Wayne McCullough, who won a silver medal for Ireland at the Barcelona Olympics in 1992 and who, as Ireland's youngest competitor, carried the Irish national flag in the opening ceremony of the Seoul Olympics in 1988. McCullough is a Protestant from Belfast's Shankill Road. As has been explained, Northern Irish amateur fighters must box under the governance of the IABA and in international tournaments, with the exception of the Commonwealth Games, must represent Ireland. This is not necessarily appreciated outside boxing circles in Northern Ireland, especially in hard-line loyalist areas such as the Shankill Road, where representing the Irish Republic is considered by some to be nothing short of treason. The glare of publicity which accompanied McCullough carrying the Irish tricolour in Seoul

---

[1] Neil Sinclair won a gold medal in the 1994 Commonwealth Games in Victoria. He turned professional in 1995 and did not box in the Atlanta Olympics.

reflected badly on his family back home, who were intimidated and beaten by hard-line loyalists elements.

More recently the politics of national division were more formally revealed by the actions of the unionist-dominated Belfast City Council. After taking (what was for them) the enlightened step of hosting a civic reception at City Hall for McCullough on his return from Barcelona, they refused to invite fellow team member and Olympic gold medallist Michael Carruth, from County Cork, even though McCullough had been guest of honour at the reception held in Dublin for Carruth a few days earlier. The Council argued that they could not honour Carruth because he was a corporal in the army of a state which still claimed constitutional jurisdiction over Northern Ireland (articles 3 and 4 of the constitution of the Republic of Ireland). With this kind of treatment fresh in his mind, McCullough ('the pocket rocket') has spurned opportunities to join professional boxing stables in both England and Ireland, electing instead to box professionally in the United States. No doubt money was a factor here, but we cannot rule out that, at least in part, McCullough made this decision to protect his boxing career from political intrusions.

Circumstances in the career of Barry McGuigan may also have influenced McCullough's decision to fight professionally in the United States. McGuigan was born and brought up in Clones, County Monaghan, in that part of Ulster which is in the Irish Republic. As an amateur, like all Ulstermen, McGuigan fought within the embrace of the IABA. However, when he turned professional he was advised by his then mentor/manager, B. J. Eastwood to box in pursuit of British rather than Irish titles – presumably because the former offered a more lucrative return than the latter and a better chance of world recognition. In an attempt to appease Irish nationalists while at the same time not offending unionists, McGuigan would enter the ring under the flag of the United Nations and to the sound of the Londonderry air 'Danny Boy', instead of having the British or Irish anthems played. However, many Irish nationalists outside the boxing fraternity never forgave McGuigan for fighting for British titles, becoming, as they saw it, a 'turncoat'. When the boxer paraded through the streets of Belfast with his world title, slogans such as 'Barry the Brit – sold his soul for English gold' were daubed on walls and gable ends in many nationalist areas of the city. Since retiring from the ring McGuigan has elected to set up home in southern England, ostensibly to be closer to his business interests. However, it is possible that in deciding whether to live in England or Ulster, the death threats which McGuigan received from nationalists helped to tip the balance in favour of Kent over Armagh.

Seamus is one of the few current senior amateurs living near to the Holy Family, but he did not graduate from the club's youth and novice ranks. As a boy he learned to box in a rival club in another part of the New Lodge estate and transferred to the Holy Family once he decided to take up boxing seriously. Seamus packs shelves in a warehouse in Belfast dock. This is a mindless occupation, but it pays his bills and gives him the financial security to continue boxing. Each morning except Sunday, Seamus gets up at first light to run through the empty streets of north Belfast and up on to the park lands of Cave Hill. Seamus's main ambitions are to get married and turn professional. He has a steady girlfriend and they have a small baby. The arrival of his small son has been an important factor in his decision to move away from north Belfast and out of Northern Ireland when he gets a chance. He has a sister living in New York and he views this as a possible avenue through which to pursue a professional boxing career in the United States.

Paul is one of the club's established stars. He is Irish senior heavyweight champion and he competed at that weight in the 1992 Barcelona Olympics. He was brought up in the same neighbourhood as Wayne McCullough, and both fighters developed their boxing skills in clubs along the Shankill Road. Like many of the rest, Paul is a member of the Holy Family because he knows that it is the best place for him to develop as a boxer and this is more important to him than the fact that the club is located in a nationalist neighbourhood. In the daytime Paul works as a courier for a bank in the city and in the night-time, when he is not training, he is a bouncer at a number of Belfast bars and nightclubs. While physically Paul is a hard man both inside and outside the ring, his experiences in boxing have given him a liberal perspective on life which is unusual among his contemporaries outside the Holy Family. He is the first to admit that, if it had not been for boxing, given his physical stature and where he comes from, almost inevitably he would have been drawn into the shadow world of the loyalist paramilitaries and their gangsters. Paul recognises that through his success in the ring he has had his horizons broadened, travelling around the world and meeting people from a wide variety of cultural, ethnic and racial backgrounds.

Billy, a twenty-one-year-old from the Shankill has walked to the club with a friend and his step-father, Bert, who is also the secretary of the Holy Family. Billy's natural father was a renowned hard man and a recognised street fighter. One night, when Billy was a child, unknown assassins burst into his house and shot his father dead while he was watching television. It is impossible to gauge the impact which this event had on young Billy. A friend took Billy to a local boxing club when he was twelve and he discovered that he had inherited some of his father's abilities as a fighter. However, Billy decided that he would develop his talent in a more disciplined fashion and became a serious boxer rather than a street fighter, and in order to achieve this ambition Billy joined the Holy Family when he was fifteen. Since then, he has been Irish junior champion and has won titles at every stage of his development. He has no time for people who become involved with vigilante politics, but so long as he continues to live on the Shankill he recognises that his life will always be bound up with sectarianism. Just as boxers from Catholic neighbourhoods must plan their training runs to avoid Protestant territory, so too must Billy select a route which keeps him away from Catholic enclaves in the Ardoyne and Oldpark estates. Likewise, when he walks to the club along the

Crumlin Road he makes sure he does not stray into Catholic neighbourhoods until he reaches the New Lodge itself, where he is recognised as Billy the boxer. Billy is a great stylist in the ring, but now that he has a steady job and a steady girl he seems less dedicated to boxing and concern is felt by his step-father and the coaches that Billy may fall away from the sport.

In certain respects Billy's step-father underlines some of the contradictions which are a part of the fabric of the Holy Family. Bert is a former prison officer who once worked within the foreboding walls of the Crumlin Road prison, which is in the heart of north Belfast and which has been temporary home to thousands of nationalist and loyalist terrorists. Prison warders are regularly targeted for retribution by both sets of paramilitaries. Outside of boxing, Bert is the chairman of the Linfield Football Club Amalgamated Supporters Club. Linfield is Belfast's biggest soccer club. Apart from achievements on the pitch, Linfield is famous for employing or fielding few Catholics and is the sporting flagship of working-class Protestantism in the city. Nevertheless, Bert seems to be more than comfortable inhabiting the cross-community world of the Holy Family while at the same time savouring the true-blue atmosphere of the Linfield supporters' club lounge. Bert's former career as a prison warder and his associations with Linfield could make him vulnerable to attacks from either section of the community, but his role within the boxing club appears to keep him safe from victimisation.

As they drift into the attic gymnasium the young men strip and change into their training gear before beginning the ritual wrapping of hands with well used strips of off-white bandage. This is accompanied by gossip and banter, which is mainly about boxing: who has fought whom on the local circuit, what calibre of fights have been on the world scene and what kind of physical condition each fighter is in. Occasionally mention is made of something going on in somebody's personal life, usually no more than a quip about a girlfriend. No matter what has been going on in the neighbourhood, the conversations in the club rarely focus on politics and related aspects of community life. Once in a while one of the boxers may complain about being 'turned over' (stopped and searched) by the security forces on his way to the club, but these comments never lead to more general discussions about the troubles. The unwritten club rule which rarely needs to be enforced. The people who are the Holy Family are united for the purposes of boxing and all other matters are left at the door of the club. In general, people in Belfast avoid speaking politics, especially in religiously mixed company. This informal regulation is in particular evidence in sporting circles, where quite a lot of cross-community mixing takes place in Northern Ireland. However, the community relations potential of these situations should not be over-emphasised, as social division and its consequences are never talked about and thus it is hard to see how attitudes are changed or prejudices reduced by this conspiracy of silence (McLauglin, 1995). It is almost as if the participants have an unspoken understanding that the very survival of their sport in Belfast depends on the capacity of the participants to collaborate with Gerry Storey's version of the

'Olympic truce' and help to insulate the Holy Family from the politics of sectarianism. As John argues, the taboo on political talk is helped by the fact that boxing is an individual sport which is not associated with one or other religious/ cultural tradition:

> Boxing is individuals as themselves coming to the best club to fulfil their potential; people from different religious denominations can take it up and come together and get on with their boxing in a fairly harmonious atmosphere. I might have my view of the political situation in which we live. Another fellah in the club may have his and they may be opposed, but as boxers we respect each other, therefore why come into conflict? Why say something that might cause offence?

Just as was the case in the MBC in the United States, at the Holy Family all the training is paced three to one (three minutes' activity followed by one minute's rest), imitating the timing of the boxing round and rest period. One of the club coaches turns on the three-minute clock, selects a tape for the ghetto blaster (Jimmy Sommerville) and the gym bursts into activity as the fighters warm up through a pugilistic form of dance aerobics. This is followed by a sequence of skipping, callisthenics, bag work, shadow boxing, sparring and warming down. The training takes no more than ninety minutes, after which the boxers shower, pack their gear and drift off to their respective neighbourhoods in all corners of the city. There is little or no socialising done among the club's members outside the gym, particularly between Catholic and Protestant members. In this respect the Holy Family, like most boxing clubs, differs from other kinds of sports clubs, which often have significant social dimensions which have an impact on members beyond the life of the sport itself. The Holy Family has no club-house for after-training or after-match fraternisation and the boxers do not go out together for meals or drinks after sharing an event. Sometimes the coaches will get together for a drink, usually after the Sunday-morning training session. However, for the fighters themselves the ascetic nature of boxing does not lend itself to the levels of conspicuous consumption which often accompany other amateur sports such as rugby and soccer. However, equally important is the fact that it is both difficult and dangerous for working-class males from different religious communities to mix socially outside the immediate boundaries of their sport. Once the fights are over it is easier and safer simply to pack up and go home.

Rites of passage 1: stepping out of the playground

As with all sports, the farm system of boxing in Northern Ireland has its gates and gatekeepers who are there in order to grade and promote quality. There are several formal career stages through which all amateur boxers must progress if they are to perform at the top of their craft. Within this structure there are three age levels:

boys and youth novice; intermediate; and senior. The boys and youth novice titles are restricted to Ulster, but intermediate and senior Ulster champions go forward to fight for all-Ireland titles. Success at national level can lead to international representative honours for Ireland in a range of one-off competitions and in prestigious multinational tournaments such as the European and world boxing championships and the Olympic Games. In addition, Northern Ireland sends a boxing team to the Commonwealth Games. Woven within this formal career structure are less formal inter-club competitions, commercial boxing 'shows' and club tours, some of which offer the opportunity for travel to other parts of Ireland and the United Kingdom and further afield. What follows is a series of snap shots of some of the lower stages of this formal and informal career progression as experienced by a sample of Holy Family boxers.

Apart from sparring with each other, the youngest members of the club get their first preview of real boxing through exchanging visits to spar with fighters from neighbouring clubs. That these exchanges continue to happen without regard to the sectarian complexion of the neighbourhoods in which various boxing clubs exist is little short of amazing. It is not unusual for groups of young fighters from clubs in working-class Protestant areas to come to the Holy Family for competitive sparring. Likewise, from time to time, Bongo and Hugh ferry Thomas, Declan and their friends for sparring experience in clubs in Tigers Bay and the Shankill. All the bravado of the New Lodge vanishes when the youngsters are driven out of their own territory and into one of these areas. Bongo tells a story of taking some youngsters to a fight in a Protestant club. One youngster had 'forgotten' the club rule and, perhaps not realising where he was boxing, he turned up wearing a Glasgow Celtic football kit (Celtic have a following which is almost exclusively Catholic and by wearing a replica kit the boy was clearly labelling himself as a Catholic). As Bongo's car entered an unfamiliar part of the city one of the boys asked him where they where. When Bongo told him that they were driving up the Shankill Road they all went silent and the boy in the Celtic kit began to strip off as quickly as he could.

Once inside the clubs, boxers and coaches are safe and are always warmly received by their hosts. It is agreed by both sets of paramilitary groups that boxing is left alone. However, once the context changes from boxing, Bongo feels that he is at risk in Protestant areas:

> During the fights there's no problems or worries at all, but when the fights are over and the boys have gone I get worried. It's rude to leave without staying for a drink, but it's then I get nervous. If something came up on the TV, some shooting or bombing, it'd only take one madman sitting in the club and I'm right there to take it out on.

During one visit to a club in Protestant Tigers Bay, Declan and Thomas recognised a boy with whom they had made friends a year before during a school-based community-relations visit to a holiday camp north of Dublin. Despite the fact that the young Catholics acknowledge that their former Protestant friend is 'dead on' (that is, a decent sort), as Declan explains, because of a deeply ingrained fear of 'the other side', they would not consider arranging to meet up other than in a boxing club or on some pre-arranged and supervised school visit:

> Meet him outside of a boxing club? Like where…? Probably he'd ask us to come into Tigers Bay, but we wouldn't go into it, there'd probably be a gang just waiting behind a wall to jump you and that; you'd get done for it. That's just the way our religions are here. It's just that we hate them and they hate us.

The youngsters' first formal test of boxing ability comes in the Ulster Boys' and Youths' Novice Championships. The youngest contenders throughout the region congregate at a single venue to fight for the title of Ulster champion. More often than not this tournament is held in Belfast, but on this particular occasion the venue is forty miles away in Coalisland, a small town on the edge of Lough Neagh in County Tyrone.

It is an exciting day out for the boys of the Holy Family, who rarely venture far away from the New Lodge. The journey takes about an hour. Unlike many metropolitan sprawls, Belfast finishes abruptly and after ten minutes' drive a drab urban landscape is replaced by the green pastures of County Antrim. Lest we forget, ten minutes further on the motorway skirts the perimeter of the Maze Prison with its the notorious H block enclosures, home to hundreds of internees in the early 1970s and which continue to host some of Northern Ireland's most feared and revered terrorists and/or political prisoners. Looking out of the windows the boys in my car seem bemused by the wide open spaces, but the Maze fits more readily into their symbolic universe. The sight of the distant concrete, barbed wire and floodlights sparks a soprano rendering of the Soldiers Song (the anthem of the Republic of Ireland) and mock salutes to 'comrades in arms'. The father of one of the passengers was shot fourteen times by a UVF hit squad and left for dead. Miraculously he survived, but the memory of the incident is etched into his son's consciousness.

Comprised mostly of good farmland, forest and heath and a scattering of small towns and villages, County Tyrone has the appearance of a prosperous shire. In fact Tyrone is the rural equivalent of north Belfast and is another of Northern Ireland's deadliest killing fields. The area is referred to by the security forces as 'murder triangle', because of the level of activity among the paramilitaries, particularly the PIRA. The boys from 'murder mile' should feel right at home here. Union flags and tricolours fly atop of silos and barns declaring the denomination and national allegiance of farm owners. Many villages and towns are either Catholic or Protestant. When a hamlet is shared each community has its separate territory, clearly demarked by painted kerb stones, flags, murals and painted slogans. The British army has its heaviest presence in this area and seldom is the sky free from dark-green helicopters, the only safe form of transport for both army and police, who are on duty twenty-four hours a day and who live in a series of heavily fortified barracks.

The town of Coalisland is a microcosm of the county and through episodes of terrorism, sectarian violence and murder it regularly features in local and national news bulletins. It was a focus of civil rights activism in the late 1960s and home to Bernadette McAliskey (nee Devlin), a high-profile republican activist and nationalist MP in the early days of the troubles. The small town captured the national headlines again in 1991 when a gang of IRA terrorists was ambushed and killed by the British army's SAS (Special Air Service) in the grounds of a local Catholic church which was seriously damaged by fire in the incident. The following year Coalisland returned to the newsreels when, after one of their colleagues had lost his legs in an IRA landmine attack, a large group of paratroopers went on the rampage in the town, wrecking a bar and beating up many of the customers. The once prosperous town has long since lost its manufacturing base and, like north Belfast, has a high rate of unemployment, particularly among the young. This is one of the reasons why the hosts of the tournament, the Coalisland Amateur Boxing Club, has no shortage of members.

The club is housed in a purpose-built shed-like building on the outskirts of the town. A well used ring stands beneath flickering strip lighting at one end of a spartan and shabbily furnished hall. Packs of boys, mainly from Belfast, dressed in track suits, shell suits and replica football kits roam around the room waiting for their turns to be weighed in. This ritual takes place in a much smaller room adjacent to the main hall. While the dehumanised metric weight divisions for senior boxers are offset by rich linguistic descriptions such as bantam, feather, straw and welter, the thinness and lightness of the juniors defy the creativity of the English language. In temperatures barely above freezing, a shivering line of emaciated pale bodies in Y-fronts or, appropriately, boxer shorts form a snaking line in front of a set of scales. Grey-haired and balding middle-aged men in blazers call out names and weights in kilos and decimals as others make written entries on to the match card. When this document appears on the notice board it shows conflict between churches and between the sacred and the secular, as boys from Immaculata, Holy Trinity and Holy Family are matched among fighters from Albert Foundry, Dockers and Hammer.

Boxers themselves are among the fittest and most health-conscious sportsmen, but at every level of the fight game, from the Royal Albert Hall to a back-street community centre, there is something characteristically unathletic about the sport's social setting and its camp followers. Coalisland proves to be no exception as the hall fills up with a ragamuffin audience of underweight boys and overweight men, shrouded in a grey/blue pall of condensation and cigarette smoke. Meanwhile the young fighters make their final preparations in the ladies' toilet, which is the only available private space outside of a small and overcrowded changing room. When the timers, judges, the doctor and the referee are ready, the master of ceremonies welcomes the first bout into the ring, initiating a loud chorus of cheering from the partisan crowd. The lightest weights are scheduled first. They offer a studied balance in ruthlessness and valour. With scant regard to self-defence, a procession of small boys, dwarfed by their gloves and helmets, engage in a series of breathless and often bloody battles. There is a limited amount of style on display in the early contests, which offer little more than scraps in the junior school playground. However, the Queensberry rules ensure that no bully with a size and weight advantage can dominate the canvas quite like he might dominate the schoolyard. As the ages and weights of the boys increase there is an improvement in the standard of boxing. An increase in ring craft in tandem with a maturing sense of self-preservation gradually turns the playground brawlers into more stylish boxers.

The Holy Family has contestants in three weight divisions. Thomas and Declan both have to fight against tough Belfast opponents. Despite seemingly limitless aggression and bravery, Declan is comprehensively out-boxed by his opponent and is easily beaten. Thomas, on the other hand, has the edge in skill and experience over his opposite number and after three hard rounds of boxing he emerges victorious, much to the delight of his young friends and his mother and father, who have made a rare excursion out of north Belfast to cheer him on. Tom's victory provides a rare interlude of success and public honour in a young life which is otherwise low on achievement and collective acclaim. For Declan, on the other hand, while defeat is disappointing it is easily accommodated by one who is used to little else. After the fights, unshowered, the boys scramble into their street clothes and are packed into cars for the journey back to Belfast, happy to have had their day out in the country, but equally looking forward to the comforting sights and sounds of the war-torn city.

Rights of passage 2: rounds of the alehouse

Apart from the official contests organised by the IABA, the Holy Family also engages in 'one-off' boxing shows held in local hotels. These exhibitions are also integral to the process through which aspiring boxers learn their trade and coaches and managers grade their ability. A visit to 'fight night' at the Gregory Hotel in north Belfast to witness one of the local boxing 'shows' (the name given to one-off amateur boxing tournaments) is a bizarre experience. The venue for this night's show is above the New Lodge on the Antrim Road, between Cliftonville Road and Crumlin Road, and is one of Belfast's most dangerous neighbourhoods. It is a Catholic area where paramilitary groups are very active and youthful sectarian street gangs are engaged in a perpetual struggle for supremacy. Strangers are ill advised to visit this quarter, particularly youngsters and especially at night. The night's bill is a mixture of boys, intermediate and senior boxers. Some of the youngest boxers who appear on tonight's card are local Catholics, but a few of the older fighters are Protestants from east Belfast. Under normal circumstances the presence of a couple of Protestant youths here would arouse great suspicion and they would be in grave danger. However, as explained earlier, their status as boxers provides them with a relative immunity and, so long as the context is clearly associated with boxing, they are able to come and go from the hotel without fear of molestation. This immunity is also extended to the small numbers of friends and relatives who come to support them.

Access to the Gregory is controlled through a pair of automatic security doors overlooked by a television camera which provides video evidence for the doormen, who open the doors only if the visitor is recognised as a regular. Strangers must explain their reasons for wanting to get in via an intercom next to the door. Access is eased for strangers if they can give the name of a local who will vouch for them. This vetting process is designed to prevent Chicago-style machine gun and bomb attacks by loyalist paramilitaries. The hotel is no longer residential and inside consists of a warren of bars and run-down function rooms. In one such room a temporary ring occupies almost all of the small dance floor, which later in the evening will be the venue for an over-thirties disco. The ring is a place of order in an otherwise shifting social milieu. The audience is made up mainly of family and friends of the fighters. Ringside sit groups of men, women and children at tables covered with glasses of beer, spirits, soft drinks and smouldering ashtrays. A few unattached fight fans wait to be entertained in the seats further away from ringside, as closer to the bar a half-interested handful of customers sip their drinks waiting for the fighters to come and go and the disco to commence at 10 p.m. A significant number of other people wander casually around the bar-room, drinks in hand, carefully avoiding the young boys and girls who chase one another around tables and chairs.

The random noise of a Belfast lounge bar in full swing is interrupted as the master of ceremonies takes the microphone and announces the impending arrival of the night's first bout. Thus begins a familiar ritual. The referee in black trousers, white shirt and black bowtie steps into the ring ahead of two small processions which make their way from the shadows at the back of the room. At the head of each shuffle two small figures draped in ill-fitting gowns dwarfed by their retinue of coaches, corner men and well-wishers. The DJ cranks up the volume of the universal boxer's anthem – the theme from 'Rocky' – as the two thirteen-year-old straw-weight boys step under the ropes, shed their robes and begin punk-like to hop and jump around the ring. Both look as if they are easily outweighed by their equipment. Half an hour earlier both had been schoolboys sitting nervously in their school uniforms waiting to be called. But now in shorts and vests, with hands wrapped, gloves and headguards tied and mouthguards in place, they are transformed into boxers as the referee calls them to the centre of the ring to administer the traditional pre-fight admonishments. With only six minutes of action permitted (three two-minute rounds) there is little time for caution, and as the bell rings to start the contest the fighters bounce out of their respective corners to merge in a flurry of wild swings at the centre of the ring. As was the case in Coalisland, the first match rarely rises above the misdirected energy of a schoolyard brawl, but as the bout progresses Seamus, fighting for the Holy Family, shows slightly more style than Damien, representing the Dockers' Club, and Seamus is awarded the fight at the discretion of the referee. After a brief personal celebration Seamus initiates the post-fight ritual as he commiserates with the defeated opponent and accepts the congratulations of the Dockers' trainers and corner men before returning to the back patting of the Holy Family team.

During the next two hours the scene is repeated by pairs of progressively older and more experienced fighters from a range of clubs throughout the city. The last fight is close to the real thing as two seventeen-year-olds dance and skirmish around the ring before converging for frenzied ten- to twenty-second exchanges of jabs, crosses and uppercuts which invariably conclude with longer periods of exhausted hanging on. Colin from east Belfast is fighting for the Holy Family and, despite a bloody nose, throws enough measured leather of his own to get the decision. Even before the appreciative applause of the audience has died away the ring is being dismantled to the loud accompaniment of sixties music as the boxing arena is rapidly transformed into the venue for the oldies disco. Equally rapidly, the night's gladiators shed their boxing regalia and their fighters' prestige as, unwashed, they step into their street clothes, ready for the tired journey home and a few hours' sleep before work or school in the morning.

On other occasions the same venue is used for unlicensed boxing. Even at its most serious, boxing exists close to the boundary between sport and theatre. In the case of 'old crocks' night at the Gregory the frontier in question is that between music hall and bedlam as local celebrities, sundry bouncers and street fighters are given the opportunity to test their pugilistic skills against one another in the ring. Current and former amateur and professional boxers are not allowed to participate and there are no doctors or official referees in attendance. Nevertheless, with the enticing prospect of men, and occasionally women, of all ages, shapes and sizes battling it out for three one-minute rounds, 'old crocks' night really packs in the audience. Many of the bouts are pure sham as the contestants push and shove each other about the ring without throwing a single serious punch. Some contests, however, give the would-be boxers the chance to settle old scores and these fights can be brutal. Even though the fighters wear twelve-ounce gloves they are still able to give and take a great deal of punishment during the three minutes of activity. Usually, once a single blow of any weight is landed, all pretence towards the science of boxing is abandoned and a melee ensues, accompanied by the shouts and roars of the packed alehouse. This is pre-Queensberry stuff and the whole scene would not be out of place in a Fielding novel or a Hogarth cartoon.

Rights of passage 3: a show at the showgrounds

In middle England, approximately 200 miles distance and a million light years in culture away from the Gregory Hotel in north Belfast, is the Three Counties

Showgrounds on the outskirts of Malvern, Worcester. Each year the Holy Family takes part in a competitive exhibition of boxing with the Worcester Sporting Club. This is one of the few occasions when the senior members of the club have the chance to travel together outside Northern Ireland. One of the main attractions of fighting for the Holy Family is the fact that the club makes an effort to take its boxers abroad, quite often to England and sometimes to the United States. While the members of the club may know each other well enough as boxers, their mutual understanding usually does not go much beyond the boundaries of the north Belfast gym. As we have seen, the senior boxers tend not to be friends in the general sense that they interact in a range of situations such as exchanging home visits, going out socially or engaging in other leisure activities together. Boxing is their only binding interest and their only point of collective contact.

However, there are unintended social consequences of arranging boxing competitions in places such as Malvern. The Holy Family is not a rich club and in order to minimise expenditure the journey to Worcester involves an overnight sea passage and a long drive in a minibus along motorways through shifting urban and rural landscapes. The visit also involves spending three days in a guest house in one of England's more picturesque shires. This allows plenty of time for the team to get to know one another more fully by exploring interpersonal avenues which have little or nothing to do with their shared sporting experience. It also creates the space for more intimate periods of self-reflection and social comparison.

One fighter, gazing out of the windows of the minibus, watching the picture postcard English countryside pass by, is able to voice some of the feelings of the whole group:

> It's not like Belfast. It's different. So nice, so peaceful and everybody looks so well off. I wouldn't like to live here though. I prefer to live in Belfast. You can have better crack [fun] in Belfast. The people are friendlier. I would like to live in the likes of Malvern, but I wish it could be somewhere in Northern Ireland.

Whether Protestant or Catholic, loyalist or nationalist, once in England the Holy Family boxers become Irish. They are referred to as the Irish team and are more or less content to view themselves as such. In situations such as this it is quite common for people from Northern Ireland to focus on what they share geographically and culturally rather than dwell upon that which separates them at home. This process of mutual affiliation is greatly assisted by the lack of awareness of people not from Northern Ireland, who neither understand nor, in most cases, want to understand the nuances of the Province's political divisions. The subtleties of accents from Cork, Dublin, Derry and Belfast are lost in most English ears, which simply register that the speaker is Irish. One of the boxers on this particular trip is from the loyalist Shankill district of Belfast and has been brought up to see himself as British. At home, outside the context of boxing, his sense of Britishness sets him apart from many of the other fighters who live in nationalist areas and who see themselves as Irish both inside and outside the ring. However, when in England he realises that, for the most part, he is viewed as Irish by his hosts. Often Irishness is given negative connotations, particularly by the English. John, the university undergraduate, is philosophical about the effect of travelling to England on the collective identity of the team from the Holy Family:

> When we go away we realise that we've got more in common with each other because we are from the same part of Ireland or at least Northern Ireland. I've got more in common with Neil than with somebody from Limerick or Cork and Neil's got more in common with me than someone from Glasgow or London.

Paul's assessment is similar, but he expresses it in the vernacular:

> It's a joke really. At home we're either Protestant or Catholic, British or Irish, loyalist or nationalists. Over here, to them, we're all the same, just a bunch of thick bloody Paddys!

This sense of belonging to a different world is highlighted by the social setting of the boxing competition with the Worcester Sporting Club. The centrepiece of the Three Counties Showground is a huge hangar-like building, designed to host almost anything from an agricultural fair to a rock concert. On this particular evening the hub of the arena is a boxing ring, radiating away from which are forty or fifty long tables bedecked with crisp white linen, cut glass and silver service. Seated at these tables are up to 400 prosperous-looking men, all formally attired in dinner jackets, dress shirts and black bowties. The dinner guests are nearly all white males, who are mostly businessmen and professional people drawn from throughout the Midlands. The only non-white guests are the famous test and county cricketing father and son Basil and Damien D'Oliveira. The guests have paid good money for a seat at this charity event which entitles them to eat, drink and gamble their way through a five-course meal while watching poor working-class lads from Birmingham and Worcester do battle with poor working-class lads from Belfast.

There are many women present, but not as guests. They perform most of the service functions, such as working in the kitchens, serving behind the bar and waiting on tables. The more shapely and glamorous among them are assigned special tasks such as selling raffle tickets and, accompanied by the catcalls of the audience, two scantily clad professional models are used to carry the numbered signs around the ring at the end of each round of boxing. This is a man's world within a man's world.

As the guests get tucked into the main course, the cast for the night's performance engage in a familiar backstage routine as they wait for their respective bouts to be called. A single room has been set aside for both teams to change. The

Holy Family occupy one corner. The boxers' back-chat diminishes as the time for the show nears and the opposition begin to arrive. The atmosphere of the room changes from leisure to work. The semi-naked men step into their costumes, have their hands wrapped and adorn their props. The teams engage in a mute exchange whereby likely opponents are identified and sized up. The Irish fighters look paler and generally skinnier than their English opponents, several of whom are black. Once changed, like so many caged big cats, the boxers begin to pace and dance around the crowded room, stopping occasionally to throw a speedy collection of jabs and hooks towards an unseen assailant.

Finally coffee and dessert are served and the call comes for the boxers to enter the *circus maximus*. Two by two the fighters and respective corner men weave their way through the seated dinner guests to the apron of the ring. The polite ripple of applause initiated by the dinner party is drowned by the roaring and shouting of the public gallery, an area set aside in the arena for the fighters' relatives, friends and local fight fans. Here T-shirts, leather jackets and jeans seem to be the appropriate dress code and best bitter and lager rather than fine wines are the preferred after-dinner tipple. The master of ceremonies steps into the ring and initiates the pre-fight ritual. The sight of the boxers limbering up promotes a flurry of private wagers among the audience. These side-bets are in addition to the 'official' gambling cards which most of the guests have already subscribed to as part of the overall charity night. These small investments add a bipartisan dimension to the support of the largely English audience and throughout the evening shouts of 'Come on Paddy!' are heard echoing around the arena. John finds it hard to come to terms with performing in front of such an audience:

> Boxing here for me is like a fish out of water. I can appreciate that these people have the money, but they don't appreciate boxing for what it is. Their main purpose in going to boxing is to try and get some business deals and have a night out with their business partners. It's not to go and watch boxing matches which they don't understand.

Boxing is a hard and often violent sport but its real brutality lies in the relationship between the fight and its audience, particularly when that audience is largely made up of those who are fans in the modern rather than the traditional sense. The term 'fan' has a dual heritage. The traditional concept has its origins in the activities of the 'Fancy', who were a loose-knit subculture made up of those who followed, supported and gambled on horses, cocks and pugilists in the late eighteenth and early nineteenth centuries. The Fancy's knowledge of and expertise in the turf, the cock pit and the ring set them apart from the heterogeneous mobs who occasionally turned out to watch a good scrap, but were more often to be found in the vicinity of cruder exhibitions such as bear-baiting, dogfighting and public executions. The activities and devotion of the Fancy laid down the institutional roots for succeeding generations of informed supporters or fans across a range of sports, including boxing.[2] In this context the fight fan is the man (fight fans are almost exclusively male) who appreciates boxing as a sport. While acknowledging the power of a well delivered knock-out blow, the fan can also applaud good defence and recognise the value of attributes such as stealth, speed of hands and feet, stamina and heart. He also keeps himself informed as to the progress of boxers locally and worldwide through the electronic and written media and, while he may follow a local favourite, the fan will also have developed an appreciation for good boxers regardless of their nationality, creed or colour.

It seems that the less a spectator knows of a sport the more he is likely to be attracted to those activities which emphasise display over subtlety of content. Equally, those who do not appreciate the finer points of skill and craft in a given sport are entertained most when that sport produces displays of physical confrontation and outbursts of violence. They seek crude sensationalism through a medium which affords many opportunities for the stimulation of a full range of emotions. Often, they attach themselves to a particular sport and identify with an individual or a team of participants, thus augmenting the emotional experience. Such people become fanatical about sport and are fans in a modern and entirely different sense from that outlined above. Football hooligans are extreme examples of modern sports fans. In terms of boxing, such spectators are not interested in the sport as a 'sweet science'. Rather, these fans like to see their man win by what ever means at his disposal and if this involves beating his opponent to a bloody pulp, so much the better.

In the Three Counties Showgrounds, traditional fight fans seem to be outnumbered by those casual spectators who judge the worth of a contest according to the quantity of blood spilled. The audience clap politely as the lighter weights box through a series of close encounters. The real support is kept for the heavier men, whose punches can have a more obviously devastating impact. In a particularly one-sided middleweight battle, Jim from Ballyclare in Northern Ireland has his nose split open by Dave from Wolverhampton. The crowd roar their approval as the referee permits the fight to continue. Blood from the Irishman's nose soaks into his emerald green vest and sprays about the white canvas. The crowd get to their feet cheering wildly as Dave punches his rapidly weakening opponent into a neutral corner. Momentarily, the distinction between this scene and fight night at the Gregory in north Belfast becomes blurred as divisions of class and culture are overwhelmed by the common expression of primordial emotions. The enchantment is broken when a towel is thrown from a more detached Irish team manager, preventing Jim from taking further punishment. This is greeted with spontaneous howls of derision from the overexcited audience.

[2] For further details of the Fancy see chapter 1.

The Worcester Sporting Club wins the night's competition by a single bout. Rugby songs begin to ring out as the dinner guests finish the last of their wine and drain their brandies. Meanwhile, backstage, the cut and bruised boxers sit quietly on the floor tucking into fish and chips served on paper plates, looking forward to tomorrow and with it the familiar and comforting sights and sounds of north Belfast.

Normal sport in an abnormal society?

At one level, the presence of young working-class Protestants in the heart of a Catholic community such as the New Lodge is very surprising. After all, while the troubles pervade all quarters of Northern Ireland's social terrain, the most bitter and violent manifestations of the Province's political crisis generally occur within and between working-class communities, and it is here that sectarian polarisation is most intense. Moreover, it is working-class young men who are most likely to be at the giving and receiving ends of sectarian violence. This is the same social context which provides the setting and raw material for boxing, arguably the most violent sport in the modern world.

Take a violent sport such as boxing and locate it in the heart of a violent society and one would not be surprised to discover evidence of the sport exacerbating existing community divisions and worsening conflict. However, evidence suggests that while boxing is an intrinsic part of Belfast's inner-city culture, to some extent the boxing fraternity manages to remain apart from those forces which promote cross-community conflict. In short, in a context where most other sports are deeply involved in the politics of community division, boxing appears to remain true to those Corinthian principles which enshrine the separation of sport and politics. How can this be so?

The notion that sport *per se* promotes peace and understanding globally and locally is largely a myth and nowhere is this more evident than in Northern Ireland, where participation in and allegiance to the range of sports played tends largely to be organised according to distinctive cultural and religious traditions (Sugden and Bairner, 1993). Nevertheless, the capacity of boxing to attract people from both communities is helped by the fact that the sport is not automatically associated with one or other cultural tradition. Even though the English may have been responsible for the initial development of boxing in its modern form, in no way could the sport be described as Anglophile. The social roots of boxing travel deeper and wider than James Figg and the Marquess of Queensberry, and forms of organised hand-to-hand combat have been recognised throughout the world from time immemorial. Boxing has been able to develop as a genuinely universal sport, which is not intrinsically bound up with a particular nationalist or post-colonial tradition. The same cannot be said of sports such as cricket, rugby union or hockey which, although played in many different countries, are still redolent of their distinctively English heritage and as such do not attract Catholics in significant numbers in Northern Ireland. Similarly, Gaelic games are so clearly bound up with the symbols and traditions of nationalist Ireland that very few Protestants are inclined to become involved. In contrast, boxing is perceived as a neutral sport, participation in which cannot be taken as an indication of a person's religious or political persuasion. As a result Catholics and Protestants can mix in the name of this sport without fear of sectarian stigma.

Also, while amateur boxers are members of and often compete for particular clubs, boxing is more of an individual than a collective sport. While there is an obvious camaraderie among the youngest members of the club, this is not necessarily generated by their affiliation to the Holy Family. Most of them live side by side in the New Lodge, play together in neighbouring streets and go to the same Catholic school. Their friendship in the gym is simply an extension of their social relationships outside it. The quality of the minimal cross-community contact experienced by the club's youngest members is usually limited to exchanging punches with Protestant boys in the ring. Very few of the younger members of the Holy Family graduate to become serious boxers and are thus deprived of regular contact with Protestants.

However, while the more senior members of the club come from both sides of the sectarian divide, it is wrong to claim that the Holy Family provides the venue for shared and collectively meaningful cross-community experiences. Teams are not built in boxing clubs in the same sense that they are when the context is association, Gaelic or rugby football. The further a boxer advances in his career, the more individualistic he becomes and the further away he gets from identification with groups of other fighters. Much of a serious fighter's training is conducted alone, outside the gym. Even though he may train regularly at his club in the company of fellow members, the nature of that training is quite individualistic and there is little time set aside for social bonding. Very little intimate social interaction takes place among senior fighters within clubs such as the Holy Family and even less occurs outside the boundaries of the sport. It is only on the few occasions when a club travels away from home to box as a team that any significant socialisation takes place, and even then the themes for communication are invariably selected from the world of boxing and other non-aligned aspects of sport, such as the goings on in the English football leagues. The lack of an intimate social dimension to boxing means that there is no serious exchange of the views and values which have a bearing upon social and political division.

Thus, while boxing does have a measure of cross-community support, it is a mistake to overstate the contribution that the sport can make to community relations in Belfast. If fighting for the Holy Family has any impact on the politics of division in north Belfast, then it is at the level of the individual and of relevance only to the serious boxer. Along with a decision to become a serious boxer comes an implicit rejection of many of the degrading aspects of life in north Belfast, including terrorism and the subculture which has sustained boundless violence.

Also, the more successful a serious boxer is in his career the more opportunity he will have to travel and experience longer-term relationships with people of different religious, racial and national backgrounds. However, the individual fighter's rejection of the sectarianism and political violence which are characteristic of north Belfast has little impact on the structure underpinning cross-community conflict there. The most likely result of a serious fighter from north Belfast having his horizons broadened by fighting for the Holy Family is that he will move out of the neighbourhood.

There is a final note to be made when theorising in this area. Boxing in Belfast is sustained by old-fashioned working-class traditions and values. It is a sport for 'hard men', but in a pre-1950s rather than post-1960s vintage. The 'hard men' of the pre-1950s were those who worked in the shipyards, mills and factories, inhabiting a proud, physically tough and exclusively male occupational culture which cast a long shadow over popular recreation outside the workplace. From an early age boys learned to stand up for themselves physically. They also learned an ethical code which valued disciplined toughness but admonished gratuitous violence. Disputes in the playground or street fights featured punches not kicks or head-butts and never weapons. It was from this environment that the pre-1950s 'hard men' emerged. Some, including the legendary Rinty Monaghan, took their talents into the ring while others such as Buck Alec and Silver McKee were content to fight for informal neighbourhood titles in bars and alleyways throughout the city. Many of the factories have long since closed and, like so many other de-industrialised landscapes, Belfast's working-class neighbourhoods have lost much of their traditional cultural cement. The city's post-industrial working-class culture remains tough, but endemic unemployment, sectarian polarisation and enduring political violence ensure that toughness is edged with suspicion, cynicism and ruthlessness. The status of today's 'hard men' is measured in terms of their capacity to engage in boundless violence and there is no place for their appetites and attitudes in the boxing fraternity. In this regard boxing in Belfast is a reminder of a bygone era when, for the majority of people, life in the city was hard but fair and relatively safe, and when local heroes earned respect in terms of a creed rooted in the morality of natural justice rather than the jungle.

Thus, while there is a surface logic to the fact that boxing, by reputation one of the world's most violent sports, thrives in the heart of a famously violent city, under closer scrutiny this logic breaks down. The central core of boxing is physical aggression, but its existence as a sport is dependent on the strict delineation and control of the boundary between aggression and violence. These are the conventions of truce, which characterise the boxing subculture worldwide and demand of its members and followers a high degree of self- and collective control. Ascetic qualities such as self-denial, personal discipline and deferred gratification are held in high regard in the boxing world. In addition, while the ultimate focus of the fighter's consciousness is the defeat of a given opponent, respect for that opponent is also one of the boxer's enduring principles. The boundless violence which seems to be endemic within the modern inner city, whether it be random, gang warfare or politically motivated, has no place within the subculture of the boxer, and this is as true in Belfast as it is in Chicago, Detroit and Mexico City. Boxing thrives in Belfast not because of the city's violent heart, but despite that violence. The gatekeepers of the Holy Family and other boxing clubs in Belfast are well aware of this and they carefully police their boundaries to ensure that the malevolence, wildness and disrespect often associated with street youth culture are not allowed to contaminate the atmosphere of their sport. In addition, because politics and sectarianism are such close relatives of violence in Belfast, great efforts are made to ensure that politics and sectarianism are left at the gymnasium door. Without these conventions of truce and their careful policing, boxing in north Belfast would surely degenerate into barbarism.

5

Havana, Cuba: fighting for the revolution

Two island peoples, united in the same sea of struggle and hope: Cuba and Ireland.
(Plaque on a wall in O'Reilly Street, Old Havana)

A thin drizzle permeates Dublin's night sky, adding dampness to the chill air and causing the tarmac to shine back at the bright street lights outside the National Stadium. Opened in 1939, this was one the first purpose-built amateur boxing stadia, and through its doors have passed some of the world's finest amateur boxers (Shipley, 1989:88). Rarely, however, has the National Stadium played host to a finer array of talent than is gathered for these two nights when Irish boxers take part in an international challenge match consisting of twelve bouts, featuring no fewer than ten world champions, eight of whom are Cuban. The skill, speed and grace of the Cubans are particularly impressive and set them apart from the other fighters. They do not shuffle or pace around the ring like the boxers from Germany, Bulgaria or Ireland. Rather they dance around it, leading their opponents from corner to corner, occasionally boxing their ears with quick-fire combinations, as if chastising a dancing partner for missing a step or clumsily standing on a foot.

Watching them one can understand how they were able to dominate the Barcelona Olympics in 1992, winning seven of the twelve gold medals and two silver. In fact, since the 1959 revolution, Cuba has grown to be the world's leading amateur boxing nation. The first Cuban to box in the Olympics was Estaban Aguilera in Rome in 1960, but it was not until 1968 that Cuba won its first Olympic boxing medal, when Enrique Regueiferos was beaten in the final of the 63.5 kg contest by J. Kulej of Poland. Since then Cubans have won thirty-four Olympic medals, nineteen of them gold. This statistic takes on greater significance when it is considered that, for political reasons, Cuba boycotted both the 1984 Olympics in Los Angeles and the 1988 Games in Seoul, when they were at the height of their power as a boxing nation.

The superiority of the Cubans has not been lost on the Irish. Seated ringside is Nicholas Hernandez-Cruz, the Cuban who coaches the Irish national boxing squad. Cruz is seconded to the IABA from the INDER (Institute of Sport, Physical Education and Recreation), which, in all but name, is the Cuban ministry of sport. He is vague about the financial arrangements between the two associations, but it is certain that a sizeable proportion of his 'salary' goes directly to the Cuban government. The Cuban peso is worthless in terms of international exchange and, during these times of economic crisis at home, the government will do almost anything to earn 'hard' currency, including exporting athletes and coaches.

The IABA provides Nicholas with an apartment in St James Gate, Dublin, for the duration of his secondment. By European standards the flat is small and functional. By Cuban standards, it is roomy and luxurious. An extended family of two or three generations of Cubans may live in the same space in Havana without any of the standard utilities and appliances available in Nicholas's Dublin home. Like most Cubans, Cruz is friendly and happy to talk about his homeland. As the rain splashes against the windows of his Dublin apartment, Nicholas explains how boxing developed in Cuba. His knowledge of his chosen sport goes beyond ring craft. He was taught to box and also about boxing by Enrique Gamury Lopez, who was Cuba's first sports coach to earn a doctorate in biochemistry and sports science, which he achieved after a period of study in the former Soviet Union. However, before the revolution Lopez had fought first as an amateur and later as a professional in the United States. In many ways he personified the dual roots of Cuban boxing, which owes much both to the traditions of the sport in North America and the system through which athletes of all descriptions were produced in the former Soviet Union and allied states.

Cuba's rough ride

For more than a hundred years the United States has exerted considerable influence on political, economic and cultural development in Cuba. In the second half of the nineteenth century Cubans struggled to rid themselves of Spanish colonial rule. In 1892, Jose Marti, a young poet and journalist in exile in the United States, pioneered the foundation of the CRP (Cuban Revolutionary Party), which in 1895 spearheaded the most serious challenge to Spanish authority in Cuba. However, Marti himself was killed in an early skirmish with Spanish soldiers and it is unlikely that the rebellion he helped to inspire would have succeeded had it not been for the intervention of the United States, precipitated by a spectacular failure in gunboat diplomacy.

Disturbed by political unrest so close to its own shores and concerned for the welfare of US citizens living in Havana, the US government sent the battleship *Maine* to Cuba, where it was promptly sunk by saboteurs in the Bay of Havana, going down with all hands. The identity and allegiance of the terrorists remain unknown. However, this incident gave the United States a pretext to declare war on Spain and join the rebellion on the side of the CRP. The Spanish–American War lasted less than a year, when it ended with Spain withdrawing from Cuba, leaving it in the hands of the Americans, who by that time had 24,000 military personnel stationed throughout the island (Thomas, 1971).

In 1902 the United States formally withdrew from Cuba, but not before the Platt Amendment, a treaty guaranteeing them the right to intervene in the island's internal affairs if they were considered to run counter to US interests, was pressed upon the fledgling Cuban government. In addition, the naval base at Guantanamo Bay was ceded to the United States on a ninety-nine-year lease and US business people were granted unhindered access to the island's sugar and power industries. Although formally independent, in many respects the Cubans had merely exchanged direct servitude under an old colonial power for indirect dependency on a new empire.

The influence of Americans was highly significant in the establishment of boxing on the island. The American occupation of Cuba occurred at a time when sport in the United States was enjoying rapid growth. At the same time Cuban sport was very underdeveloped and hitherto had been centred around the pre-modern Spanish imports of bullfighting, cockfighting and jai alai or pelota, a traditional Basque courtyard game for two players involving racquet-like slings, a hard ball and a considerable amount of off-court gambling. When they came ashore in Santiago de Cuba, Guantanamo, Cienfuegos, Matanzas and Havana the US sailors and marines brought with them a knowledge of and an appetite for the games and pastimes of home, which they would play in their spare time. Among them was future president Theodore Roosevelt, who was captain of a cavalry troop known as the 'Rough Riders'. Roosevelt personified the American passion for sports and was a particular devotee of boxing (Gorn, 1986: 195–7), and it was the influence of the likes of him and his men which catalysed the emergence of modern sports in Cuba. Of course, even before the US 'invasion' there had been a considerable amount of commercial and cultural contact between the two countries, and North American sports and pastimes would have already been familiar to many Cubans, who were particularly attracted to two of these activities: baseball and boxing, both relatively simple sports requiring little in the way of equipment or facilities. Led by these activities, sport became part of a general and gradual process through which Cuban society adopted many of the cultural preferences of the United States.[1]

The military occupation of Cuba was followed by the arrival of commercially minded entrepreneurs who viewed post-colonial Cuba as a land of opportunity in much the same way as the 'carpet baggers' had regarded the southern states of the USA after the Civil War. Among them was an itinerant boxer and trainer, John Budinich. Originally from Chile, Budinich had spent many years in the United States, where he boxed professionally and worked as a trainer in New York. Budinich realised that money could be made both by promoting professional boxing and through training would-be contenders in Cuba. To this end he opened

---

[1] There is some debate over the extent to which baseball was a developed form of the native Cuban game of *batos*. For more on this see Pettivo and Pye (1994: 25–7).

Havana's first boxing academy and arranged boxing promotions for the entertainment of the city's elite in places such as Vedado Tennis Club and the National Hotel. In 1912 Budinich promoted and participated in Cuba's first professional boxing match, against the American Jack Ryan, which brought professional boxing to the attention of a wider Cuban audience. Budinich then went on to train Cuba's first home-grown professional fighters. The island's first national champions, Victor Achan, Tomas Galiana, Manolo Vivancos, Juan Suarez and Anastasio Penalver, all trained under the guidance of Budinich. In 1915, after he had been knocked out by the formidable American champion John Lester Johnson, during a bout in Havana, Budinich left Cuba for France. However, during his brief stay in Cuba he had laid the foundations of a sport which was to grow to become second only to baseball in popularity among Cuban males (Alfonso, 1988).

Boxing proved to be particularly popular in the cities and among Cuba's poorer classes, who were almost exclusively of African descent. Indicative of the degree of racial tension which still existed in the former slave colony, boxing was banned by the Cuban authorities for a brief period after Budinich's departure because they believed it created unseemly opportunities for blacks to fight against whites. However, the sport continued underground, effectively making the ban meaningless. As a result, the government did not object when the Comision Nacional De Boxeo (the National Boxing Commission) was established in Havana in 1921 with the aim of codifying and centralising the administration and regulation of the sport in Cuba. A year later La Comision de Boxeo de la Union Atletica Amateur, the professional body's amateur equivalent, was established, paving the way for the introduction of nationwide amateur boxing championships, which in the 1930s were superseded by Los Guantes de Oro Cubano (Cuban Golden Gloves). Havana, with its grand hotels and gambling casinos, became established as a leading location for international boxing promotions, and a strong professional boxing subculture thrived around boxing clubs such as the Black Cat Ring, Ring Cuba and Recreo de Belascoain. From these foundations Cuba grew to become a force in world professional boxing in the 1930s and 1940s (Alfonso, 1988).

Abject poverty ensured that at this time few Cuban boxers lingered long in the ranks of the amateurs. As soon as an opportunity presented itself, poor young fighters entered the ranks of the professionals and were particularly attracted by the money on offer in the United States. The flow of Cuban boxers into the American professional ring was accelerated in the 1950s when the Cuban Golden Gloves was subsumed within the rubric of its counterpart in the southern states of the United States. Despite the fact that the mainly black Cuban fighters experienced discrimination while participating in American Golden Gloves competitions, their uncivil hosts were only too willing to pass the most successful of the Cubans off as Americans once they turned professional. During the 1950s many Cuban boxers fought on the North American and world professional circuits (Pettivo and Pye, 1994: 65). Most were underpaid and a few suffered serious injury and even death in the ring. This form of national exploitation was stopped in its tracks when Fidel Castro and his guerrilla army seized power from President Batista on New Year's Day, 1959.

Before the 1960s, Cuba's sports culture was as underdeveloped as that of most Third World nations. A small minority of mainly 'white' Cubans – those of direct Spanish descent – participated in elite sports such as sailing, equestrianism, hunting, and tennis, while the masses played and watched baseball and boxing. There were fewer than 800 teachers of physical education for a population of 10 million. Many youngsters received no formal education and of those who did, few received instruction in sports and games. Significantly, before 1960 Cuba participated in only three Olympic Games (1900, 1904 and 1948), winning a total of thirteen medals in two activities which were played by only a small minority of wealthy Cubans, fencing and chess. With the ascendancy of Fidel Castro, this situation rapidly changed.

As a young man Castro had an appetite for sports which remains with him to this day. His father, Angel Castro, was born in Spain, but had remained in Cuba after serving in the Spanish army during the Spanish–American War. Fidel was brought up on the family's sugar plantation in Oriente Province, where he led a robust life, hunting and fishing with his brothers Raul and Ramon. He went to a series of parochial schools before being transferred to a Jesuit boarding school in Havana. In this environment Fidel's mastery of sports soon became apparent and in 1944 he was awarded the prize for being the nation's most outstanding young athlete.

The influence of Castro's education at the hands of the Jesuits should not be underestimated, and this included the passion they nurtured in him for organised sports. While at school he rejected the doctrines of Catholicism, but he accepted the moral and rational principles of muscular Christianity as preached by the Jesuits. In this regard, Castro was something like an Hispanic Tom Brown. As Huberman and Sweezy (1968: 26) report, his graduating yearbook foretold something of whom the young Castro would grow into:

> His record was one of excellence, he was a true athlete, always defending with bravery and pride the flag of the school. He has known how to win the admiration and affection of all. He will make law his career and we do not doubt that he will fill with brilliant pages the book of his life. He has good timber and the actor in him will not be lacking.

The University of Havana provided Castro with a proving ground for his intelligence, his physical ability, his charisma and his bravado. In one famous incident, as a freshman he publicly challenged the President of the Students' Union to a boxing match over a point of order in a debate. In another, he rode a bicycle at full speed into a brick wall in front of a crowd of on-lookers – just to prove that he had the willpower to do something which they could never do (Thomas, 1971: 809). Throughout the early stages of his college career, before he

135

turned his attention, full time, to political activities, Fidel displayed his athletic prowess on the track, the basketball court and the baseball diamond. With regard to the latter, there are claims that as a young man Fidel had a try-out for a US major-league baseball team, the Washington Senators (Pettivo and Pye, 1994:16 and 246). What is more certain is that, in later years, he never lost his appetite for hard physical training, and this helped to sustain him through the arduous years spent in the Sierra Maestra fighting against Batista's army from 1956 to 1959.

The record of the Cuban revolution and Castro's role in it reads like a fairy story. It begins with the brave but forlorn attack on the police barracks at Moncada on 26 July 1953, after which he was imprisoned before being exiled to Mexico. Then in 1956 came the voyage of the *Granma*, a fifty-eight-foot US motor cruiser in which Fidel and eighty-two rebels set sail from Mexico to invade Cuba and take on Batista and his army of over 30,000. The *Granma*, which is preserved in a glass case and is on view to the public in Havana, looks like the sort of vessel that was designed for sleepy Sunday afternoon cruises for a couple of well-off families and not as an invasion craft for half a regiment. Only twelve survived the landing. The rest were either killed or captured by Batista's troops, who had been forewarned of the 'invasion'. Among the twelve survivors were Fidel Castro, his brother Raul and the rebel's doctor, the charismatic Argentinian Ernesto 'Che' Guevara.[2] As they lay resting deep within the Sierra Maestra, the mountain range into which they fled, it is reported that Castro announced to his exhausted colleagues that now they had returned to Cuba, the dictator Batista's days were numbered. The others looked back at him in disbelief. That Castro's prophecy came true is a matter of historical record (Thomas, 1971).

Operating from their mountain base the revolutionaries gradually won the confidence of the peasants, many of whom joined the rebel army, as did increasing numbers of students and disillusioned workers from the towns and cities. Gradually, the small motor of twelve grew into a substantial guerilla engine, which was able to inflict a series of relatively minor military defeats on Batista's demoralised army. At the close of the last day of 1958, less than three years after the *Granma*'s landing, under pressure from trade unionists, political dissidents and urban terrorists in Havana and besieged by Castro's rebels in the provinces, Batista lost his nerve and fled the country, leaving the capital and the country in the hands of the revolutionaries. A week later, on 8 January, as Castro gave his victory oration to the people of Havana, outlining the brightness of their future, somebody in the crowd released two white doves. Spontaneously, one circled in the air above Castro before alighting upon his shoulder. They all lived happily ever after.

Well, not quite. Some argue that Castro was a communist from the beginning. Others say that he was forced into the embrace of the Soviet Union by the

[2] Che Guevara was also a keen sportsman. As a young man he played soccer and was particularly adept as a goalkeeper (Guevara, 1996).

belligerent attitude of the United States and its allies who, after a brief honeymoon period, imposed a trade embargo on the fledgling republic. Certainly, both Castro's brother Raul and Che Guevara were Marxists and were sympathetic towards the Soviet model. For its part the Soviet Union was only too grateful to have an ally so close to the shores of its bitterest Cold War enemy. The massive subsidy of the Cuban economy seemed but a small price for the Soviets to pay for a huge and permanently moored aircraft carrier seventy miles east of Florida's Key West. It was largely on the strength of this subvention that in the early years of his reign Castro was able to finance the reform of Cuba's political, institutional and cultural order.

That he followed the Soviet example when doing this is not surprising, since Moscow held the purse strings. This was a model which emphasised collective goals over individual freedoms, the dictatorship of the proletariat over democracy, and a command economy over market forces. It was justified by a Marxist–Leninist ideological principle that true communism had to be dragged from the womb of capitalism and, in its infancy, nurtured by a cadre of committed and informed revolutionaries who would seize the apparatus of the state and use it for the benefit of the people until such a stage that the economic and social foundations for genuine collectivism had been securely laid. Once this point was reached the dictatorship of the proletariat would end and the state would gradually wither away, leaving a community of committed socialists within which the government of people had been displaced by the administration of things. However, a combination of factors, including the American-led trade embargo, the pre- and post-Cold War international balance of power and Castro's own populist/ Peronist tendencies, have ensured that the Cuban government continues as a socialist dictatorship and retains many of the features of those Eastern European totalitarian states which collapsed with the Berlin Wall.

From the 1930s the Soviet Union had a declared commitment to the development of physical education and sport which became manifest through success in Olympic competitions in the post-war era (Riordan, 1978). Once he had established himself in power, Castro likewise committed himself to the wholesale reform of Cuban society, and this included physical education and sports. His background suggests, however, that it is an oversimplification to assume that, once Castro fell within the Soviet embrace, the island's sports development was dictated totally by ideas and structures borrowed from Eastern Europe. As has been pointed out elsewhere, the gradual alignment with the Soviet Union provided Castro with an even stronger pretext to do with the island's sport culture what he wanted to do anyway (Sugden *et al.*, 1992).

The remainder of this chapter presents a critical evaluation of Castro's sporting reforms as they appear through the particular lens of boxing, as a lived aspect of Cuban culture. Necessarily this is an ethnographic journey which begins and ends in Cuba, among ordinary Cubans and shoulder to shoulder with those who go on to become perhaps the finest amateur boxers the world has ever seen.

Havana

It is 5.30 a.m. and as the Aeroflot jet banks for its final approach to Havana it is hard to believe that it hangs above a city of more than 2.5 million people. Apart from the lights of the runway at Jose Marti Airport, Cuba's capital is shrouded in darkness. Because of the country's economic crisis and the high cost in hard currency of the oil which fuels the power stations, most parts of the city are allowed electricity for only two hours each night. Even the airport terminal is only dimly lit, adding to the aura of mystery which greets the already apprehensive traveller. Airport guards, immigration officers and policemen wearing steel blue and khaki uniforms, droopy moustaches and mirror shades, hang around the terminal, waiting for the aircraft to disgorge its passengers while outside the tourist taxis wait to deliver this latest batch of hard currency to the capital.

Even in the pre-dawn gloom, the people of Havana are already on the move. The highway into the city centre is already crowded with an assortment of Ladas, ancient trucks, Chinese bicycles and motorbikes with sidecars. Our sparkling, new minibus makes a sharp contrast to the ancient American limousines, relics of the 1940s and 1950s and held together with spit and sticking plaster, which creep along, usually in the slow lanes. At regular intervals clusters of Cubans wait at the side of the road for one of the city's buses to pick them up. These are generally decrepit vehicles, made somewhere behind the iron curtain before it was drawn, and are usually packed way beyond their official capacity. Train-buses, the name given to the largest form of public road transport, trundle by, pulled along like a container on the back of an articulated lorry.

Havana's architecture reflects the city's history. Old Havana is dominated by mostly dilapidated Spanish colonial buildings while further out the Art Deco influence of the North Americans is unmistakable. The central square of the city is dominated by the Capitolio, the former state house of pre-revolutionary Cuba, which is a replica of the Capitol Building in Washington, DC. The island's more recent neo-colonial past is evidenced by the utilitarian, Soviet-style high-rise office buildings which are scattered across Havana, disturbing an otherwise picturesque skyline.

The Bay of Havana is a spectacular vista by any standards. On top of a rocky plateau on the Casablanca side of the inlet which leads to Havana Harbour is the sixteenth-century Castillo de Morro, constructed by the island's Spanish conquerors who, led by Diego Velazquez, colonised the island in 1511. It was constructed as a deterrent to pirates, such as Sir Francis Drake, who sailed these waters in the 1580s, but who dared not sail his ships beneath the powerful cannons of Morro de la Habana and el Castillio de la Punta on the opposite bank. At 9 p.m. each night a single cannon shot would be fired to indicate that the harbour was now closed. This was achieved by dragging a huge chain across the 300-yard mouth of the estuary, thus preventing privateers sneaking into the harbour under cover of darkness. The cannon is still discharged each night, in a ceremony designed to attract tourists rather than deter pirates.

Beyond the inlet, running south is the impressive six-lane Malecon highway and sea wall, which stretches for eight miles, as far as Mirimar, formerly the city's exclusive and plush suburb. For its first mile or so the city side of the Malecon is fringed with the outer facades of Habana Viaja (Old Havana). Here are three- and four-storey apartment buildings, at least a hundred years old and look not to have been decorated or refurbished for at least half that time. Blue, pink, tan and grey crumbling plaster, ancient oaken doors, hanging louvre doors and windows, rusted wrought iron railings on tiny balconies, glassless windows and gloomy interiors. The facade of Habana Viaja provides a great photo opportunity for tourists, but the place must be hell to live in.

Havana is horribly crowded. The population is crammed into a city designed for less than half its 2.5 million inhabitants. In some cases two or three generations of families share a single three- or four-room apartment. The old, the middle-aged, the mature, the young and the children all live on top of one another. In the words of Cuba's most famous salsa and sol band, Los Van Van, 'there is no room in Havana'. Apart from the squalor to which such overcrowding inevitably leads, these living conditions force *Habaneros* to live much of their lives, day and night, in public. The public person may have disappeared in the United States and Western Europe, but not in Cuba. Because of the economic crisis, television viewing is limited to two hours in the evening. Cubans are forced to make their own entertainment through socialising in the narrow streets or in the city's parks and squares.

The broad sea wall of the Malecon is the most popular location for *Habaneros* to socialise in and is the nearest thing the city has to a public leisure centre. During the day it is dotted with fishermen, sun bathers, courting couples and thousands of children who play in the watery shallows in the rocks at the bottom of the sea wall. But it is at night that the Malecon really comes alive. There is hardly a spot which is not claimed by Cubans in pairs or small groups, chatting, courting, listening to music, dancing, smoking and drinking cheap rum as the waves from the Atlantic crash against the promenade.

Eventually the facade of Old Havana gives way to that of Vedado, the city's commercial district, which also housed some of the more prosperous middle classes before the revolution. Here the post-colonial skyline is broken by some ugly high-rise offices and apartments and several pre-revolutionary luxury hotels. Notable among them are the Habana Libre (Free Havana), formerly the Havana Hilton, which towers forty or more storeys above the horizon, and the Nacional, a wedding cake of a building overlooking the Malecon. The Nacional, like one or two other exclusive hotels, is an oasis for tourists in Havana. When it was built in the early years of the twentieth century it was Havana's finest hotel, but after the revolution it suffered from neglect and fell into disrepair. To this day it is still scarred with bullet holes, relics of the failed putsch of 1933 when 300 dissenting army officers were flushed from the hotel by soldiers loyal to Batista's first government (Thomas, 1971).

As Vedado gives way to the township of Marianao, the Riviera Hotel, with its huge globe-like cabaret club and casino, towers over the surrounding one- and two-storey dwellings. Reputedly, like so many of the city's hotels before the revolution, the Riviera was owned by the Mafia. American gangsters and racketeers like Lucky Luciano are said to have been frequent visitors here and Frank Sinatra, who had a villa a few miles away in Mirimar, pre-revolutionary Havana's most exclusive suburb, appeared in several cabarets.

In a park next to the Riviera a small plaque commemorates the most infamous boxing match ever to take place on Cuban soil. It occurred in April 1915, in el Hipodromo Oriental Park, and involved a world heavyweight title fight between two North Americans, Jack Johnson, the first black world champion, and Jess 'Cowboy' Willard, a white challenger. At a time when racial discrimination was widespread, it was controversial enough that a black man and a white man should box at all. Indeed, one of the reasons why the fight took place in Havana was that it was highly unlikely that a fight of this nature would have been sanctioned anywhere within the United States. The racial dimension was augmented by the fact that shortly before the fight Johnson had married his white girlfriend, Lucille Cameron. This so much enraged white America that a warrant was issued for Johnson's arrest on the pretext that he was a pimp. The world champion was forced to flee the country, another reason why it was appropriate for his encounter with Willard to be held in Havana. Worldwide interest in the fight and support for the boxers was split according to the colour of the skin of the fight fans.

After more than twenty rounds the fight was even, without being spectacular. Then, in the twenty-sixth round, Johnson seemed to slip rather than be punched to the canvas. To the amazement of the audience he failed to rise and was counted out, leaving Willard as the new, white, world champion. Later Johnson explained that a combination of sweat and sun in his eyes and heat exhaustion had caused him to fall. However, there was also a popular view that Johnson faked the knock-out because the fight promoters promised him that if he threw the fight they would use their influence with the US authorities to ensure that Johnson would be allowed back into the United States without facing criminal charges. There are even suggestions that the Mafia, which, among other things, was renowned for its racism, threatened to kill him should he beat Willard (Alfonso, 1988: 25). Following the fight there was a huge public outcry, as a result of which the authorities in Havana banned professional boxing within the capital. This set back the development of the sport in Cuba, and although boxing continued in the provinces, it was not until 1921 that the Havana embargo was lifted after a national commission for boxing in Cuba was established there.

Now a new hotel is being constructed on the site of the Johnson–Willard encounter. In early 1990, in a partnership deal with a group of Spanish entrepreneurs, many of Cuba's foremost hotels and restaurants, including the Nacional and the Riviera, were extensively refurbished and new luxury hotels were constructed. Most of the best tourist facilities have been developed in partnership with foreign capital, usually Spanish, Canadian or British. In return for its investment, a foreign company gets 49 per cent of any profit, while the Cuban government gets the remaining 51 per cent. How much profit this arrangement generates is hard to discern. The advantages of low local wages must be more than outweighed by the disadvantages of expensive raw materials, food and other luxury items essential to a modern tourist industry. Because the total tourist infrastructure in Cuba remains underdeveloped and because of the country's reputation for radicalism on the international stage, insufficient numbers of tourists come to the island, making profit generation a difficult business. Nevertheless, there is a view that it is only a matter of time before Cuba goes the way of most former communist countries and embraces capitalism and Western-style democracy. When this happens, those who have already invested in the island's tourist industry will be best placed to take advantage of the inevitable boom in tourism as the island reverts to its former role as North America's playground. Ironically, Cuba's tourist industry is particularly attractive to European investors because, under existing circumstances, they do not have to compete with North American companies, which are not allowed by their government to invest in Cuba.

There is an incongruity about the pink and bewildered elderly visitors from Basingstoke and Toronto who fry on the white sand, shy away from the locals and complain about the food – even though their daily intake would feed an average Cuban for a week. Opening Cuba up to tourism is fraught with political risks for Castro's government. From the early 1960s until the middle of the 1980s Cuba was virtually closed to foreign visitors other than those from friendly communist nations. In terms of relative affluence there was little to distinguish most Cubans from tourists from Moscow, Prague and Hanoi. In fact tourists from the former Soviet bloc often used their trips to Havana as opportunities to buy consumer goods which were not available in their own countries. However, since the virtual collapse of international communism, the pressure to earn hard currency has forced Cuba to open itself up to visitors from anywhere and to develop a vigorous tourist industry modelled on that of neighbouring Caribbean islands. While this may help the economy, it is a strategy which has led to tensions building within the social system. The highly visible presence of thousands of tourists with a daily spending capacity often in excess of $100 in an economy which supports an average local wage of $5 per week has an impact on the perceptions and expectations of the local population, who observe them enjoying a lifestyle within Cuba that the vast majority of Cubans can only dream of.

Currently, most Cubans exist on next to nothing. Food rationing, which was introduced as a temporary measure in the mid-1960s, continues in the 1990s with a vengeance. A Cuban is allowed one bread roll a day, four eggs a week, 1 lb of fish per fortnight and 5 lb of rice a month (Calder and Hatchwell, 1993: 111). In other words, most Western Europeans consume in a day what most Cubans are officially expected to live on for a week. This diet can be supplemented by growing one's own vegetables or keeping one's own livestock. But where can one do this in Havana, particularly in the old part of the city? *Habaneros* are thankful for the versatility and durability of the chicken. The number of cockerels which crow at around 4.30 a.m. is testimony to the fact that even in the city, chickens are relatively easy to keep and are a good source of eggs and meat. The only other way of getting extra food is to enter the black market, within which virtually everything is sold in US dollars at a value four or five times higher than the peso price. Consequently, many Cubans presently subsist on one meal a day, which usually consists of *moros y christanos* (rice and black beans) mixed with an egg.

In 1993 Castro's government made it legal for Cubans to possess dollars. Before this time, only tourists could use American currency and any Cubans caught with dollars in their pockets faced imprisonment. Even though possession of the dollar has been legalised, Cubans are still paid in pesos, which are virtually valueless against the dollar inasmuch as nothing of any real worth can be bought with pesos. As mentioned above, the average Cuban monthly wage, when changed from pesos to dollars, is around $5. For many Cubans life is a constant scramble for dollars, and for a small minority of successful black marketeers the legalisation has brought a huge windfall. This has created an embryonic commercial class, whose wealth and access to consumer culture sets them apart both from ordinary Cubans and from the relatively better off party bureaucrats. It is easy to understand why tourists, with an average spending rate of between $50 and $100 per day, are the targets for so much unsolicited attention in Cuba.

It is, of course, bizarre that the currency of Cuba's greatest enemy, the United States, dominates the Cuban economy, despite the fact that there are no formal trade links between the two nations. No matter how steadfast Fidel has been with regard to his revolutionary principles, it has proven impossible to insulate Cuba from the tide of international consumerism, and this is a dollar-led phenomenon. Cuba still needs to import most of its raw materials and almost all of its consumer goods and is forced to trade in hard currency. The island earns most of its money by selling sugar and other home-grown produce. This is one of the main reasons why, in such an arable and verdant country, it is almost impossible to find and buy any decent vegetables: they have all been exported. The hard-currency issue was less of a problem for Cuba when the island was being supported in various ways by the USSR. Since the demise of the Soviet Union, which itself was caused in no small measure by the clash between a Western-style consumer culture and the collective logic of communist economics, Cuba's economic situation has become progressively worse. Another means of bringing in hard currency has been to encourage the subvention of dollars donated to individual families by Cuban expatriates. It is estimated that more than 2 million Cubans live in the United States, mostly in Florida. The problem with this strategy is that it gives many indigenous Cubans a regular and direct link with the United States, with all its consumer trappings, causing them to feel even more frustrated by their own relative deprivation.

Manifestly, the United States continues to cast a long shadow over Cuba. A few hundred yards along the Malecon from the Nacional Hotel is the US Interest Section. Cuba and the United States have no formal diplomatic links and as such have neither embassies nor ambassadors in one another's countries. They do, however, have interest sections, through which the barest levels of diplomatic contact can be maintained. The US Interest Section is a modern and architecturally uninspiring oblong building bristling with satellite dishes and aerials. It is heavily guarded, at the perimeter by Cubans and closer to the inner compound by US marines in white helmets. There is a perpetual line of visitors waiting to get in, the vast majority of them in pursuit of precious visas or other documents which will give them access to the United States.

Despite official attempts to control emigration, since 1959 Cuba's population has been haemorrhaging. Many of Cuba's wealthiest left Cuba as soon as Castro assumed power in 1959. Most of the middle classes watched and waited to see how the new republic would develop. Once it became clear that Cuba was to become a socialist dictatorship many of them also left, usually for the United States. Between 1959 and the beginning of 1962 more than 200,000 Cubans left the country. Because most of these emigrants were professional people or highly qualified technicians, their departure proved to be catastrophic for an economy which was desperate to diversify away from an almost total dependence on sugar cane. Castro's government reacted by placing draconian restrictions on emigration and making life very difficult for those who expressed a desire to leave. It was possible to leave Cuba, but the price became higher the longer the revolutionary government stayed in power. Nevertheless, a further 200,000 left between 1965 and 1971 under the Freedom Flights Programme, a scheme set up by the US government. Then, in 1980, in the Mirimar boat lift, more than 100,000 Cubans were allowed to sail in small crafts to the United States as illegal immigrants. The Carter administration allowed them in without realising that Castro had used this exercise as an opportunity to make room in his gaols and asylums by exporting some of his most unstable criminals, mental patients and dissidents. Significantly, athletes were not allowed to leave then or thereafter.

Since then there has been a small annual quota of Cubans officially permitted to emigrate to the United States, a number far outstripped by the demand (Gebler, 1988: 187–8). In recent years US policy on Cuban immigration has been ambivalent. While they have restricted the number of visas given to those who wait patiently in line outside the Interest Section, until the middle of 1994 they granted automatic political asylum to any Cuban who 'escaped' from the island and made it safely on to American soil. Such escapees were used by the US authorities and elements of the Cuban community in exile in anti-Castro propaganda exercises. In retaliation for this and the continuance of the trade embargo, in the summer of 1994 Castro decided to turn a blind eye to illegal immigration. In less than two weeks it is estimated that more than 10,000 people attempted to escape to Florida in a variety of craft, the vast majority of which were perilously unseaworthy. Some made it to the US mainland and many were picked up by the US coastguard and sent to holding camps at Guantanamo, the US navy base on Cuba. Untold thousands are believed to have perished at sea. This latest wave of illegal emigration has led to renewed tensions between the United States and Cuba and, at the time of writing, the situation is unresolved. However, the fact that so many Cubans have been prepared to risk death in the shark-infested waters of the Florida Straits or imprisonment for trying to escape in small boats or inner tubes testifies to the degree of contempt which many people hold for Cuba's current political and economic regime. As we shall see, it may also help to explain why for many young Cubans a career in the ring can seem very attractive.

Facing the US Interest Section is a huge advertising hoarding with a cartoon scene depicting a Cuban peasant wagging his finger at an aggressive-looking Uncle Sam. Beneath it runs a slogan which, roughly translated, reads 'Mr imperialist we have absolutely no interest in your media'. This is a reference to the daily bombardment of Cuba by American radio and television stations. Some of this is random, but some is not. Most significant is Radio Marti, broadcast by anti-Castro elements from Florida which, in between rock music, sports news and consumer advertising, conducts a constant anti-Castro propaganda war. An attempt to follow Radio Marti up with television Marti has largely failed because of the strength of Cuba's Soviet-built electronic jamming devices. Indeed, when television Marti was first broadcast to Cuba in 1991, Castro retaliated by using his own powerful transmission facilities to put himself on American television sets during prime time up and down the south-east coast of the United States! Nevertheless, through the efforts of Radio Marti, many Cubans know as much about and are more interested in the professional sports scene in America as they are aware of the affairs of their own, amateur performers. They are especially eager for information about the handful of Cuban baseball players and boxers who have escaped from Cuba and who are performing in the United States.

For the love of my country

The heightened awareness in Cuba of the lifestyles associated with a successful sporting career abroad is beginning seriously to threaten the stability of the island's self-contained sports system. For a long time the siege mentality of Cubans who remembered the Batista years and who supported Castro's revolution in the face of North American hostility was sufficient to keep the nation's top athletes loyal to the Cuban flag. However, more than thirty years after the revolution, with the economy in tatters, it seems that patriotism alone is an insufficient guarantee that Cuban athletes will remain fully committed to the revolution, and defection has emerged as a serious problem for Cuban sport. Consequently, getting access to Cuba's boxers involves some tough negotiations. As a precondition for any research in this area it is necessary to assure senior boxing officials that the investigator has no interest in identifying Cuba's best young boxers and persuading them to defect to the professional ranks overseas. This is a real fear in Cuban sporting circles. In recent years, almost every time there has been an international sporting competition, such as the Good-Will Games, the Pan American Games or the Olympics (when the Cubans have not boycotted them), numbers of Cuban sportsmen and women have defected.

Athletic defections are a particular problem for the Cuban authorities because sport has been developed not just for its own sake, but more importantly as the country's ideological ambassador. Borrowing from the old Soviet model, success in Cuban sport is viewed as a wider indicator of the health and wellbeing of the whole system. However, this image becomes seriously tarnished if the athletes themselves begin to reject the system which nurtured them. Since 1991, seventy athletes have defected from Cuba (Powers, 1995). More than forty fled during the Central American and Caribbean Games in 1993. Under the headline 'Winners run out on a loser', Hugh Davis, writing for the *Daily Telegraph*, claimed that:

> the defection of the cream of Cuba's athletes at a track and field championship in Puerto Rico is sending shock waves through Havana, where they were the privileged elite of the generation born after the 1959 revolution. The exiles in America are now looking to the young people in Havana to help sweep Castro from power. (Davis, 1993)

As was the case in East Germany, the Cuban government invests a disproportionate amount of resources in its athletes – educating them, feeding and clothing them, paying for their equipment and travel with precious currency and so forth. To see an athlete defect in his or her prime must be particularly irritating because in both a real and a metaphorical sense it helps to bankrupt the system.

The temptation to defect is somewhat offset by the fact that successful Cuban sportsmen and women experience a marginally better lifestyle than the average Cuban. While they are training and competing all their needs are taken care of by the State. Once they leave the school system they are given a reasonable apartment and, for the most successful, a car, albeit a second-hand, Soviet-built Lada, as well as being given an allowance and access to better food, clothing and so on. Once they retire from top-class competition they are more or less guaranteed employment within the sport/physical education system as coaches, sports development officers and the like. Talking to John Powers of the *Boston Globe*, Olympic and world heavyweight champion Felix Savon justifies his long-term amateur status with a mixture of patriotism and pragmatism:

> One reason that I don't want to turn professional is that I want to keep a revolutionary Cuban and keep on doing what I am doing. I already have my title and I have a physical education degree. I prefer to stay the way I am right now. (Powers, 1995)

However, none of this seriously competes with the kind of riches associated with a successful sporting career in democratic countries. Even erstwhile 'amateur' sports such as athletics offer tremendous rewards for successful competitors in direct monetary terms, in kind (cars etc.) or through product endorsement and advertising. Cuban athletes, for instance, rubbing shoulders with their American and European counterparts on the summer Grand Prix tour, must become acutely aware of these differences. If nothing else they get a first-hand glimpse of how ordinary people live in First World countries and must realise that even this far outstrips the domestic experiences of Cuba's sports stars. Being a top athlete gives an opportunity for foreign travel denied to most Cubans and with it the opportunity to defect likewise denied to most Cubans – apart from those foolhardy enough to risk the inner-tube across the Florida Straits. One such person is Ramon Ledon, a bantamweight and former member of the Cuban national boxing team whose makeshift raft was picked up off Florida by the US coastguard in September 1994. His views contrast sharply with those of Savon:

> There is no respect for athletes in Cuba; athletes can't decide for themselves what they can and can't participate in. The money you get for competing, the government keeps, and after you're done, you get nothing. (Price, 1995: 64)

Cuban baseball players and boxers are the most vulnerable because of the massive appeal of the professional versions of these sports in the United States, coupled with the fact that the Cubans excel in both. There has been a steady flow of baseball players into the US major and minor leagues and several Cuban boxers have turned professional in the United States and Japan (Price, 1995: 64). On the surface, given that top boxers are the highest-paid sportsmen in the world, it is surprising that not more have taken this option. There may be several reasons for this. First, we have to admit the possibility that most Cuban athletes, including boxers, are loyal Cuban citizens who love their country and will not leave it at any price. It is worth remembering that the greatest Cuban boxer of recent memory, triple Olympic champion Teofilo Stevenson, turned down a handsome offer to defect and turn professional in the United States, rejecting a multimillion dollar offer with the famous words 'ningun dinero del mundo puede tener el valor de los millones de Cubanos' – not any money in the world is worth losing the love of millions of Cubans (Ruiz, 1980: 8). Stevenson may have been sincere when he said this, or he may have been under considerable pressure to reject the offer with a fanfare which could be used as an element of the anti-American/capitalist propaganda campaign (for instance, what would have happened to his family had he defected?). In a famous public oration in Havana in 1972, Fidel Castro used Stevenson's rejection as a theme through which to glorify the revolution and the purity of spirit of the Cuban people in comparison with the corruption of their American neighbours (Ruiz, 1980: 47). Suffice it to say that, whatever the boxer's motivations, it is widely believed that the Ali versus Stevenson match was the greatest fight never to happen. Today it is generally believed that several of the country's top boxers, such as Juan Hernandez, Roberto Balado and Felix Savon, would be world title contenders should they ever defect to turn professional. This view is supported by the fact that one of their less fêted contemporaries, the heavyweight Jorge Luis Gonzales, who defected in 1991 to box within the MGM stable in Las Vegas, has been undefeated in his first thirteen professional fights and is ranked in the world's top ten by both the WBC and the WBA.

Another, and perhaps more plausible, reason why more do not defect was given by a senior boxing official:

> I think that there are too many risks involved, particularly in boxing. OK, life in Cuba may not be so good right now, but at least as a boxer you are well fed and have some basic comforts. Also, when you are finished fighting your health-care needs are looked after and the state gives you a job. In Cuba a boxer is guaranteed security for life, albeit at a basic level. If he goes to the United States and boxes as a professional none of this is certain. What if he doesn't make it? What if he gets seriously hurt? Who looks after him and his family?

Senor Martines has a good point. Sporting careers are notoriously short-lived and few are shorter than that of the boxer. One punch can finish a man's career, if not his life. While Cuban amateur boxers are among the world's best, the professional ring is of a different order altogether. It is by no means certain that a champion amateur boxer will successfully make the transition into the prize ring. Even if he does 'make it', there is no guarantee that this will bring him security for himself and his family for life. In the annals of pre-revolutionary Cuban professional boxing, the ring's success stories are matched only by the numbers of fighters who were ruthlessly exploited by managers and agents and who fought their way from rags to riches and back to rags in the United States (Pettivo and Pye, 1994: 143). Conversely, many top professionals never made it as top amateur champions. There are considerable differences in terms of duration, pace, technique and rhythm between amateur and professional boxing, and while they are close relatives they are definitely not the same. Thus, the jump from Cuban amateur to American professional is a considerable leap and one which is highly risky.

Finally, boxers, like all Cuba's athletes, are very carefully monitored, both at home and particularly when they are overseas, to make sure that the opportunities for defection are minimised. The fears of the Cuban officials are not without foundation. During the Dublin international tournament in March 1994, mentioned at the beginning of this chapter, the author encountered a lawyer from Chicago whose avid interest in Cuban boxing was tied up with his desire to act as their agents if/when they chose to turn professional. With people like him waiting in the wings, no wonder the gatekeepers to the boxing subculture seem a little suspicious of foreigners, and this helps to explain why negotiating access is such a difficult task. Only the fact that I had visited Cuba several times before and had established good relations with senior sports administrators enabled me to get permission to spend time close to the inner circle of Cuban boxing.[3]

Boxing, sport and physical education in Cuba

In order to get detailed information about the structure and processes which accompany the development of Cuban boxing it is necessary to visit the Boxing Commission's offices, which are situated within the headquarters of INDER at Ciudad Deportiva (Sports City), about four miles from the centre of Havana. INDER is housed in a huge flying-saucer-like building which used to be the country's main indoor sports auditorium before the Pan American village was built in the early 1990s. Ciudad Deportiva was opened in 1958 by Batista. Indicative of the status of boxing in Cuba at that time, Batista and his entourage were entertained by a boxing match between the Cuban welterweight Orlando Echevarria and the North American world title holder Joe Brown. Inside, the auditorium has a distinctly American college 'field house' (sports hall) atmosphere. One wall is dominated by a mural of Che Guevara, who occupied the building in the early months of 1959 and used it as his headquarters while the new, revolutionary government took control of the capital. It is still an impressive building. It holds about 12,000 spectators and surrounding the auditorium are two concentric circles of offices from which Cuba's sports system is organised and administered.

INDER was the instrument which Castro used to reform all aspects of physical culture in Cuba. It was set up in 1961 with the twofold task of bringing sport to the masses while at the same time overseeing the development of Cuban champions. This was to be achieved through forging an institutional alliance of educationalists, health-care specialists and governing bodies of sport within the rubric of INDER. Faced with a situation of almost total neglect, this involved the construction of a cross-institutional pyramid within which the educational, recreational and health-care needs of Cuban citizens would be catered for from 'the cradle to the grave' (Pickering, 1978).

In the context of sport the foundations of this pyramid are laid early. When a baby is forty-five days old mothers are encouraged to take their infants to physical manipulation classes at the *matrogymnasium* (mothers' gym), during which babies are stimulated to explore their bodies through the fullest range of limb movements and kinaesthetic experiences. From the age of one year, pre-school education is available for all Cuban toddlers. Playful forms of physical education are given a high priority within the pre-school curriculum. An appreciation of rhythmic movement is central to this process and almost all activities are accompanied by a

---

[3] Joel Casamayor, the 1992 Olympic bantamweight gold medallist, and Raymond Garbey, the 1993 world amateur light heavyweight champion, defected from the Cuban pre-Olympic training camp in Guadalajara, Mexico, shortly before the commencement of the 1996 Olympics in Atlanta.

simple percussion instrument. Dancing is likewise emphasised during these formative years. Thus, when the five-year-old child arrives at primary school, she or he already has a foundation in physical literacy unsurpassed in most fully developed countries.

In 1958 there were less than 1,000 physical education teachers in Cuba: a ratio of one per 10,000 of the population. Thirty years later, through reforms initiated by INDER, officials claim that there were 28,000 PE teachers, one for every 360 members of the population. Every primary school has at least one full-time physical education teacher to supervise classes which are an integral feature of the child's early learning experiences and which continue to emphasise rhythm and movement. In addition, outside the regular PE programme, exercise is used as a cross-curricular theme, with interludes of calesthenics being practised regularly in classrooms during other subject periods. In the secondary school, physical education is third behind mathematics and sciences as a priority subject, and out of a forty-hour school week, twelve are dedicated to PE and organised sport. During secondary school, Cuban children specialise in a range of team sports and individual events, including boxing, which feed into a network of regional and national inter-scholastic championships.

Running parallel to the school physical education curriculum is physical activity within the Pioneer Movement, a uniformed youth organisation falling somewhere between the old Soviet Lenin Youth and the British Boys' Brigade. The patron of this organisation is Che Guevara who, before his death in the forests of Bolivia, had a particular affinity with young people. Despite their disillusionment with many aspects of the current regime and its guardians, most young Cubans still hold Che in high esteem. The Pioneer Movement engages young Cubans outside school hours in a wide variety of quasi-military activities. Sports, including boxing and related forms of physical activity, are central features of this organisation, the overall objectives of which are related to fitness for national defence and labour.

In Cuban schools the physical development of children is monitored alongside their progress in sports through a series of athletic examinations called *Listos para Vencer* (Ready to Win), or LPV. These examinations involve a combination of physiological, anthromorphological and technical measures which are used to assess the general level of fitness and ability as well as to single out those who possess the potential to excel in sports once they are fully developed. At this point the standard system of education overlaps with a more specialised network of schools and colleges which is designed to bring out the best in the country's most talented young athletes. There are approximately thirty EIDE (*Escuales d'Inciacion Deportiva Escolar* – Schools for Initiation into Scholastic Sport) located throughout the island. To these are sent the most promising performers who have been identified either through the standard schools testing programme or have demonstrated above-average ability in inter-scholastic competitions, Pioneer and/or community-based sports programmes. The EIDE are purpose-built boarding schools within which the normal school curriculum is followed alongside an extended and increasingly specialised sport and physical education programme. Depending on the sport, after several years in an EIDE academy those who have demonstrated the highest potential graduate into one of Cuba's ESPA (*Escualas Superior Perfeccion Atletismo* – Superior Schools of Athletic Perfection), which are located in each of the island's thirteen provinces and in the capital. At the age of sixteen (this may vary with sports such as gymnastics or synchronised swimming for which smallness is considered a virtue) the best in each sport are selected and sent to the junior national training camp in the Pan American village on the outskirts of Havana. Two years later the best of the best are inducted into the various senior national squads and are sent to an elite training camp, the peak of Cuba's pyramid of sporting achievement, appropriately situated in the shadow of INDER's headquarters at Ciudad Deportiva. Those who do not make the grade at this stage usually move on to one of the *Escula Provinciale de Education Fisica* (Provincial Schools of Physical Education) to train to become teachers of physical education.

Before this revolutionary structure could be properly introduced, the remnants of the old system had to be purged from the island. As one of its first tasks INDER was charged with dismantling professional sport in Cuba. Boxing was the first casualty, as in January 1962 the revolutionary government issued resolution 67D abolishing professional boxing, because it was 'una actividad totalmente nociva y contraria al desarrollo y estado de salud de los atletas que practican este deporte' – a harmful activity which is very damaging to the health of those who take part. The death of the Cuban Bernado Kid Paretes, after he had been knocked senseless by Emile Griffith in Madison Square Garden, two months later was seen to justify the abolition of prize fighting. The outlawing of professional boxing was rapidly followed by the closing of Havana's Jai Alai Fronton (stadium). Jai alai or pelota was more than a sport. It was chiefly a medium for gambling and along with the island's numerous gaming casinos was viewed as a corrupting product of capitalism which had no place in post-revolutionary Cuba. Ultimately, in March of the same year, all professional sports were banned in Cuba because they 'pugna con los objectivos fundamentales que inspiran nuestra Revolution Socialista' – ran counter to the fundamental principles which inspired our socialist revolution.

Amateur boxing survived and flourished, however, because it was a high-profile Olympic sport and, as in the Soviet Union and other client states, the Cuban government elected to invest heavily only in those sports which afforded opportunities to produce Olympic champions. At least rhetorically, Olympic achievement provided a showcase for Castro's and Che Guevara's vision of the 'new Cuban', an athletic hero who was nurtured through socialism and who participates purely for the love of his or her country. After the revolution the deepening hostility in the relations between Castro's government and the United States increased nationalism within Cuba. There is nothing like an enemy at the gates for cementing solidarity within, and the failed invasion of American-backed, counter-revolutionary partisans at Playa Giron (the Bay of Pigs) in 1961 and the missile crisis the following year helped to consolidate Cuba's new, socialist identity. Castro realised the potential which sports have to act as a surrogate theatre for the enactment and projection of nationalism. In honour of the victory at Playa Giron, in April 1961 Castro held a vast sports competition which, for the first time, revealed his vision of the future for Cuban sport and its intimate relationship with national identity and loyalty to the revolution.

Boxing for the Bay of Pigs

The boxing tournament was held in a former jai alai fronton, the Vicente Ponce Carasco Stadium in Havana, where every year the victory at the Bay of Pigs is celebrated with a high-profile senior boxing competition. This is an ideal venue to begin looking at the practice of the Cuban system. The Ponce Carasco is in a narrow street behind Havana's main hospital (Hospital Amejeirar). Before the revolution Ponce Carasco was a jai alai fronton, but has been used for boxing for many years. Jack Dempsey fought Eddie Cutter at this site in an exhibition bout in 1926. It is dusk and, as usual, all life is out on the streets. As a European it is impossible to walk ten paces without being offered cigars, women or being badgered by street urchins for 'chicklets' (chewing gum), cigarettes or money. The area surrounding the sports hall is as squalid and run down as anywhere in the city. If Havana has a ghetto, then this neighbourhood must be it. The buildings are all crumbling, the road is dirty and dusty except where some unmentionable liquid happens to be seeping up through the cracks in the pavement or cobblestones. Children play in and out of the doorways and in the gutters while adults lounge on doorsteps or in open windows idly chatting or simply gazing into space. Over their shoulders can be glimpsed familiar sights of crowded and cluttered rooms with mixtures of ancient and cheap plastic and formica furniture. Bicycles weave in and out of this moving human landscape with bells ringing or 'pssst pssst' hissed warnings from cyclists and their passengers. Three or more to a bike is not an unusual sight in Havana. One man peddles by with a dead pig strapped to his saddle. As a fuel-saving measure Castro imported tens of thousands of bicycles from China and the streets of Havana have more bone shakers on them than Amsterdam, Holland, or Cambridge, England.

Take a deep breath and stroll into the auditorium. Outside the main hall, in the foyer and underneath the galleries, ragamuffin children are scampering and playing everywhere. Like the surrounding neighbourhood, or indeed like anything which has not been purpose built or refurbished for tourists, the stadium is pretty dilapidated and there is no sign that it has been maintained since the revolution, more than thirty years ago.

The main hall is a long oblong room, half of which is taken up by bench seating for about 2,000 people behind a wire mesh divide. The other half seems to be marked out for some kind of wall tennis game. Tonight, however, the activity half of the hall is dominated by a large boxing ring. In the spotlights the white ropes and canvas of the ring contrast sharply with the grey gloom of the rest of the building. The seats are about half full and the audience is mainly black and Creole, including a few women and girls and lots of little boys. Ringside in rows of seats are the in-the-knows of Havana's boxing fraternity. Stocky middle-aged men with puffy faces and gnarled muscles. Many of them are smoking; one or two puff away at long Havana cigars. Hardly an atmosphere to inspire athleticism, but hardly any different from boxing crowds anywhere else in the world. A visiting boxing team from Mexico sits in their midst.

This particular night the cream of Cuba's boxers are on display in an inter-provincial boxing tournament marking the thirty-third anniversary of the Bay of Pigs victory. The evening's card is given added significance by the fact that the competition will also serve as a selection guide for the team which will compete in the 1994 World Amateur Boxing Championships in Kuala Lumpur. There is a ripple of applause as the first boxers enter the auditorium and are announced into the ring. The chaos outside the ring could not contrast more sharply with the order in it. The corner men in their colourful track suits, the boxers in their satin shorts and red or blue vests, ebony skin (most of the fighters tonight are black) and the referee, gleaming whites and a black bowtie.

Once the bell sounds for the first round we are treated to an exhibition of studied determination and breath-taking rhythm, coordination, timing and power. In this particular bout the world super heavyweight champion, Roberto Balado, makes short work of a younger and less experienced opponent. Roberto is a real hero in Cuba, having won fifty-six contests in a row, including the Olympic gold in Barcelona in 1992. Despite his bulk, Balado seems to glide about the ring as if a half-inch cushion of air separates the bottom of his calf-skin boots from the canvas.[4] With the possible exception of dancing, Cubans do nothing better than boxing. Meanwhile, in the dungeon-like changing area: bam-bop-bam; biff-biff-bumph are being whacked out as the next contestants warm up by driving combinations into the padded hands of their trainers. Others sit alone, rhythmically inhaling and exhaling like bellows, with far-focused eyes, concentrating on the task ahead. Nobody challenges me as I sit and take notes and snap the odd photograph.

There is a stir in the audience with the arrival of Cuba's world heavyweight champion Felix Savon. He seems to know everybody and as he makes his way to the changing rooms, like the Pied Piper, he accumulates a growing train of children. I inadvertently break up this scene by producing a packet of chewing gum out of my pocket. Immediately I am surrounded by six or eight children demanding 'chicklets'. I make the near fatal mistake of dividing up my single

---

[4] Two months after this field work was completed, Roberto Balada was killed when his car collided with a train at an unattended level crossing on the edge of Havana.

packet and handing the pieces out. Suddenly every child in the place cascades down out of the stands and I am engulfed by thirty or forty urchins chanting 'chicklet, chicklet, chicklet'. This seems to amuse the audience more than the fight taking place in the ring a few yards away. So much for the researcher not disturbing his field.

After about an hour, I step outside the stadium for a break and to take in the scenery. By now it is pitch dark outside and the atmosphere feels slightly more sinister. I have no sooner set foot outside than I am once more set upon by the chicklet kids. Older youths and men approach me with the standard sales patter about cigars: 'Habana cigar ... bery gooood, Monti Cristo? Cohiba?' Ten yards from the stadium door across the street a young girl is smiling at me from her doorway. 'My sister,' I am informed by a smiling, black youth, 'ten dollar?'. During such times of extreme economic hardship it seems that there are few things that are not for sale for hard currency in Cuba.

I retreat into the relative sanity of the auditorium to discover Savon warming up in a side room. There are some half-hearted attempts to exclude the children from this area, but a few manage to slip in. The fact that Savon's warm-up area is also the entrance to the snack bar severely reduces the potential for his privacy. Not that the procession of men, children and bicycles seems to worry any of the fighters or their coaches. In the crowded warren that is Havana creating privacy in public spaces is a well practised art form.

All the fights are of the highest quality. When you are watching the top ten Cuban amateurs fighting their nearest domestic rivals, you are probably watching sixteen or eighteen of the top amateur boxers in the world. The quality of the fights bears witness to this. When Savon enters the ring for his contest the audience comes alive. He is a real favourite. Ding ... round one. The fight is a bruising one. Two big men moving with such speed and elegance. It could almost be ballet if it were not for the hammer blows with which they keep assailing one another. In the early stages the challenger shakes Savon with some aggressive inside work and a couple of thunderous uppercuts. First round even.

The tide turns in the second round as the challenger, on his approach for an attack, is caught by a sweeping right hand from the champion. He does not go down, but he wobbles and this gets him a standing eight count. The challenger recommences showing a little more respect for Savon. The latter senses this and begins to move forwards with more purpose. A rapid-fire left jab snaps back the challenger's head and before he has time to gather his defences an over-arm right catches him on the cheek, sending him reeling – another standing eight count. Second round: Savon by a distance. Third and final round. It goes no more than a minute before the weakening challenger is tagged again. He still does not go down but the referee decides that enough is enough and stops the fight. After the usual courtesies in the ring Savon leaps out and goes around the auditorium thanking almost everybody personally. He is hugely popular and likes his public, particularly the children who throng around him as he makes his way triumphantly back to the changing rooms with the chant of 'Savon, Savon, Savon' echoing around the cavernous auditorium.

I have witnessed this combination of popular adoration and common-man humility before in Havana, once while in the company of Juantorena, a former double gold Olympic champion for Cuba in Montreal in 1976, and a second time during a meeting with Sotomayor, the world champion high jumper and gold medallist at the Barcelona Olympics in 1992. Like Savon, both men exude the personal aura of stars, but this does not seem to keep them from being accessible to the community which has sustained them. As one US journalist put it, 'there is none of the resentful awe that attends the arrival of an American superstar, no distancing *celebrity*' (Price, 1995). One is left in little doubt that, regardless of how their achievements are used for propaganda purposes, Cuba's top sports performers are without doubt the people's champions.

As soon as the final bout is over up to fifty children swarm into the ring. Even the renowned tolerance of Cubans for children is tested by this invasion. As the hoard continues to shadow box and perform all manner of gymnastics, helpers are attempting to dismantle the ring. One man leaps in the midst of the children waving his jacket wildly, but as fast as he is chasing them out one side, others are boarding from another. Only the virtual collapse of the ring sends the children scurrying home.

I walk back to my hotel with Ajo, the commissioner of boxing for Havana. He too has a Chinese bicycle, on the back of which he straps the two stools which were used for the night's bouts. He tells me that some of the same children who invaded the ring will reappear the next evening at a local boxing club as they take their first, tentative steps along the road which leads to Savon and Balado. He offers to take me there the following evening.

Observations from the grass roots

The local boxing club is about ten minutes away from my hotel in the heart of Old Havana. Unlike the newer parts of the city, which have a US-influenced grid-pattern design to the street layout, there is no particular logic to the geography of the old part of the city. It is a maze of narrow winding streets which criss-cross one another at irregular intervals and odd angles. The streets are lined with dilapidated three- and four-storey colonial buildings which, apart from a few empty shops and the odd workshop, contain a warren of apartments. Because the streets are so narrow, apart from at midday when the sun is high in the sky, Old Havana exists in a chequered twilight of dark shadows and piercing shafts of bright sunlight reflecting off the chrome fins of abandoned Chevrolets and Cadillacs.

School is over for the day and there are children scampering about everywhere, shrieking and laughing as they play a variety of time-honoured street games. There are a few rusted basketball rings here and there which receive a little attention from one or two older boys, and where roads meet or in one of the small squares stick and ball games resembling baseball are under way. The locals play baseball in the most dangerous locations, impervious to the dangers to passersby or the danger to themselves from the traffic. In one instance I witnessed a game taking place alongside the busy, six-lane Malecon and one of the out-fielders was placed amid the traffic in the middle of the highway! Occasionally you can come across small knots of boys hacking at something which resembles a football. However, other than these rare pick-up games, there is minimal evidence of a formally organised sports culture in and around these teeming streets and this makes one doubt some of the extravagant claims for the scale of popular participation (*masividad*) made by INDER's officials.

Finally we arrive at Trojo (the name of the gym/club, which means something like barn) which is located in Calle Cuba (Cuba Street). The entrance is an archway which admits the visitor into a small hallway, beyond which is the main body of the club. The 'gym' turns out to be an old, open-air amphitheatre which was purpose built for boxing in the 1920s. It is how I imagine James Figg's boxing booth in Oxford Street, London, must have looked in the eighteenth century. The central floor is about twenty meters square and is dominated by a full-size boxing ring under a hanging canopy which, like everything else in the vicinity, has long since seen better days. The canvas has huge rips in it, through which the pieces of chipboard that have been used to patch the actual floor can be seen. At the east and west ends of the amphitheatre, raised ten feet off the ground are sets of wooden bench seats which angle back and upward for twenty rows. Formerly the place must have accommodated more than a thousand spectators, who decades ago would have crowded in here to see some of Cuba's best up and coming professional boxers make their reputations. The legendary 'Kid Chocolate', who lived locally and went on to become junior lightweight champion of the world, trained and fought here in the 1920s. The bleachers would have been packed to watch the Kid make a name for himself by beating the likes of 'Young Chico' Wallace, Willi Jimenez and Jose Santos.

It is not difficult to imagine the crowd half a century ago, dark suits under their white Panama hats, smoking cigarettes and long Havana cigars, buzzing in anticipation of the Kid's fight and the rest of the evening's card. That was a long time ago, during an era belonging to a different boxing subculture in Cuba. These seats have not been used for many years. They all seem to be rotten and have been cordoned off to prevent the children climbing on them and injuring themselves. High along the north side of the hall, directly above the ring, is an old press box which looks as if it has not housed a journalist for many a year. Like the bench seats, it looks to be on the verge of collapse. This does not deter local children from climbing into it for a good vantage point to view the afternoon's proceedings. The whole place is like a fading relic of and monument to professional boxing in Cuba.

The faded glory of the auditorium contrasts markedly with the vitality of the young members of the club. Training sessions take place from 4 p.m. to 8 p.m.

Monday to Friday. Sometimes on Saturday mornings there are inter-club boxing contests. On this occasion there are about twenty youngsters and an elderly coach taking part. The age range is from about ten to sixteen, although a few six- and seven-year-olds have sauntered in off the streets to go through the motions with their elders. While the club operates an open-door policy – any youngster can walk in and train – the vast majority of participants are referred to the club from local schools. Unlike in the United States and Europe, boxing is a central part of the school games curriculum. From an early age Cuban boys are introduced to boxing and the basic techniques of ring craft. The physical education teacher, supported by the local INDER boxing expert, will identify the youngsters with the most potential and they will be strongly 'advised' to attend training sessions at a nearby gym after school. Through their application in training and their progress in local and provincial tournaments the INDER coach will assess their development and, in consultation with other boxing experts, will recommend the best of the best for admission to the provincial EIDE (for eleven- to sixteen-year-olds).

As with most aspects of life in Cuba, it takes a while for things to get started. For the first half hour the older boys lounge around chatting, joking and laughing with one another. The younger ones dash about playing a variety of impromptu games. One child circles the yard surrounding the ring at speed on a home-made scooter. At the end of each lap he leaps with his scooter over the prone body of one of his friends, two of his friends, three of his friends ... before the coach steps in to stop anybody getting hurt, indicating that it is now time to box.

Once the older boys have wrapped their hands and, in some cases, put on their gloves, in customary fashion the coach shouts '*Tiempo!*' (time) and the action begins. Despite the fact that the batteries for his Chinese watch ran out long ago, years of experience enables the coach to judge within two or three seconds the three-minute rhythm and beat of the training session. The atmosphere in Trojo changes as the formal action begins. The older boys seem to have their own routines well worked out. Two begin to shadow box in the space between the entrance and the ring. Another, with torn gloves, begins to dance around and stab at a patched punch-bag as it swings from the press box. Two more take turns to pummel a midriff-height padded board which is screwed to the wall next to the changing rooms.

Meanwhile, in the ring some serious sparring gets under way. One of the first contestants is fourteen and is the provincial champion at his weight. Ajo considers that he has sufficient potential to be recommended for admission into the provincial EIDE. These special schools have permeable boundaries to ensure that talented athletes can gain access at times appropriate to their physical development and the needs of the particular sport. At the shout of '*Tiempo!*' the contestants dance towards each other across the torn canvas like images reflected in a misted mirror. The footwork, punching technique, defence and hand spread are all impressive. The provincial champion looks particularly adept and has to be restrained by the coach from giving his partner too much of a beating. 'At the youngest age we like to concentrate on technique, technique, technique,' explains the coach. 'The youngest boys are too light to hurt each other seriously, so you can let them mix it a little and this helps you to coach more effectively than in simulation outside the ring'. The boys in the ring are fourteen and are at the stage when childhood is giving way to adulthood and, just as in boxing gyms in Hartford and Belfast, punches are thrown with more power and received with more pain. However, because their overall ring craft is so good, it is unusual for too many telling blows to be landed in these sparring sessions.

Outside the ring the coach takes the younger boys in hand. He lines them up in a single row and begins to teach them basic punching techniques and associated movements. Like a drill sergeant major he barks out commands and the row of boys dances forward, rag-wrapped hands simultaneously snapping punches at the body and head of an unseen adversary. He grabs the arm of one, tilts the head of another and points to the feet of one more as he issues general instructions to his class while still keeping half an eye on the proceedings in the ring. These younger boys seem to have no special equipment and are dressed in their shabby, torn, grey street clothes. The worst of their attire is on their feet. Most have battered and ripped baseball boots or fake-leather sneakers. Several have odd shoes on and one boxes barefoot.

The poor dress of the boys, the paucity of the equipment and the general dilapidation of the auditorium are a source of embarrassment to the trainer. He uses Cuba's standard excuse for the poor state of affairs. 'It is the economic crisis,' he explains, without attempting to qualify what this is and why it exists. Like talking about the 'troubles' in Northern Ireland, in this one phrase (the economic crisis) responsibility, both collective and individual, is abdicated, the onus is taken off the internal political system and a sense of hopeless inevitability and permanence is communicated. As I look at the poor state of their clothes and equipment I am reminded of what an Irish amateur champion had told me. He had been beaten by a Cuban in the last world championships in Montreal, Canada. After the fight he had paid with dollars for the shorts, vest and boots belonging to the Cuban fighter. Apparently this was not an unusual practice, which, he claimed, was sanctioned by the Cuban coaches, who took their cut. Ironically, the Cuban government has to buy this equipment in the first place with precious hard currency. If this trade in equipment does go on, while it can be viewed as a 'perk' for the boxers it is also indicative of the poverty of their circumstances in comparison with other amateur fighters, particularly those from Western Europe and North America.

After about one and a half hours of sustained practice things are wound down and the young pugilists drift outside to join the throngs in the narrow streets of the old city. As I walk outside, as usual I am assailed by the 'chicklet' hunters and I notice some of the formerly disciplined boxers are in their midst. Once more I am struck by the poverty of the surroundings, the lack of material possessions, the vitality of the people and the high quality of the boxing which I had just witnessed.

A pictorial history of Cuban boxing

It is 8.30 on Saturday morning. A training session/competition has been arranged in Trojo between the provincial ESPA and a team of young boxers from one of Havana's municipal districts. The streets feel less intimidating in the brightness of the morning. Also, being Saturday, most people seem to be enjoying a late morning sleep. The entrance to Trojo is locked behind a metal grill. Outside there is a cluster of youths, most of whom are clutching plastic bags in which they are carrying their modest boxing kits. I step back down the street hoping to use the zoom on my camera to get a better shot from greater distance. As I adjust my position I bump into an old man coming in the opposite direction. I apologise – '*de nada*' (it's nothing) he shrugs his response.

He is clearly interested in my camera and also intrigued by my interest in the young boxers opposite. 'I used to be a boxer,' he tells me in Spanish. 'When I was younger, I too boxed over there,' he says, gesturing towards Trojo. 'Come with me, I will show you some photographs,' he commands, pulling me towards the huge oak door of the apartment directly opposite the auditorium. Trojo remains closed so I have little option but to follow him into his home. Inside, his ground-floor apartment is surprisingly spacious, consisting of one large room, with very high ceilings and a tiled floor, subdivided into a kitchen/dining area and a lounge. There is a small bedroom at the rear of the kitchen area. It is dark and musty until he opens a rear door, allowing in a bright shaft of sunlight and some welcome fresh air. Unusually for crowded Havana, we are alone except for a small, threadbare, scrubbing-brush-like dog which jumps off an old sofa when we enter and scuttles off into the bedroom to resume its snooze on its master's bed.

The old man invites me to sit down and begins to burrow in an old dresser. As I look around the room it appears like a shrine, the icons of which are divided evenly between Christianity and boxing. Here and there are symbols of Catholicism – the Madonna and child, Jesus with his Sacred Heart, scenes from the crucifixion and so forth. Next to them are relics from Cuban boxing. Faded photographs of long-dead fighters and yellow and brown newspaper cuttings telling of their triumphs and tragedies. An old certificate is pinned to the wall, testifying to the fact that my host, Senor Miguel Sanchez, has been certified by INDER as a qualified boxing trainer.

He returns to the table with a black plastic bag, the contents of which he empties on to the formica surface. Dozens of old photographs and newspaper cuttings spill out. He dons a pair of spectacles which, with one arm missing, balance at a precarious angle along the bridge of his nose. Finally, the old man begins to pick his way through his album, every now and again pausing to select a faded image of a forgotten hero. His otherwise tired eyes sparkle with renewed life as each image takes him back fifty years to his own youth. 'Nino Valdes y Kid Gavilan … dos de los mueto en el cuadrilatero,' he says, pointing to the images of two healthy-looking former champions who lost their lives in the ring. His album is a jumbled history of boxing in pre-revolutionary Cuba. 'Ah, Kid Chocolate, Cubano, campeon mundal'. He waves a photograph of Kid Chocolate and his entourage taken after his triumphant return from the United States, where he won the world junior lightweight title against the odds in Madison Square Garden, New York, defeating Toni Canzonari in front of 20,000 partisan spectators. 'Kid Chocolate bibio cera de aqui,' he says, explaining proudly that Kid Chocolate was brought up near to the apartment in which we now sit.

As he produces photographs of other pre-revolutionary professionals, some with names like Kid Charcoal and Black Bill; it is obvious that the social basis of boxing then, as now, was Afro-Caribbean Cuba. The island was one of the last places in the Americas to abolish slavery. In 1841 it is estimated that over 40 per cent of Cuba's population of just over a million were black or mulatto slaves brought to Cuba by the Spanish to work in the sugar and tobacco plantations. It was not until 1886 that slavery was finally abolished. In economic terms, freedom meant little and for the remainder of the nineteenth century and for much of the twentieth blacks have been rooted firmly at the bottom of Cuba's class structure.

The ranks of both the rural and urban poor have been dominated by those of African descent. Until the revolution in 1959, for this group of people life was a harsh struggle against hunger and deprivation. Opportunities for self-expression and personal advancement were extremely limited. Most sports in Cuba were elitist and bound up with an education system which catered primarily for the privileged (Pettivo and Pye, 1994: 23–5). It is not surprising, therefore, that boxing, a sport which asked no questions about social background or certified intelligence, which opened its doors to all those who were brave enough to try and offered a chance for the best to raise themselves above the poverty line, became very popular with pre-revolutionary Cuba's black under-class. To this day the vast majority of Cuban boxers are black. Despite official claims to the contrary, through the eyes of a neutral observer, Cuba's black population continues to have second-class status. Most of the country's senior bureaucrats seem to be fairer skinned, as do most of those who hold publicly visible positions of responsibility, such as the tourist guides. In contrast, most of those who are out of work or who occupy menial positions and work the front-line of the black market are Afro-Cubans and, significantly, the bulk of those who attempted to flee the island in the latest exodus of rafts came from the same social stratum. Surely it is more than a coincidence that it is also Afro-Caribbean Cuba which continues to provide most of the island's top sports performers?

Next the old man produces a brown and faded photograph of a large white boxer standing over the prone form of a black man on the canvas of an open-air ring. The referee, who is dressed in a white shit and dark trousers, is in the process of sending shock waves around the boxing world by counting out Jack Johnson in his sensational contest with Jess Willard. He fishes out another handful of photographs of foreign champions who boxed in Cuba: Jack Britton (1922); Jack Dempsey (1926); Panama Al Brown (1930); Freddie Miller (1936); Henry

Armstrong (1939); Joe Louis (1947); Sugar Ray Robinson and Sandy Saddler (1951); and Joe Brown (1958). Apart from a very favourable climate and its proximity to the United States, until the 1959 revolution Cuba had a very liberal approach to gambling, alcohol, prostitution and all of the other trappings of a decadent holiday resort. The Mafia, which controlled much of the vice and crime throughout the United States, had considerable influence in Cuba, particularly in Havana, where many of the largest hotels and gambling casinos were run on behalf of North American gangster 'families'. Cuba really blossomed as a resort in the 1920s when the prohibition of alcohol was introduced in the United States. The fact that the Chicago-based racketeer Al Capone had a holiday home in Varadero (it is now a 'salsa palace') illustrates the importance of the island in relation to organised crime.

In the United States, from the 1920s to the 1950s, professional boxing was virtually run by infamous Mafia gangsters such as Al Capone, Lucky Luciano, Legs Diamond and Frankie Carbo. As Butler (1986: 115) argues, these gangsters 'did not need boxing financially but it gave them a kick to be seen at ringside and talking to the champions'. Because it was outside US jurisdiction and because the Mafia already controlled much of the entertainment infrastructure there, Havana was an ideal venue for professional boxing, and many of the world's greatest boxers fought in Cuba's capital at least once in their career.

The penultimate image produced by my host is that of a young Teofilo Stevenson landing a crushing right hook to the temple of the besieged US heavyweight Duane Bobick, on his way to winning his first Olympic title at the 1972 Munich Olympics. Stevenson repeated this feat in Montreal in 1976 and in Moscow in 1980. Finally, Senor Sanchez reveals his proudest possession, a photograph of himself and Teofilo taken after the champion had given up competing to dedicate himself to coaching younger Cuban boxers.

The old man gathers his photographs and cuttings and with a gnarled hand shovels them back into the black plastic bag before burying them once more in the depths of his dresser. Outside his front door he raises his chest proudly as I take his photograph. Then he turns and disappears once more with his memories into the gloom of his apartment.

A gathering of hopefuls

By now Trojo is open and a crowd of twenty or thirty youths has gathered inside along with Ajo and several other coaches. Mingling and playing in their midst is an equal number of local children in their ragamuffin shorts and T-shirts. As usual nobody pays too much attention to these children, who roam freely about the gym or crowd into the rickety press box waiting for the fights to begin.

I wonder how different this scene would have been in the 1950s, when the old man across the street frequented this gym? Then as now this was one of the poorest parts of Havana and it is likely that the children would have been no better dressed. Just as today, many would have also been barefoot. While there are no obvious signs of child hunger in contemporary Cuba, given the current 'economic crisis' and the ever-contracting rationing system, levels of nourishment must be low and it is unlikely that the children of the 1950s would have been any worse off in terms of food. Today's children are certainly better educated. In 1953 it was estimated that almost 25 per cent of the population over ten could neither read nor write. Even though since 1940 education between six years and fourteen years was mandatory for Cubans, through lack of facilities, lack of interest and the need for child labour, almost 50 per cent of the population never attended the *escuela primaria elemental*. By 1990 adult literacy was close to 100 per cent and all children over the age of five attended school, most of them after having several years of pre-school care and education. All the children present today are in full-time education and it is inconceivable that this would have been the case in the 1950s.

Likewise, despite chronic shortages of medicines, standards of health care for children and adults alike are considerably better than they would have been under Batista's regime. After the revolution Castro and his close allies made a conscious decision to invest in the people of Cuba, and wide-ranging reforms in education, health and welfare are a testimony to these policies. Thus, while there is an obvious lack of material comfort for young Cubans there is an equally obvious lack of evidence of any serious physical suffering. Rather than compare contemporary Cuba with pre-revolutionary Cuba or with highly developed nations such as the United States, it is perhaps more useful to compare the country with neighbouring island states such as the Dominican Republic, Jamaica and Haiti. In the last, the nearest of Cuba's neighbours, all the indicators of extreme poverty such as hunger, infant mortality, illness, and illiteracy are very high. To a lesser extent, this applies also to the Dominican Republic and Jamaica. Thus, most young Cubans are much better cared for than many of their near neighbours.

Nevertheless, as I cast my eyes around the gym, watching the sparkling brown eyes of the youngest children as they play their games and the determination on the faces of the older boys as they wrap their hands in preparation for the morning's competition, I wonder what the future holds for them. What is the point of having an extensive and democratic education system if intellectual endeavour goes largely unrewarded? For instance, why should a young person work hard at school or university to become a doctor if doctors can only earn the equivalent of less than $10 per week? It is tragic to think that as things stand the strongest ambition which parents can have for their children in Cuba is that, once they are old enough, they will find a way of leaving the country. Sadly, it seems, the revolution, which attempted to construct a society around the maxim which Lenin borrowed from Rousseau, 'from each according to his ability, to each according to his needs', has succeeded only in, more or less, equalising lack of opportunity. In most instances, no matter how bright they are and no matter how hard they work, it is difficult for Cubans to better their lot. Unlike becoming a 'model worker', or working one's way up through the communist party bureaucracy, or being a vigilant member of one of the numerous committees for the defence of the revolution (and being permitted to buy a second-hand Soviet car!), boxing, sport in general and other aspects of popular entertainment, such as dancing and music, are rare avenues for self-expression, self-fulfilment, relative prosperity and, in some cases, exit and exile from Cuba.

In contrast with the lazy interaction taking place outside the ring, once the competition begins the fighters acquit themselves with focused determination. In the first bout one contestant boxes barefoot and I am mesmerised by the agility of his brown feet as they dance quick-step patterns across the torn canvas. As usual, irrespective of the poor equipment, the standard of boxing in all the contests is very high. As could be expected, the team from the provincial ESPA has the edge in most contests. But the local team are highly motivated and, by and large, give good accounts of themselves. Ajo explains that it is in contests such as this that he and his colleagues assess the potential and development of Havana's pool of talent. For those who are not at the provincial ESPA a skirmish like this gives them an opportunity to be recognised as somebody worthy of a place there.

Despite the fact that there is a lot at stake and that the fights themselves are conducted with furious intensity, the young boxers show incredible self-discipline and emotional restraint. There is little overt sign of anger, even in the most bruising encounter, which has the small crowd baying and leaves one boxer badly cut. After the fight the two boxers hug one another, thank the referee and the opposite corner men and skip out of the ring without further ado. Ajo tells me that while winning and losing have some significance, at this level he is more interested in combinations of technique and temperament, believing that if the balance between these can be established early in a fighter's career, then the victories will follow automatically later. He goes on to explain that in the 1960s, before the educational and welfare reforms of the revolutionary government took effect, most of Cuba's boxers were the rough and ready children of the poorest classes who had endured the Batista regime. Today, while the majority of boxers in Cuba still come from marginal areas of the towns and cities, because the sport now takes place within an educational setting, it is easier to produce contenders who, beyond having a passion for fighting, are good technicians and can also appreciate the moral and ethical dimension of their favoured sport.

As I manoeuvre myself around the ring attempting to take photographs of the action and its surrounds I feel a tug at my shirt. A small boy with a toothy grin and big brown eyes who can be no more than four years old appeals for a 'chicklet'. I give him my standard 'no tengo' (I have none) reply. This does little to deter him and he stays by my side for some time continually pulling at my shirt and repeating his request for chewing gum and entertaining himself by swinging beneath the apron of the ring.

At the end of each round he scrambles into the ring to entertain the audience with furious bursts of shadow boxing before returning to my side and demanding gum for his efforts. Even though I have two sticks of gum in my pocket, I dare not give him any, knowing from experience that if I produced a pack in this setting I would be engulfed by a mob of children. Instead I let him have a look through the lens of my camera. The experience of seeing the world through a zoom lens has a strange calming effect on him and while he stays by my side for the duration of the contest he no longer tugs at me demanding gum. I have let him do something different and it seems that this small gesture of kindness is enough to make him content. At the end of the final bout the referee comes across to me and whispers 'chicklet?'. I laugh, reach stealthily into my pocket and palm him a pack of gum out of view of my new friend and the other chicklet hunters. What price making it as a sports star in a country where a look through a camera lens or a stick of gum can mean so much?

Afterwards I walk back to the hotel with Ajo and his young son Juan. Ajo tells me that alongside regular 'one-off' competitions like the one we have just witnessed there is a nationwide competitive structure, coordinated by INDER, through which fighters can be gauged, graded and the best of them sent to the appropriate training academies. There are five levels to this competitive structure and each level has provincial and national tournaments.

At age eleven to twelve years the youngest boxers take part in the Pioneer Movement's championships. The second and third levels of competition, for thirteen- to fourteen-year-olds and fifteen- to sixteen-year-olds, are orchestrated within the school system and it is at these stages that most of those with greatest potential are identified and sent to the provincial schools of sporting excellence. Moreover, performance at the third level of competition has a considerable bearing upon which boxers will progress from the EIDE schools to the ESPA academies and the National School in Havana. The fourth or juvenile level, for seventeen- to eighteen-year-olds, is organised outside the school by INDER, and it is at this stage that those who will join the national junior team are identified. The final, senior level, for those who are over eighteen, is the show case within which those who have successfully endured the rights of passage up to this point can stake a claim to be considered for the national senior team and where those with established reputations earn the right to continue to represent Cuba internationally.

While the structure of these amateur competitions is similar to that found for amateur boxing in the United States or Ireland, there are two very important contextual differences which have a significant bearing upon the way boxers develop in these different cultural settings. In the first place, at every stage of development, amateur boxing in Cuba is closely supported by the education system, and this considerably reduces the wastage of talent. In the United States, for instance, once a talented youngster reveals himself at the Silver Mittens or the Golden Gloves the development of his potential is left in the hands of local clubs, which exist largely outside the public gaze. Given the precocious social context of the boxing subculture in the United States, there is little guarantee that this talent will attain its full maturity. Similarly, in Ireland, because of the underground ambience of boxing and the voluntary nature of the sport, there is a huge wastage of ability. In Cuba, on the other hand, potential is recognised early and protected within special schools of excellence where, in the hands of well qualified coaches, talent can be maximised, with a single goal in mind – to produce amateur champions who will win international honours for Cuba.

Secondly, in Cuba, once an amateur boxer becomes established as a national and/or world champion, he remains within the amateur ranks until his career reaches its natural plateau. Elsewhere in the world where boxing is also a professional sport, a considerable number of boxers turn professional once they have proven their worth as amateur champions on the world stage. Teofilo Stevenson won three consecutive gold medals at the Olympic Games in Munich, Montreal and Moscow (1972, 1976, 1980). Had he been American it is unthinkable that he would have won more than one because he would have turned professional almost immediately after his victory over the Romanian heavyweight Ivan Alexe, in the Olympic final in Munich 1972, just as Cassius Clay, Joe Frazier and George Foreman had before him after respective triumphs in Rome in 1960, Tokyo in 1964 and Mexico in 1968.

The grooming of the excellent

Willi – my interpreter and odd-jobber – is despatched that evening with instructions to return the following morning with a car and a driver. We have to return to Ciudad Deportiva, from where we will be taken to the national sports school in the Pan American village on the outskirts of Havana. A clap of thunder announces the arrival of the new day as a tropical storm sweeps over Havana from the Gulf of Mexico. The wind howls around the narrow streets of the old quarter of the city and one particularly strong gust bursts open the shutters leading to the balcony of my room, scattering papers everywhere. Downstairs Willi is waiting with the car, which turns out to be a 1953 Chevrolet driven by an elderly man who is willing to spend the whole day with us and take us wherever we want for $16. It is like a scene from a 1950s B-movie as we head out of the city centre looking over the dashboard and through the split windscreen of the old Chevy. The driver looks tiny behind the huge steering wheel. In vain, a lonely wiper struggles to beat clear a section of the window for him to see through the torrential rain. Cubans on their way to work scamper across the road to shelter beneath the arches and arcades of Old Havana. In the square surrounding the Capitol Building tall palm trees bend in the furious gale and people waiting for buses huddle beneath plane trees for protection from the storm.

By the time we reach Ciudad Deportiva the storm is beginning to move away. Romilio Vichy, an assistant commissioner for boxing within INDER, is waiting for us. He has no car and since INDER cannot afford to run executive cars we are grateful for the 1953 Chevy to take us to the national sports school in the Pan

American village, about five miles east of the city, on the coast. On the way there Romilio tells me that there are approximately 15,000 registered boxers in Cuba and 570 qualified coaches. Confirming what Ajo has already made clear, he says that each of Cuba's fourteen provinces has two specialist sports schools, from which the best seventeen- and eighteen-year-old boxers are sent to the national school in Havana. Currently, out of a total of 340 athletes there are thirty-four boxers enrolled in the national school and they are serviced by a minimum of eight senior boxing coaches and a full range of back-up services. Following the Soviet model, the Cuban sports system invests most of its resources in coaches and related support personnel such as doctors, physiotherapists and sports scientists (Pettivo and Pye, 1994: 126–97). Boxing, it seems, conforms to this pattern.

The Pan American village was completed for the staging of the Pan American Games, which were held for the first time in Cuba in the summer of 1991. Its centrepiece is an impressive athletics stadium with all-seating capacity of 70,000. It is surrounded by a variety of other sports facilities, including a swimming pool complex, a velodrome, a basketball arena and several multipurpose halls and gymnasia. Spread further afield is a jigsaw of apartment blocks, in the midst of which is the Pan American Hotel. In places the accommodation blocks have been allocated to the families of the workers who were involved in their construction. Otherwise the whole site has an eerie, unused feel about it. The prospect of playing host to the likes of the United States, Canada and Mexico proved to be irresistible to Castro. However, if he had known in 1987 when he broke the ground to begin the construction of these facilities that Cuba's main trading partner and financial backer, the Soviet Union, would collapse, leaving his own economy in tatters, it is doubtful that he would have sanctioned a project of this magnitude. Already the sea-salt air has begun to corrode the buildings and long, rough grass and weeds have reclaimed almost all open spaces. It reminds me of one of those ghastly English 'new towns', built in the 1960s and half-deserted in the 1980s.

We reach our destination at 10 a.m., about an hour before the main training session of the day for the boxers. The training hall is nothing more than a long rectangular room, about fifteen metres wide and forty metres long. The impression of a much larger room is created by a mirror covering the wall at one end of the hall reflecting the boxing ring immediately in front of it and the people and things gathered beyond. There is a team of six boxers from Algeria pounding away at a row of punch-bags under the watchful eye of three coaches, two Algerian and one Cuban.

For a decade or more after the revolution Cuba either sent its athletes abroad to receive training in the Soviet Union, East Germany and Bulgaria, or brought in experts from these places to work with Cuban athletes in Cuba. However, by the mid-1970s, Cuba had developed its own sporting infrastructure and coaching methodology modelled on the Soviet system. The traffic in coaches and athletes began to flow in the opposite direction as Cuban expertise was demanded, particularly by underdeveloped socialist countries such as Ethiopia and Angola. In the late 1980s and early 1990s the need to earn hard currency had displaced ideological solidarity as a rationale for marketing Cuban expertise in sports. Now it is not unusual to see athletes from all over the world (excluding the United States) taking part in coaching clinics in Cuba. As exemplified by Nicholas Hernandez-Cruz, the coach of the Irish amateur boxing team, Cuban experts can be enlisted by governing bodies of sport from other nations, provided that 70 per cent of their hard currency salaries are paid to the Cuban government. No fewer than nine nations employed the services of Cuban boxing coaches at the 1992 Barcelona Olympics (Pettivo and Pye, 1994: 150) and it is estimated that in 1995 more than 500 Cuban coaches and trainers from more than thirty sports were working as advisers in thirty-eight different countries (Powers, 1995).

While we are waiting for the Cuban boxers to commence their training we wander down to the athletics stadium where athletes from the track and field teams are practising. In the entrance to the stadium a brand new, unregistered, metallic gold Mercedes is parked. Shortly, an identical vehicle, this time in bright red, pulls up. Sotomayor, the Cuban world high-jump champion, uncurls himself from the driver's seat. It turns out that both vehicles had been won by Cuban athletes on the European Gran Prix circuit at competitions sponsored by Mercedes Benz. As well as winning cash prizes, the victor of each event was presented with a new Mercedes. While all prize money won went to the Cuban government, the athletes were allowed to keep the cars. In a country where a ten-year-old Lada is a status symbol, owning a new Mercedes is like driving a top of the range Rolls Royce anywhere else. The fact that the best of Cuba's aspiring athletes walk past these vehicles each day on their way to and from practice must have increase their motivation.

. As the short-sprint hurdlers go through their routines on the 100-metre straight they are passed at 50-second intervals by a group of six middle-distance runners who are cantering lap after lap on the rubberised, rust-coloured running track. Even doing something as straightforward as running, the Cubans display a sense of rhythm which I have not seen matched anywhere else. There is a fluidity and elegance about them which makes even the hardest physical task appear effortless. It would be easy to pass this off, stereotypically, as an innate characteristic associated with the African heritage of most of Cuba's top sportsmen and sportswomen. (Like suggesting that black people are better dancers than white people because they are black or that West Indians are superior cricketers because they have natural reserves of timing and rhythm.) While sociobiological theories of physical performance should not be dismissed out of hand, they are often so overstated as to be worthless. As we have seen, INDER sees to it that the development of rhythm is not left to chance in Cuba. Whatever natural advantages Cuban athletes may have, the Cuban system of physical education ensures that physical literacy, balance and timing are key elements of the maturation process and this can be seen just as easily on the running track or in the boxing ring as on the dance floor.

At 11 a.m., back at the boxing hall the Algerians have gone and the young Cuban pugilists are beginning to gather. Typically, the atmosphere is laconic as the boxers and their coaches drift into the gym, slapping hands and going through elaborate US 'brother'-style greetings rituals before finding a spot to sit and chat to the accompaniment of a North American rock band blaring from a small ghetto blaster which one of the coaches has plugged in. They wear a rag-tag jumble of old training clothes, much of it carrying fading symbols of American colleges and US and European sports goods manufacturers' logos. One or two wear beaten-up boxing shoes, but most wear battered baseball boots. There is obviously considerable trade in these within the class as many of the fighters wear odd pairs, no doubt having dealt for a left or right one from a colleague whose other shoe was so worn it had to be thrown away. It could almost be a scene from a gym in New York or Detroit and my earlier observations about the social base of Cuban boxing are confirmed as out of approximately thirty boxers there are only four who are not Afro-Caribbean. Like all the other athletes, the fighters live on site.

This sleepy group have just left their dormitories having taken a few hours rest after the early morning training session which went from 6 a.m. to 7.30 a.m. Breakfast is at 8 a.m., after which most of the boxers take to their beds until the 11 a.m. session is due to begin. Once this period is over, at around 12.30 p.m., they will take lunch before attending school until 6 p.m. After dinner they are free to catch up on some studying or just relax. During the week bedtime is at 11 p.m., a curfew which is not difficult to enforce given that the boxers have to be up before 6 a.m. the following day for the morning training session. Weekends are free unless an important boxing tournament is imminent, in which case extra training may be scheduled. Otherwise the students are free to go home or, if home is too far away, they can travel in and out of Havana to shop, go to the cinema or stay with friends or relatives. As with all schools in Cuba, the national sports schools are closed during the holiday months of July and August and the athletes will go home unless there are major international competitions scheduled during the summer months.

Eventually the senior coach arrives and the formal proceedings begin. The session begins with a long and leisurely warm-up, the content of which is left up to the fighters themselves, who display an ingenious variety of stretching and loosening exercises. After ten minutes the coaches take over and get the boxers to jog and dance their way in single file around the room, practising footwork, punching combinations and coordination in sequence. The head coach stands in the centre of the gym calling the shots while his seven assistants orbit the revolving boxers issuing individualised pieces of advice. I am mesmerised by the hand speed of some of the fighters. The pace of the delivery of a punch is critical to success in boxing. If I had to face some of these fighters, I am certain that I would be hit by their third punch before I saw their first coming. As each lightning combination is thrown, thirty fighters force lungsfull of air through clenched teeth and the music from the ghetto blaster is stifled by a sound like an old steam train. After a further ten minutes of this the gloves are dished out and the real work begins.

Once gloved up the boxers spread around the hall, taking up different stations at punch-bags, wall punching pads and in the ring itself. Others in pairs find a space in the centre of the room and prepare for mock sparring. In obedience to the traditional and universal beat of the boxing gym, the head coach glances at his stopwatch before calling *'Tiempo!'*, beginning three minutes' deafening and frenzied activity. This session lasts for about ten rounds, during which the fighters rotate around the stations, pausing every four rounds or so to take on water to compensate for the gallons of sweat which they are producing in the hot and steamy gym. During each round the lieutenant coaches mingle among the jittering throng, cajoling and encouraging the boxers as they mercilessly attack and defend against imaginary adversaries.

After almost forty minutes of exhausting, high-quality work and a short water break the boxers move on to a period of callisthenics, most of which are dedicated to hardening the stomach and diaphragm. At one point, the boxers are laid out in a circle around the room like the intervals on a misshapen clockface. With toes pointed they raise and hold their straight legs twelve inches off the floor while one of the coaches walks around the room using the stomach of each fighter as a stepping stone as he passes. After ten minutes of sit-ups, leg raises, body crunches and more sit-ups, the boxers move to a warm-down, which involves slow jogging around the room and gentle limb and body movements.

The whole episode is brought to a conclusion through a ritual whereby the boxers line up on one side of the gym facing their coaches. The class leader stands apart from the rest of the boxers and invites them to thank the coaches for providing the morning's training. This is done lustily with a collective voice. In turn the head coach thanks the class for their efforts and follows with a short homily on the value of hard work and personal sacrifice.

Once the ceremony is over the head coach explains that he expects that between fifteen and twenty of these fighters will join the national team within the next twelve months or so. They will then move to the national senior training school where they will join the five or six top Cuban boxers in their weight class, becoming part of an elite team of forty to fifty fighters, many of whom will be national, regional and world champions. With a system like this producing and supporting them, I am hardly surprised. The question is, given Cuba's prevailing political and economic circumstances, how long can it last?

At first sight, Cuba's pre-eminence in amateur boxing is a marvellous achievement for a small country with a collapsing economy, which is barely above the degrading title of 'Third World'. There again, boxing and poverty have always gone hand in glove. Nevertheless, history suggests that too much poverty impedes the development of athletic talent of any kind, and this includes boxing. In the modern world sporting prowess is not a random product. On the contrary, unlike in days gone by when champions were either groomed in public schools or recruited from farms, blacksmiths' shops or coal merchants' yards, towards the end of the twentieth century, sports stars of all complexions have to be systematically nurtured if they are to compete credibly on the world stage. Despite their sport's rags-to-riches reputation, boxers are no different.

Boxing is one of the few sports which Cuba has been able to compete effectively in on the international stage both before and after the revolution. With the possible exception of baseball it is the only sport which before the revolution was non-elitist and which the largely black urban poor had access to. The glory days of Kid Chocolate and his contemporaries are retained in the collective folk memory of places like Old Havana and this helps to sustain a subculture which encourages young Cubans to dedicate themselves to the ring. Boxing is valued deeply in Cuba, particularly in neighbourhoods such as that surrounding Trojo, where the concept of the local hero is particularly strong. In Old Havana, like in most inner-city locations, having the status of a boxer can be the cornerstone of a young man's identity and something of which a young Cuban can be particularly proud.

Of great importance is the system through which sporting ability is reared and nurtured from a very early stage in an educational context. Little is left to chance in the farm system which underpins all of Cuba's post-revolutionary sporting achievements. Athletic potential is identified early in elementary school and those with the greatest potential are sent to special schools for sporting excellence. Within these institutions, alongside the regular school curriculum, young athletes spend many hours learning and practising those sports for which they have been earmarked. All of their needs are taken care of in these schools and they are relatively well fed.

Apart from the fact that practice does make perfect, this system also helps to reduce significantly the numbers of talented teenagers who drop out of sport as they pass over the adolescence threshold. In most countries this is a problem for almost all sports and particularly for boxing. Once boys get to their mid-teens the demands of the ring increase as their bodies begin to take on the shape of grown men. At the same time a whole range of vocational and leisure activities become available outside the boxing subculture. Going out with friends to bars and discos, getting involved with other, less demanding consumer-driven pastimes and finding jobs to pay for these diversions, and experimenting with alcohol and drugs are all common reasons why, elsewhere, young boxers leave the sport in their mid to late teens. In Cuba, few if any of these diversions are available. If a young Cuban does not keep up with his boxing, what else does he do with his spare time? As was expressed to me so many times by young people, 'life in Cuba is boring' (because they have no dollars to engage in a consumer-oriented leisure culture). For those boxers who are in the schools of excellence there is even less chance that they will drop out. To where can they drop? Moreover, they are aware that if they make the national team this will open up new horizons and improve their lifestyles. They will experience foreign travel and local fame and will enjoy a standard of living which is far higher than that of the average Cuban.

The power of this as a motive should not be underestimated, especially when, for most Cuban boxers, their formative years were spent in and around the mean streets of places like Old Havana. The impact which this experience has on a young fighter's consciousness is a critical element on his development as a boxer. Like all cliches, 'you can take the man out of the ghetto but you can't take the ghetto out of the man' contains an element of truth which is as important to a successful career in the ring in Havana as it is in New York, Detroit, Hartford or, indeed, Belfast. Moreover, because relative deprivation is a fact of life for the vast majority of Cubans, the chance of making it as a boxer is one which is not lightly squandered.

There is little doubt that the Cuban system, which has produced sporting success immeasurably beyond that which could be expected of a country of its size and economic resources, has much to be commended in purely sporting terms. Nevertheless, having a good system cannot guarantee success. The raw materials which enter that system have to be of an appropriate standard and, of equal importance, must have the correct level of motivation. Hitherto, the Cuban system has worked because Cuban society, by First-World, Western standards, has been poor, but not poverty stricken; has fed the population on limited resources, which ironically, may have increased their health; has pumped limited resources into education, health and welfare; has encouraged population growth and has celebrated increases in longevity. Among other things, this has resulted in the creation of a younger generation which is fit and lean, well educated, creative, argumentative and hungry for achievement, the expression of which vacillates between nationalism and escapism.

Conclusion: *tiempo!*

It is doubtful that under existing fiscal restraint Cuba will be able for much longer to finance the system which produces world-class athletes and sustains them while they are at their peak. Already the indications are that the system has peaked and output, measured in terms of international honours collected, is beginning to decline. In 1991 Cuba won its highest total of 265 medals in the Pan American Games in Havana. In 1995, in Mar del Plata, Argentina, Cuba won 229, a reduction of 10 per cent, and as conditions continue to deteriorate it is hard to imagine that Cubans will match their achievements in the 1992 Barcelona Olympics in Atlanta in 1996 (Powers, 1995).[5] Moreover, it is increasingly obvious that, as happened in the former East Germany shortly before its demise, the relative pampering of sports stars at a time when the vast majority of the

---

[5] In Barcelona Cuba came fifth in the overall medal table, winning a total of thirty-one medals: fourteen gold, six silver and eleven bronze. Cubans won seven of twelve gold medals available in the 1992 boxing competition and two silver. As predicted, in Atlanta the Cubans were in decline, coming eighth, with a total of twenty-five medals: nine gold, eight silver and eight bronze. This time Cubans won just two gold medals in boxing.

population stands in line for scarce and low-quality food is becoming a source of widespread resentment.

For centuries sport and other forms of popular entertainment have been used by dictatorial regimes as a means of placating and distracting oppressed peoples. But we learn from history that bread and circuses can offset the desire for liberty only for a limited period and that despite the integrity of those who would elevate the status of collective goals, once the circus leaves town and bread runs short it is impossible with words alone to quell the appetite of a population long starved of freedom. In today's Cuba this is especially true for those who were born after 1959 and who neither experienced the corruption of the Batista regime nor shared the euphoria of the revolution which overthrew it. For them, Cuba's boxing champions are a testimony to what they see as a constraining past rather than an enabling future, and can anyone who has not lived there and shared their deprivation blame them? Nevertheless, for those of us who grew up in relative affluence and, albeit from a distance, came to view Cuba as a bright light in the otherwise gloomy appearance of international socialism, it is to be hoped that Castro can reform and liberalise the island's political economy while retaining the more positive, humanistic, features of the existing system. This includes approaches to education, health care and, of course, sports.

Unfortunately, judging by what happened in Eastern Europe during and since the demise of communism and given the continuance of the US-led trade embargo, it seems highly improbable that Cuba's road to reform will be a smooth one and even less likely that Castro can win his battle to maintain socialist structures while gradually edging towards a free market economy. For all good boxers, there is always one fight too many and, with nobody left in his corner, the odds on Fidel keeping his title must be slender. Of one thing we can be certain, however, and that is that he will not throw in the towel.

6

Boxing and society

By the middle rounds it was no longer a question of power, but of guts and stamina. How Benn survived the eighth round is a mystery. Stiffened by a right, he was in desperate trouble. Two more rights sent him down. Benn rode the subsequent storm and in the ninth round McClellan began to indicate that something odd was happening to him. Still ahead on two of the three official scorecards he rose wearily at seven after Benn put him down in the tenth. When McClellan went down again, this time on one knee, he showed no inclination to beat the count. But, contrary to popular supposition at the time, the challenger had not simply given up. He was in desperate trouble. After walking slowly to his corner he sat on the floor and slumped against the cushion. Alarm bells were ringing. (Jones, 1995)

Twenty thousand people packed into Wembley Arena had roared their approval as Benn and McClellan hammered one another for ten rounds, producing one of the greatest boxing matches in the history of the British ring. A television audience estimated at 11–12 million shared the spectacle which had left one man close to death and the other badly hurt. The challenger had suffered severe brain damage as a consequence of the pummelling which his head had received at the hands of Benn. McClellan was rushed to hospital to undergo emergency neurosurgery to remove a blood clot from his brain. Not long afterwards the champion, whose swollen and battered face revealed that he had taken almost as much punishment as he had dished out to McClellan, was admitted to the same hospital for overnight observation and treatment for concussion, cuts and bruises.

The following day, as McClellan's life hung in the balance, the future of the sport for which he lived and which defined his very being was called into question just as it had been less than a year before when bantamweight Bradley Stone died from a massive blood clot on the brain after losing to Richie Wenton. Similarly, in 1991 in a world super middleweight title fight, which rivalled Benn versus McClellan for sheer courage and brutality, Michael Watson finished up paralysed and wheelchair-bound after suffering brain damage at the hands of Chris Eubank, and the place occupied by boxing in a 'civilised' society was the subject of earnest discussion. In this concluding chapter it is my intention to summarise the positions taken in this debate, locate them in a wider theoretical context and judge them from the vantage point of boxing in the lived cultural settings as depicted in the preceding chapters.

Death in the ring

> If boxing is a sport it is the most tragic of all sports because more than any other activity it consumes the very excellence it displays – its drama is this very consumption. To expend oneself fighting the greatest fight of one's life is to begin by necessity the downward turn that the next time may be a plunge, an abrupt fall into the abyss. (Oates, 1980: 16)

Since the Marquess of Queensberry rules superseded the London Prize Ring rules in 1884, according to official records approximately 500 people have died in the ring worldwide. However, in terms of fatalities, boxing is a relatively safe sport. In England and Wales, for instance, between 1986 and 1992 there were 412 fatal accidents related to sport. Only one of these deaths was as a consequence of boxing, whereas eighty-seven people had died while taking part in motor sports, eighty-two when flying or parachuting, forty-six while playing ball games and sixty-five on mountainsides or in caves (Rodda and Weale, 1994). In the United States, for every 100,000 participants, the chance of a death in boxing has been estimated at one, compared, for instance, with scuba diving at eleven, hang gliding at fifty-five and horse racing at 128 (Cantu, 1995). Statistics on injuries are much more difficult to come by, but, while it is certain that all sports carry with them the risk of both minor and serious injuries, there is agreement that there are few sports to compare with boxing when it comes to injuries to the body's most vital organ: the brain.

When they elect to step into the ring, boxers risk two categories of injuries to the brain. The first are the product of the 'killer punch', the big knock-out blow which rotates the skull faster than the brain inside, causes one or more of the delicate bridging veins between the cranium and the brain to become detached and, sometimes, snaps the head back against the top of the backbone, leading to unconsciousness, paralysis and, in the worst cases, death. No one has described the observable effects of such a blow better than Norman Mailer:

> the head smote the spine with a lightening bolt and the legs came apart like falling walls. On the night Foreman took his championship, who could forget the film of Frazier's urgent legs staggering around the ring, looking for their lost leader? (Mailer, 1975: 98)

The second category of injuries involves the debilitating effects caused by repeated blows to the head, not only in a single fight, but also accumulated over the length of a fighter's amateur and professional career. This leads to the so-called 'punch drunk' syndrome whereby a fighter's physical and intellectual capacities gradually become impaired as the brain suffers cumulative damage. Often it is only after a boxer has retired that the long-term effects of his profession become manifest. After he gave up the ring Muhammad Ali, perhaps the greatest boxer ever, was diagnosed as having Parkinson's disease, a condition which Ali's chief medical consultant is convinced was brought on by his career in the ring. The former world heavyweight champion who was famed not just for his speed and skill in the ring, but also for his nimble wit and silver tongue ('move like a butterfly, sting like a bee'), now moves about slowly and suffers from slurred speech (Hauser, 1991).

The question here is whether or not such injuries can be considered accidental. While points can be scored for hitting below the neck and above the waistline and while body-shots can have a devastating effect on one's opponent, the main target in boxing is the head. Moreover, an accumulation of points can and often does lead to victory, but this is usually the residual consequence of the pursuit of a knock-out, a condition which, by definition, leads to some degree of brain damage. Whereas in almost all other sports serious injuries are the result of unintentional actions (or wilful actions outside the rules of the sport), in boxing it is argued that the better and more successful a fighter is, the more likely it is that he will seriously injure his opponents. In other words, the *raison d'être* of boxing exists on a continuum which can and often does lead to infirmity and death. The Benn versus McClellan and Eubank versus Watson fights bear testimony to this: they were great fights because they bordered on the deadly.

While over the years the various governing bodies have been receptive to suggestions for changes at the margin of their sport to make it safer – shorter fights, mandatory brain scans, enforced lay-offs after knock-outs and better on-site medical attention – they have steadfastly refused to countenance changes which undermine the pursuit of and defence from the knock-out as the central, defining aspect of boxing. They argue that boxing without the potential of a knock-out would be like football without the potential of a goal and they perceive, probably correctly, that just as football crowds turn out to see goals or at least action around the goal mouth, the boxing audience is attracted mainly by knock-downs and the skills which accompany their pursuit and avoidance. There are even suggestions that, albeit an unlikely occurrence, the potential for death is a subliminal factor which compels the boxing crowd. Given this, while the debate surrounding boxing is often conducted in medical terms and, at least on the surface, appears to be concerned with the welfare of the fighters themselves, at a deeper level the issue is more concerned with what the durable popularity of boxing tells us about society in general. As Jack O'Sullivan (1991) put it, 'the debate about the future of boxing should not be just about its safety, but about what on earth are we doing watching it'.

Boxing and civilisation

Boxing is often accused by its detractors of being 'uncivilised': their argument being that the sport encourages manifestations of brutality which have no place in a morally advanced or civilised society. A useful starting point for theorising on this issue is Elias and Dunning's (1986) typology of the civilising process. This model suggests that the development of sport and its central position in our society can be understood as part of a process through which, over the centuries, our appetite for violence has decreased. In the dark ages and before, people were born into and matured within quasi-tribal social networks characterised by functional independence, subsistence and self-reliance. Social relations were narrow in scope and traditional. Political authority was closely allied to physical force and what law there was centred on punishment and retribution. This harsh and threatening world was reflected in the barbarity of the culture which it spawned, including the violent and blood-thirsty activities which were regarded as sports. At a time when life for many was 'nasty, brutish and short', so too were their sports.

However, beginning in the late Middle Ages, a related series of developments, particularly the change from an agricultural to a commercial and industrial economy and the emergence of a centralised political and civil authority (the State), led to a gradual, but nevertheless wholesale, change in the mechanisms through which individuals are socialised into and maintained within society. In this regard, according to Dunning, a homologous relationship grew between institutional apparatuses of social control and psychological processes of self-control, leading to:

> a more or less continuous elaboration and refinement of manners and social standards ... together with an increase in the social pressure on people to exercise stricter and more even self-control over their feelings in more and more fields of social relations. (Dunning, 1993: 45–6)

Consequently, culture develops a more genteel appearance, within the embrace of which people no longer feel impelled to take part in or watch blood-thirsty and violent sports.

The durability of boxing as an entrenched feature of popular culture casts doubt upon Elias and Dunning's typology, for several reasons. It has been argued that their thesis implies a more or less unilinear imperative to historical progress and in doing so ignores the uneven facts of social change and development (Hargreaves, 1986; Horne and Jary, 1987). While as a collective endeavour societies may develop in one direction or another there can be nothing preordained about their ultimate destination. The Hegelian model of society on a long march towards Utopia is undone by the facts of modern history. As Curtis (1986) observes, events such as the Holocaust, the Dresden fire storms and atomic bombs dropped on Nagasaki and Hiroshima severely damage the optimistic dynamic underpinning the civilising process. More recently, ethnic cleansing in the former Yugoslavia and genocide in Rwanda and Burundi help to confirm that societies are just as capable of moving backwards as they are of moving forwards. Also, the internecine violence which exists behind the facade of civilisation in all advanced societies, and particularly in the United States, suggests that we remain part of a species which, under certain circumstances, is capable of manifold acts of social degradation.

While the form of boxing has changed over time, as argued in chapter 1, the sport has a submerged historical continuity which connects today's ring with the booths of Regency England and the amphitheatres of ancient Rome. Elias and Dunning (1986: 136–40) argue that boxing as it was practised in Ancient Greece was more brutal than its modern counterpart and they use this as evidence of a society at a 'less advanced stage in the civilising process' than our own. Their original thesis is taken further by Sheard (1990), who argues that after the Marquess of Queensberry, boxing became rationalised and rule-bound, resulting in a de-emphasis on violence. However, although Virgil wrote around 70 BC, there is nothing in his account of a mythical boxing match between Dares and Entellus to suggest that his experience of boxing in the ancient world was more or less violent than fights between Dutch Sam and Jem Belcher in 1807, James Corbett and Yankee Sullivan in 1892, George Foreman and Muhammad Ali in 1974, or Nigel Benn and Gerald McClellan in 1995. Indeed, in Virgil's account Aeneas, 'having decided that Entellus must cease this show of vindictive savagery, stopped the fight and rescued the exhausted Dares' (Virgil, 1956: 133) perhaps earlier than a contemporary referee might have done and certainly before the contest would have been stopped had it been conducted under Broughton's eighteenth-century rules. There is a danger here that in looking for civilising trends (or vice versa) one can misread and/or misinterpret historical evidence.

For instance, it is generally considered that the introduction of the Marquess of Queensberry rules in 1884 made boxing a more genteel sport. But, as Gorn (1986: 205) argues persuasively, boxing under these rules is, in fact, more dangerous than fighting according to Jack Broughton's rules. Today's boxers are physically fitter and stronger. Boxing gloves are not like the *caestus*, but neither are they like pillows. They are both heavy and hard. Gloves protect the antagonist's hands more than the defender's head and they extend a boxer's reach, helping him to throw more and harder punches than ever before. Thus, despite technical changes, the spectacle of the ring has lost little of its potential to thrill audiences, who turn out or switch on to appreciate the dexterity and athleticism displayed in the foreplay, but who are particularly electrified by the final moments of a toe-to-toe encounter when one fighter weakens and the other moves in for the kill, usually metaphorically, but occasionally literally.

As I wrote this chapter (19 March 1995) the radio chattering in the background told of a police operation in northern England which had broken up a cockfighting ring, taking away the carcasses of a dozen or so savaged birds for forensic examination. Cockfighting, along with bare-knuckle prize fighting, was outlawed in England 150 years ago, but it appears that the sentiments which draw certain groups of people towards both sports, whether in the public domain of the reformed version of the latter or in the underground networks of the proscribed former, have yet to be socialised away (Ingram, 1995). Perhaps even more revealing is the global revival of free-for-all prize fighting in the form of the UFC (Ultimate Fighting Championship), described by Marcus Trower as a form of 'human cockfighting':

The modern sport combines the striking techniques of Thai and Western boxing with the throws and takedowns of amateur wrestling and pro-wrestler's painful submission holds. Again there are no gloves, rounds (fights are scheduled for between 15 minutes and an hour) or weight categories. Opponents can hit with the palms to the head (more a concession to the user's fragile hands than the receiver's face) and with their fists to the body; they can bludgeon each other with the forearm, slam in kicks, pump away with knees, and wrestle. (Trower, 1995: 21)

This depiction is very similar to Elias and Dunning's (1986: 136–7) invocation of the ancient Olympic game/contest of pancration, a sport which they claim belonged to pre-modern and less civilised society. The persistence of violent sports such as UFC and cockfighting is hard to square with the notion that society, including its sports, is trundling inexorably along civilisation's super-highway.

The relationship between the contests mentioned above suggests not only a continuity in boxing itself but also a continuity in the appetite of humans to appreciate and share in the celebration of life and death which is at the core of a boxing match. In this sense the appeal of boxing goes beyond the search for excitement in unexciting societies (Elias and Dunning, 1986). Oates (1980) argues persuasively that boxing is compulsive viewing for many because in dramatic form it captures this timeless human struggle for survival and mastery. Two men alone in a ring with nothing more than strength, courage and wit. Neither may leave until the fight is over. Only one can win and the other must lose. The fight is viewed as a parody of the human condition and as a reminder that even the foundations of post-modernity are themselves buried in antediluvian soil:

While it is plausible that emotionally effete men and women may require ever more extreme experiences to arouse them, it is perhaps the case too that the desire is not merely to mimic but, magically, to be brute, primitive, instinctive, and therefore innocent. One might then be the person for whom the contest is not mere self-destructive play but life itself; and the world, not in spectacular and irrevocable decline, but new, fresh, vital, terrifying by turns, a place of wonder. It is the lost ancestral self that is sought, however futilely. (Oates, 1980: 44)

I am not a fight fan, but I have had this dormant passion roused in me in dirty back-street halls in Belfast, in decaying sports palaces in Havana and ringside at Madison Square Garden. I have also noticed how it spreads like a concentric wave from those closest to the action to those at the back of the theatre, accompanied by a collective baying for the despatch of the weakening victim. This seems to connects us to a more barbaric past. It may be as Oates suggests, that 'civilisation's trajectory is to curve back upon itself' (Oates, 1980: 43) and that we are not so far removed from those who thronged into the coliseums of Ancient Rome as some would like to think:

When the boxing fan shouts, 'Kill him! Kill him!' he is betraying no individual pathology or quirk but asserting his common humanity and his kinship, however distant, with the thousands upon thousands of spectators who crowded into the Roman amphitheatres to see gladiators fight to the death. That such contests for mass amusement endured not for a few years or even decades but for centuries should arrest our attention. (Oates, 1980: 42)

Elias and Dunning (1993: 47) attempt to accommodate observations such as these by talking of 'de-civilisation', implying that just as people in institutionally secure settings can, over time, be socialised to exercise voluntary self-restraint, if those settings are disrupted, then under-socialisation will ensue and 'counter civilising developments will occur' (p. 47). However, this fails to take account of the rapidity with which the vestments of civilisation can be shed when social consensus breaks down in circumstances such as the civil war in the former Yugoslavia, sectarian conflict in Northern Ireland or a badly executed police arrest in Los Angeles. The global resilience of boxing serves to remind us that the relationship between the individual and society is an exceedingly complex one and that not all social behaviour is learned in a single generation. Furthermore, the existence of a sport like boxing may signal the need to maintain a balance between individual needs and social expedience.

While we must reject the notion of an invisible hand manipulating the pace and direction of history we can accept that all societies seek to progress. In this sense progress can be understood as improving the material wellbeing, the collective security and the cultural production of a given community. To borrow Elias and Dunning's term (divested of its over-determinism), communities aim to become progressively more civilised. However, there is a price to pay for civilisation – for the greater good of the whole social order we may have to suppress certain basic urges and desires and keep sheathed deep-seated physical and emotional energies. In this regard it may be useful to view sport as having an asymmetrical relationship with its host society. In important ways it both reflects and is a part of a given cultural flow which itself is predicated upon prevailing socio-economic, political and institutional arrangements. However, it is also clear that sport is a relatively autonomous theatre within which the conventions of the socio-cultural mainstream can be temporarily suspended, permitting modes of behaviour which as a rule, in terms of physical and emotional expression, lag behind the conventions of conduct which govern everyday life. The underlying thesis here is that through both participation and spectatorship, sport provides opportunities for people to express repressed potentials and feel basic human urges in settings which do not pose a threat to a given social order.

Nevertheless, the autonomy of sport is not limitless. There is an ongoing dialogue which ensures that the canons which determine acceptable behaviour within the boundaries of sport do not trail too far behind generalised conventions of good taste. As Elias and Dunning themselves acknowledge (1993: 51), the current debate about boxing can best be understood as part of this dialogue, as can discussions over the future of fox hunting and campaigns to rid soccer of violence on and off the field. Through this dialectic we construct sport in such a way that it follows the contours of rather than completely mimicking the standards which govern most other areas of our lives.

Boxing and social class

These propositions concerning the place of boxing in society assume that all segments of society participate equally in debates about sport. This is far from the case and a further problem arises when we look at the boxing debate in the context of social stratification. With echoes of both of Parson's structural-functionalism and Gramsci's Marxism, Elias and Dunning (1986) argue that society is plural and hierarchically structured according to socio-economic status and derived power, which in turn influence each social stratum's contribution to the processes through which dominant ideologies are constructed, transmitted and received. During the twentieth century, rising affluence in concert with the extension of the State and related public bureaucracies has given more people a material stake in the existing social order while at the same time exposing them to top-down institutional influences, 'increasing incorporation into dominant values of more and more sections of the working class' (Dunning, 1993: 63). Civilisation in modernity, Dunning argues, begins as a bourgeois formulation:

> Between the middle-ages and modern times, powerful elites standing at the nodal points of complex networks of interdependence, above all royal courts and large trading and manufacturing establishments, have been the principal standard setting groups, the initial model-makers in this long-term civilising process from which subsequent standards have subsequently diffused. (Dunning, 1993: 46)

However, this civilising process does not emanate from all segments of society and neither does it permeate all levels evenly. According to this view, there are social groups who have had a limited say in the dialogue between material and moral improvement and, as such, have neither contributed to the substance of the civilising process nor fully consumed its message. These are referred to as the 'rougher' working classes, a significant minority who are relatively impoverished and who, from early in life, are faced:

> not only with economic insecurity but also with the regular interruption of violence from a variety of sources: when they are children, from their parents; as they grow up, from their peers in the street and the school; as adolescents, from gangs within their own and neighbouring communities. (Dunning, 1993: 46)

This argument has a superficial appeal for anybody wishing to understand the social location of boxing. In the preceding chapters a strong case has been made for locating the sport's epicentre in the ghetto, which is also the habitat of those

179

referred to by Dunning as the 'rough' working class. Both ethnographically and theoretically the ghetto can be understood to be a violent habitat. Boxing is a violent sport and the ghetto is a violent environment and as such one could easily jump to the conclusion that the former is the natural product of the latter. However, under close scrutiny this logic breaks down for several reasons, discussed below.

While the overwhelming majority of those who box, particularly professionally, are from marginal working-class environments, the same cannot be said for those whose commercial interests in and vicarious appreciation of the sport ensure that it continues to exist as an important component of the sport entertainment industry. There is little new in this. In Greece and Rome all gladiators, including boxers, were supported by the elite. In Regency England, without the patronage of the gentry boxing would not have developed at all. In both cases the mass popularity of boxing illustrates downward stratified diffusion. Likewise, throughout the twentieth century the economic viability of boxing has been predicated on its appeal to people from the full cross-section of society.

Despite a powerful moral crusade against bare-knuckle prize fighting in the second half of the nineteenth century, boxing continued to have a wide appeal among the middle classes. In the United States in the next century boxing can viewed as a symbolic event within which the tensions among rugged individualism, masculinity, bureaucratic rationality and liberalism were worked out. Business people, politicians, actors and movie stars, 'classy dames' and stars from other sporting arenas regularly rubbed shoulders at the 'big fight. To be seen at the 'big fight' was as much a statement of status confidence as it was a confirmation of sporting affiliation (Gorn, 1986: 250). In this regard, professional boxing differs little from many other professional sports where the performers are drawn mainly from the lower classes and their performances, particularly those viewed live, are consumed by middle-class audiences.

That many of those who call for the sport's abolition are middle class should not be allowed to obscure the fact that many middle-class people pay to go and watch boxing and even more are armchair spectators. As Luis Bunuel's (1972) savage social satire *The Discreet Charm of the Bourgeoisie* illustrates so well, the outward sophistication of the middle classes often conceals dark secrets, not the least of which are a liking for violence and related behaviour. Following Elias and Dunning's (1986) arguments, it could be that a vicarious interest in boxing offers a legitimate and risk-free refuge within which such tastes can be indulged without openly flouting the more binding canons of bourgeois respectability. Jennifer Hargreaves is sceptical about the soothing effects of violent sports on the male persona and expresses serious concerns that domestic violence against women is connected to male notions of power and domination which can be stimulated by violent masculine sporting images (1994: 15–16).

It may be that not only do the bourgeoisie struggle for ideological dominance over the attitudes and appetites of the lower orders, but also, from time to time, experience a fracturing of 'civilised' hegemony within their own rank and file.

Indeed, as exemplified by the contest between the Holy Family and the Worcester Sporting Club described in chapter 4, sometimes the boxing audience is an exclusively middle- to upper-class affair. As they sat in their evening suits and relished a five-course, silver-service meal, there can be no doubt that they also enjoyed the combat between the spare young men from Belfast and the local boys from Birmingham. So they should, because, at £30 per head (not to mention side-bets), they had paid for it. It would be easy to dismiss this as an example of 'one-off' *nouveau riche* largesse if it were not for the fact that gatherings such as this, with its broad cross-section of middle- and upper-class support, have been regular features of boxing in Britain for more than a century (Shipley, 1989). While participation in and/or being victimised by violence may now be the preserve of the 'rough' working class, it would appear that violence as spectacle has a much wider appeal and it is this, not the generic push of the ghetto, which has enabled boxing to survive so long.

Boxing as rational recreation

The view that boxing is the natural product of inner-city poverty and violence is further undermined by a closer look at the value system which lubricates the inner workings of the boxing subculture. The notion that boxing is a social good has been critical to its survival in the twentieth century. This is rooted in the sport's late-nineteenth-century history, when a rationalised and reformed version of boxing re-emerges from the ashes of pugilism to be used by urban missionaries as a means of improving the health of the poor and diverting them from more antisocial activities (Gorn, 1986). However, the practice of making a living out of one's fists has an even longer history and it was not long before young working-class men who had learned to box in amateur clubs found a commercial outlet for their talents in a reformed professional ring (Shipley, 1989).

In this regard, amateur boxing, almost from its inception, has been incorporated into the farm system which recruits and trains professionals. The amateur boxing club provides the link between these two worlds. In this regard, while amateur boxing can be, and perhaps should be, viewed as a sport in its own right, it must also be seen as a means for the development of professional boxers. Because this relationship is ingrained within the deep structure of the subculture, the submerged status of amateur boxing as a vital stage in the occupational socialisation of professionals is rarely questioned. Moreover, amateur boxing works as a pre-professional training ground irrespective of whether the fighters themselves or the managers and trainers who handle them realise it or, indeed, want it to be so.[1]

---

[1] Officially, boxing in Cuba remains an exception to this process of occupational training. However, as noted in chapter 5, the defection of Cuban amateurs to the United States to fight as professionals is significant.

The belief that boxing keeps young people off the streets and out of trouble is axiomatic of the boxing subculture and is also accepted by many people in the wider society. The fact that the police are happy to sponsor boxing in the United States and that the criminal justice system, at least informally, views time spent learning to box as a viable and more rehabilitative 'sentence' for young offenders than custody bears this out. Likewise, the RUC justify their involvement in boxing in Northern Ireland in terms of community relations and as a means of diverting young people away from the paramilitary gangs. In Havana, Ajo, the district boxing commissioner, speaks of his sport as an alternative to drinking rum and hustling tourists. Throughout the world, the gatekeepers of the boxing subculture project an image of their sport as an antidote to crime, delinquency, drug abuse and moral decline.

This view is so deeply structured within the boxing fraternity that everybody, especially the fighters themselves, believe it to be true. Boxing has the appearance of being a self-constructed coping strategy through which young men from disadvantaged backgrounds can 'make something of themselves'. Even if they do not make the big time, as Wacquant points out, something might stick and at least they are physically out of the way for significant periods during dangerous ghetto nights:

> If for no other reason boxing is experienced as a positive force in the life of those who make it their career by dint of the prophylactic function it plays with regard to street crime and related social ills. Even when they make little or no money and end up in an occupational impasse, shorn of readily transferable skills and useful contacts for professional reconversion, the gym and the ring have taken them off the streets and sheltered them for the timebeing from the dangers they harbour. So that fighters have at least avoided the worse fates too often visited upon their non-boxing peers and childhood buddies, encapsulated by the macabre triptych of imprisonment, drug abuse or trafficking, and violent death. (Wacquant, 1993: 42)

Boxing and the ghetto

A ghetto environment may imbue a youngster at an early stage of his development with some of the foundation skills and attitudes upon which the physical and mental attributes of a boxer can be built, but it is the degree to which the boxing subculture can suspend some of the images of the ghetto and negate others which determines whether or not he will make the transition from the street corner to the professional ring. The boxing club needs the ghetto for initial recruitment and also as a back-cloth against which to remodel the physical and spiritual dimensions of its members. (In Charter Oak, Mack chides his young apprentices, warning them that beyond the gym door, if they forget that they are boxers first and foremost, they will fall prey to the drugs and violence which lurk in the housing project, and in Belfast, Morris and Hugh banter their boys about what trouble can befall those who hang around the lethal streets in the New Lodge estate.) The subculture needs kids who are 'tough-tough' and who have little else going for them, but they must also be willing to learn and to adapt their lives, both inside and outside the club, to the disciplined rhythms of the ring.

As I have argued elsewhere (Sugden, 1987) boxing is a hard regime which contrasts sharply with the 'quick fix' environment of the ghetto. It demands time, physical effort and mental discipline and it requires dedication, isolation and self-sacrifice, as Wacquant terms it, 'the drab and obsessive routine of the daily work-out' (Wacquant, 1989: 2). Every second spent in the limelight has to be earned through countless hours of physical and mental preparation. Norman Mailer compared the life of a boxer to that of a prisoner inasmuch as 'the prisoner or the fighter must give up some part of what is best in him' (Mailer, 1975: 12). Generally, only a small minority of those who inhabit the ghetto can surrender themselves to the total institution of boxing and it is only those with the strongest will and greatest determination who can see that commitment through. This, according to Wacquant, who observed young boxers in one of Chicago's ghetto gymnasiums, tends to exclude the roughest of the rough working class:

> Youngsters from the most disadvantaged families are eliminated for lack of the habits and inclinations demanded by pugilism: to become a boxer de facto requires a regularity of life, a sense of discipline, a physical and mental asceticism that cannot take root in social and economic conditions marred by chronic instability and temporal disorganisation. (Wacquant, 1989: 11)

Continued membership of the boxing subculture necessitates the acceptance of a value system which emphasises respect for oneself and for others: not just physical respect, but equally respect for one's own and an opponent's character. It also requires the acceptance of a work ethic along with the principles of self-sacrifice and deferred gratification: qualities not usually associated with the ghetto experience. Boxing requires a certain deference to authority and appreciation of fairness and, despite what goes on in the ring, it demands controlled aggression and a renunciation of vicious violence which is so familiar in neighbourhoods beyond boxing-club doors. In short, boxing inculcates in its adherents the value system and behavioural trappings of a 'civilised' society. The irony here should not be lost. Those who regularly call for boxing to be banned are often the same people who abhor the rough working-class culture which boxing, at least on an individual basis, seems best placed to counteract. In this sense it could be argued that boxing is one of the few harbingers of bourgeois civilisation to penetrate into the heart of the ghetto experience.

However, the relationship between the ghetto and the boxing gymnasium has to be lived out by the boxers themselves. Their individual characters and life experiences will have a telling impact both on careers inside the ring and lifestyles adopted outside it. Shortly before he became world welterweight champion, Marlon Starling explained to me that even though he no longer lived in a ghetto, his heart and soul still belonged there and that this awareness was essential to his continued success in the ring. A deprived and often criminogenic environment may be necessary to provide the motivation and frame the consciousness of 'hungry' fighters, but how this is subsequently harnessed and tied to the disciplines of the ring is a complex process which can have negative as well as positive outcomes. The career of heavyweight champion Mike Tyson illustrates this well.

Tyson has a cliched, Hollywood boxer's pedigree. He came from a broken home and was brought up in some of the roughest sections of Brooklyn. By the time he was twelve, Tyson's reputation for thuggery went before him and he had been arrested forty times. He was sent to a juvenile correction facility in up-state New York where he was spotted by Cus d'Amato, a legendary trainer of boxing champions. In his biography of Tyson, former light-heavyweight champion Jose Torres (1990) explains how d'Amato was able to shape Tyson's character in the ring by constantly invoking images of Mike's former life in Brooklyn's slums while simultaneously keeping him protected from the physical influences of the ghetto in an isolated training camp in the Catskills. It is very doubtful that Tyson would have made it as a boxer had he trained in an inner-city gym. Given his personality, it is highly unlikely that he would have learned to protect himself from the more pernicious influences of the ghetto. In their mountain retreat d'Amato froze the ghetto experience in Tyson's consciousness and was able to trigger its thaw in the ring. It was a method through which Tyson's anger, predatory viciousness and natural athletic power could be preserved and focused on opponents in the ring and which would see him before his twenty-first birthday crowned as the youngest-ever world heavyweight champion.

However, it is possible that this strategy had an adverse effect on Tyson's already fragile personality. His successes in the ring gave him wealth and celebrity status which rendered his position as an isolate increasingly untenable. Tyson's physical development was matched only by the size of his ego, which was inversely proportionate to the underdeveloped state of his super-ego (social conscience). After the deaths of his guardian and mentor Cus d'Amato and his manager Jim Jacobs, Tyson appeared to lose the ability to distinguish between himself as predator in the ring and his persona outside it. The 'ghetto as jungle' metaphor, preached by d'Amato for Tyson's application as a boxer, seemed increasingly to inform his approach to life in general as he lunged from one personal crisis to another. If you did not have what you want, you took it and by force if necessary. After a series of relatively minor skirmishes with the law, several involving violence against women, in 1992 Tyson was convicted of rape and sentenced to three years' imprisonment. In his case the means through which the violence of the ghetto had been harnessed to frame his consciousness as a fighter seemed to offer him inadequate guidance in how to control his aggression outside the ring.

Despite cases such as Tyson's, because the overwhelming majority of boxers learn their trade in local gyms, they also learn to live within the ghetto experience:

to keep it at arm's length, like a devious opponent with a killer punch. Wacquant contrasts the order of the boxing club with the social anarchy of the ghetto when he says it:

> constitutes an island of stability and order where social relations forbidden on the outside become once again possible. The gym offers a relatively self-enclosed site for a protected sociability where one can find respite from the pressures of the street and the ghetto, a world in which external events rarely penetrate and upon which they have little impact. This collective closure, which borders on claustrophobia, is what makes life in the gym possible and it goes a long way in explaining its attractions. (Wacquant, 1989: 8)

Farming the farm system

The boxing club is rarely a spontaneous creation of the ghetto, however. A third and final avenue for understanding boxing as more than a natural product of the rough working class relates to the externality of the forces which use the ghetto for the production of professional fighters. One of the main features of the ghetto experience is dependency, and this can be exploited for a wide range of purposes. As chapter 3 illustrates, in the United States characters such as Mack animate the relationship between urban poverty, youth culture and professional boxing. As he explains himself, it was only through his direct intervention in the routine youth culture of Charter Oak that a boxing club existed there:

> About ten years ago I decided to start my own operation. I knew it would take time and a lot of work, but I knew it would be worth it in the long run. I found this place [Charter Oak basement] and with some help from the PAL [Police Athletic League] persuaded the city to let me use it as a gym. The neighbourhood was rough, particularly then; it wasn't long after the race riots, and, as a Fed [Federal Prosecutor] I'm sure I wasn't the most popular guy on the project. While I was prosecuting for the state I used to come down here wearing my gun, but once I got the place set up, the kids came pouring in and gradually the locals have learned to respect what we're doing here. It's taken over ten years, but if you look at the record books you'll see we've got one of the strongest gyms in New England.

There can be little doubt that Mack genuinely views his boxing involvement in terms of community development and crime prevention. However, the time and money which he invests in the club can lead to other rewards. He knows that the success of his boys in the ring brings him considerable personal kudos and, ultimately, the financial rewards associated with the professional ring. Better than any sociologist, Mack is aware of the social mechanisms with which he is tampering and this is precisely why he chose to develop a boxing club in the midst of the social and environmental dereliction which is Charter Oak. Mack seeks to disguise the exploitative nature of the regime which he oversees by using the rhetoric of amateurism to justify his operation to outsiders, while inside the gym he invokes the American dream to hold the commitment of and fuel the efforts of the boxers themselves. The instrumental intervention into and manipulation of the ghetto experience has been explained in terms of Bourdieu's conceptualisation of symbolic power. Mack shields and thereby strengthens 'relations of oppression and exploitation by hiding them under the cloak of nature, benevolence and meritocracy' (Wacquant, 1993: 2). In this way, ultimately for his own ends, Mack is able to shape the career of a young fighter from the streets, through the juniors and amateurs and into the professional circus while at the same time making this progression appear to be voluntary, self-determined and merited. In this way the meaning of boxing within the subculture is constructed in such a way that fighters are led to conspire in the exploitation of their own disadvantage (Sugden, 1987).

The centre stage of the basement gym is a boxing ring. The ring is in fact square and this is symbolic of the paradox around which the boxing subculture is constructed. The main, but largely unspoken, objectives of the club revolve around the production and training of professional fighters. For the most part, this is achieved through a framework of junior and amateur boxing. The exploitation of disadvantage which takes place is made to appear laudable by locating the boxing club within a pocket of urban poverty: a declared ideology of moral and social development legitimises the club's targeting of the male youth of the urban poor, offering itself as a deterrent against juvenile delinquency and a series of related social ills. However, the states of mind and physical skills displayed by male youth in Charter Oak, which the boxing club purports to deter, are precisely those attributes required by the professional boxing stable as its raw material. In this way Mack, the manager, is in the same position as the preacher who is dependent upon the devil for the size of his congregation.

Once involved in the club, recruits share a process through which their streetwise qualities are honed and controlled in the service of professional boxing. Their volatile aggression and physical assertiveness, their courage and pride, their 'tough-toughness' are given new rhythms and disciplined around the timing of the professional ring. Their identities gradually become centred on the role of boxer and, as they mature through adolescence and become aware of a world beyond Charter Oak, it is the light of the professional ring which is construed to offer them hope in the shadow of urban poverty.

Thus, through the intervention of the likes of Mack into the social life of the ghetto, the circle is squared. Through their agency, self-improvement and character development are tied to an individual's progress through the various hurdles of a boxer's career. Going all the way to the top is appraised as a sign of moral transubstantiation, as well as commercial and occupational success. For a few, at least for a while, the squaring of the circle offers a genuine chance for self-fulfilment. But, to make one contender it takes the exploitation of many others who will not succeed. The boxing subculture takes them as boys off the streets and shows them a glimpse of the big time: a vision which can only reinforce a sense of failure when they find themselves without their gloves, without an education and without jobs, back amid the poverty of the global city.

Bring me your huddled masses: professional boxing's global network

The case study of boxing in Northern Ireland illustrates how this process continues to work even when amateur and professional boxing are not taught under the same roof. Youngsters from all over Belfast box as amateurs in their local gyms and if they prove to be good enough they are encouraged and enticed to migrate to one of the more successful establishments like the Holy Family, where they will get better training, better sparring and more opportunities to travel and fight in major amateur championships. Of course, throughout this journey, according to their mentors, these young boxers are 'kept off the streets' and out of the clutches of the paramilitary organisations. The best win national titles and the best of the best go on to win international honours. As their amateur careers progress so too do they become noticed by those who broker for the professional ring. Gerry, the manager of the Holy Family, is also coach to the national amateur boxing team and has good contacts in professional circles worldwide. Through Gerry's mediation, the Holy Family's better amateur fighters are recruited into professional boxing stables in Belfast, England and in increasing numbers in the United States.

Even in places where there is an official embargo on professionalism, amateur boxing, at least in part, dances to the tune of the prize ring. Before the 1959 revolution Cuba produced some fine professional boxers, most of whom plied their trade in the United States. This migration is more dormant than dead. Professional boxing was banned in Cuba in 1962, but high-quality amateur boxing continues to thrive there. Cubans are regularly seen on display, usually winning major international boxing competitions and as such, despite Castro's ban on professionalism, the island's best fighters are sought as recruits for the professional ring. Notwithstanding Stevenson's legendary rejection of a professional contract, several fighters have defected to the United States and, at the time of writing, one heavyweight, Jorge Luis Gonzales, is a ranked world contender. Everywhere the Cubans perform outside their county there are professional agents waiting in the wings for a chance to develop links with some of the world's most exciting young prospects (Price, 1995). The more 'open' Cuba is forced to become in order to shore up its failing economy, the more amateur boxing there will become reincorporated into the global professional circuit. Certainly, once Castro goes, and if, as is highly likely, the regime of which he was the chief architect crumbles, boxing in Cuba will once more become open and in no time at all the top ranks of every world professional weight division will feature Cubans.

The disguised structural interdependence between the amateur and professional codes of boxing is a global phenomenon. In the last century and in the early part of this, most of the United States' professional boxers were the progeny of the waves of immigrants from Europe who, before assimilation, spent a generation dwelling in the inner-city slums of cities such as Boston, New York and Chicago. As they moved on and up they abandoned the ghettos and the ring. The Europeans' places were taken by black African-Americans and, more recently, Hispanics, for whom, in the face of deep-seated and systematic prejudice, assimilation and social mobility have been exceedingly difficult to achieve. Their numbers dominate inner-city America and their representatives dominate the world ring. In more recent years, the United States has become the global clearing house of professional boxing as promising fighters from the rest of the world have been recruited into American stables. In boxing clubs in Detroit, Las Vegas and Miami, Americans from poor backgrounds sweat it out with even poorer contenders from South Africa, Nigeria, Puerto Rico, Nicaragua, Ireland, the former Soviet Union and Cuba. In this way First World and Third World poverty have become merged in the shadow of First World opportunity and affluence to produce a maximum yield for the professional ring.

Boxing as labour

Clearly, professional boxing never was and never has been the spontaneous product of urban poverty. It was one of the earliest developments of a sports entertainment industry which now has an extremely lucrative worldwide market. As a commercial endeavour, boxing has always been 'owned' and controlled by wealthy groups of people for whom the ghetto provides a reservoir of willing labour, not a residence. Professional sport is one of the few occupations for which labour and the product of labour are contained within the same physical form, the human body. Once in the ring the boxer and his opponent are both producer and product. Wacquant refers to this juxtaposition as 'body capital' and argues that the boxing subculture is a process through which the fighter's physique is trained and sculpted in such a way that its optimum surplus value can be realised:

> The fighter's body is simultaneously his means of production, the raw materials he and his handlers (trainer and manager) have to work with and on, and, for a good part, the somatized product of his past training and extant mode of living. Bodily capital and bodily labour are thus linked by a recursive relation which makes them closely dependent on one another. The boxer uses what Marx (1977: 173) calls 'the natural forces of his body' so as to optimise the growth of these very forces. Properly managed, this body is capable of producing more value than was 'sunk' in it. (Wacquant, 1995: 67)

The world's highest-paid athletes are professional boxers, but this is misleading. For every one who fights for a purse of a million dollars or more, there are thousands who fight for a pittance on the under-card of some small-town show. 'The top of the pyramid is small, the base broad, shading out the anonymous subsoil of humanity at any level of boxing' (Oates, 1980: 34). Furthermore, the winner's (and loser's) purse is divided up among a retinue of trainers, managers, cut-men, match makers and agents. In this regard the boxer's body and the capital it generates cease to be owned and controlled by the fighters themselves. With the possible exception of prostitution there can be no other profession within which alienation is so directly experienced. Joyce Carol Oates believes that boxing and prostitution are connected through deprivation:

> Impoverished people prostitute themselves in ways available to them, and boxing on its lowest levels offers an opportunity for men to make a living of a kind. (Oates, 1980: 34)

Selling your own body for the abuse and pleasure of others has been the last refuge of the poor as long as history has been recorded. In the modern world the inner city, where the rich can visit and where the poor must live, is the territory of both boxers and prostitutes. In Havana, for instance, while in back-street gyms young Cuban men strained and sweated, preparing their bodies for display in the boxing ring, young Cuban women paraded in the avenues and squares of the old city, hustling tourists for precious dollars. While the social legitimacy bestowed on each activity is markedly different, there is little to distinguish boxing from prostitution in terms of the conditions and motivations which underlie each type of exploitation of the physical form. The fact that in general women have far fewer opportunities to succeed in professional sports and virtually no chance of making a living as boxers (there are no women boxers in Cuba, for instance) means that under impoverished circumstances their options for material and personal enhancement are even more limited than men's.

Boxing and resistance

However, even as boxing exploits, it also liberates and, like most sports, it has an aesthetic quality which has intrinsic appeal to those who step into the ring. In this regard it is mistaken to view boxing as a straightforward example of exploited wage labour. Boxers take up the sport and stay involved because, first and foremost, they enjoy it as an athletic experience and, secondly, because it gives them status within the ghetto and, if they are very successful, a semblance of respectability in the wider society. Interview managers, trainers and young boxers anywhere in the world, ask them to justify boxing and, whatever the language, the message will be the same: boxing is not just a sport, it is a saviour of the oppressed and a theatre of their dreams. Colin McMillan (1991), former British featherweight champion, speaks for most boxers when he claims that:

> In a world cloaked in prejudice, the ring is the one place where all men are equal ... to us pugilists the boxing arena is a place where we can raise our self esteem; where the short can stand tall, the weak become strong, and the shy become bold. It is a place to fulfil one's dreams, aim for the stars, and better one's future.

It is possible to interpret this and the many statements like it emanating from the boxing fraternity as evidence that boxing is a site for subcultural resistance against political and economic oppression and discrimination. In the 1970s there were a significant number of theorists who focused on subcultures as sites for reaction against an imposed social order and the dominant value system (Hall and Jefferson, 1975; Robins and Cohen, 1978; Willis, 1978; Corrigan, 1979). According to this school of thought, subcultures did not just appear and languish in the cracks of society; rather, they were produced by structured inequalities and cohered around patterns of behaviour and styles which, at least at a local level, enabled members to appear to be fighting back. However, it has been pointed out that this new wave of subculture theory failed to account for the ephemeral and transient nature of most subcultures and, perhaps more significantly, underestimated the extent to which subcultures which have the appearance of resistance, like, for instance, punk rock, are incorporated into dominant cultural forms (Brake, 1980).

In this respect boxing occupies an ambivalent position. Boxing clubs do offer at least temporary sanctuary from the worst excesses of ghetto life, and a prolonged commitment to the sport often keeps 'at-risk' young males on the straight and narrow. For the small minority, prolonged engagement within the subculture can lead to a successful professional career and economic, if not social, mobility. In short, it is possible to view boxing as a positively sanctioned mechanism (at least for the timebeing) through which young men in the ghetto, with few other opportunities, can fight back against the structures which define the poverty of their existence. It is hard for anybody who has spent time in the modern ghetto not to conclude that, given what else is on offer, boxing is an extremely positive option for the young men who have to live there.

However, a note of caution must be included. When questioned, none of the professional boxers whom I met in the course of this study were eager to have any of their children embark on a career in the ring. For them boxing was the best way to exchange their 'body capital' for a livelihood, but they wanted better futures for their children. Moreover, as we have seen, even though boxing may be interpreted by fighters themselves as a form of resistance against layers of social, political and economic disadvantage, it is, nonetheless, an extremely exploitative medium. Furthermore, while boxing draws heavily on the working-class experience for participants and followers, it is a mistake to interpret the ring as a forum for ritualised class struggle against bourgeois hegemony. If anything, given the rational and proselytising value system which characterises this subculture worldwide, boxing supports rather than detracts from established authority.

A few fighters have used their renown in the ring as a stage for quasi-political activity. Once he became world heavyweight champion, Cassius Clay, who came from an impoverished background in Louisville, Kentucky, changed his 'slave name' to Muhammad Ali and proclaimed his success as a beacon for oppressed black people in the United States and throughout the world (Hauser, 1991). He often characterised himself as a 'black Henry Kissinger', and claimed that he was only using his skills as a boxer to build a platform upon which he could champion the cause of his down-trodden brothers in the face of white (American) imperialism. Thus, boxing for Ali became synonymous with political activism. The seemingly bizarre choice of Kinshasa, Zaire, for his show-down with fellow African-American George Foreman was linked to Ali's particular black internationalist cause.

Foreman, on the other hand, had different ideas. For him boxing was an end in itself and, as such, the vindication of the American dream. He was the rags-to-riches child, who, after juvenile flirtations with crime, had been converted to boxing. He had waved the flag and wept when he won his Olympic gold medal, and when he became heavyweight champion of the world he was glad to invoke God's blessing of America (Mailer, 1975).

When Barry McGuigan boxed for world titles he did so under the United Nations flag, an emblem of peace which symbolised that he was fighting for peace and reconciliation in Northern Ireland. This was interpreted by some as nothing more than a public relations exercise by his manager, Barney Eastwood, who viewed McGuigan's stance as an opportunity to raise his international profile. On the other hand, some members of the Irish nationalist community outside the boxing fraternity never forgave McGuigan for fighting for British titles, and his refusal to box under the Irish tricolour simply compounded what they interpreted as perfidy (Sugden, 1995: 212).

Albeit in a different context, the Cuban Teofilo Stevenson, arguably the greatest heavyweight boxer never to win a world professional title, became his country's most famous sportsman and greatest patriot when, after winning successive Olympic gold medals, he rejected a multimillion dollar offer to defect from Cuba to fight Ali. He had fought his way from poverty and succeeded in defeating, at least symbolically, the forces of capitalism and imperialism. His achievements in the ring and his patriotism out of it were rewarded by Castro with civic honours, a generous state pension and other material gifts such as a car and better housing for himself and his family.

In different, but sometimes overlapping ways, those who have shared Ali's, Foreman's, McGuigan's or Stevenson's successes and beliefs have been important role models for the international boxing subculture, and their photographs and records of achievements are stuck on the walls of back-street gymnasiums throughout the world. Whether it be fighting for yourself or for your country, your class, your race, or for peace, in terms of the underpinning processes, the message is the same: stick with boxing, work hard, stay out of trouble and you will better yourself. You may even become a champion. In this manner, even forms of resistance can be turned to the advantage of professional boxing's farm system.

This is the key linkage through which, both ideologically and in terms of process, amateur boxing is bound to and, in many ways, is dependent upon professional boxing. Boxing is a social good because it keeps vulnerable and potentially delinquent youngsters off the streets and out of trouble. It also gives them an opportunity to make something of themselves and if they should make it all the way – become 'a contender' – almost by definition, they will have completed an interpersonal journey which will have transformed them from urchins to decent young men. If they should so chose they and those close to them may wish to interpret success in the ring as a triumph against the tyranny of political elites, social class and racial and ethnic prejudice. Whatever the rationale – and it is usually a complex blend of all the above – the net result is an example set which will stimulate the steady production of talent for the professional ring.

The last male preserve?

In many ways the subtext of this book has been the maleness of the boxing subculture. At one level this feature of boxing should not be too surprising. In general sports are male dominated and this to some extent is related to the historical links between sport and militarism and warfare, themselves male-dominated theatres. Boxing more than most other sports resembles its ancient, martial progenitor and has proven to be very resistant to female involvement. Furthermore, the fact that violence in society in general is overwhelmingly male instigated and perpetrated (Hargreaves, 1994: 14–16) would lead one to expect that it would be men rather than women who would be drawn to a sport which has violence as its centrepiece, albeit in a controlled form.

Significantly, the only place where women featured prominently in the preceding ethnographies was at the 'black tie' affair when the Holy Family performed for an audience of Midlands businessmen at the Three Counties Showgrounds in Worcester. In this case most of the women present waited on the men while a few models paraded in bathing suits in the ring, carrying signs indicating the numbers of forthcoming rounds. The presence of women as either servants or 'classy dames', as escorts and adornments, is common practice in the staging of boxing events. Nevertheless, when they are not formally prevented from doing so, some women do attend boxing matches as integrated members of the audience. There is need for further research in this area to discover how many attend and whether they go looking for the same things as their male counterparts. Joyce Carol Oates may provide an insight into the attractiveness of boxing to women when she describes it as a symbolised form of love-making:

192

No sport is more physical, more direct, than boxing. No sport appears more homoerotic: the confrontation in the ring – the disrobing – the sweaty heated combat that is part dance, courtship, coupling – the frequent urgent pursuit by one boxer of the other in the fight's natural and violent movement toward the 'knockout': surely boxing derives much of its appeal from this mimicry of a species of erotic love in which one man overcomes the other in an exhibition of superior strength and will. (Oates, 1980: 30)

While women may be allowed in the arena they are almost never seen inside the boxing gym. Not once in the many months I spent in boxing clubs in Hartford, Belfast and Havana did I encounter a woman. It is as if the very presence of a female would threaten the masculine spell which frames a fighter's consciousness. Wacquant shows how the taboo over women is ingrained within the boxing subculture and how it is particularly powerful in the weeks and days leading up to a fight, when abstinence from sexual activity becomes one of the focal points of the boxer's training regime (Wacquant, 1995: 79). Often, boxers with partners will move out of their homes during the period leading up to a big fight to ensure that any temptation for intimate relations is removed. This taboo goes beyond any practical understanding of the physiological effects of sexual intercourse. It can be understood only in terms of a ritual dislocation between the worlds of men and women in much the same way as certain religious orders take oaths of celibacy and, in certain cases, separation in order that they may keep focused on a sacred task which they believe to be of a higher order than mortal relationships.

In the past women have boxed, but only at the margins of the sport, in freak shows, travelling circuses and as male-oriented pub entertainment (Hargreaves, 1994: 143). However, in the 1990s boxing's masculine citadel is threatened with a female invasion which is coming from three related directions. First, as a response to increased male violence and harassment, more women have taken up one of a variety of forms of martial arts as a means of improving their capacities for self-defence. For many years women were banned from boxing in many countries around the world, but recent advances in women's rights have rendered such legislation obsolete in countries such as the United States and the United Kingdom. As such, boxing has been added to judo and karate as an activity for women who feel the need to learn how to protect themselves (Hargreaves, 1994: 282).

Related to this, because women have had greater access to boxing clubs, in an era of heightened bodily awareness, they have discovered that boxing training is an excellent medium for keeping fit and staying in shape. As such, the female demand for access to boxing has increased dramatically.

Finally, and perhaps most importantly, as a result of more open access, increasing numbers of women have gone beyond training to discover that they actually enjoy and are good at the real thing and slowly but surely women contenders are chipping away at the popular perception of boxing as a sport for men only. Whether or not this movement in the direction of sexual equality represents a progressive movement in civilisation or merely offers women an opportunity to share in the uncivilised barbarity of men is an issue which requires future debate.

Conclusion: boxing, inequality and poverty

Returning to the opening theme of this chapter, on the basis of the preceding analysis, what counsel can we offer those who would ban professional boxing? Imagine a social engineer had been challenged to design two societies: the first for the cultivation of professional boxing; the second a community within which professional boxing would not be tolerated. The resulting designs may look something like this.

The first society would have a high incidence of urban poverty. In contrast it would also be an affluent society within which the accumulation and conspicuous display of wealth were prioritised. Abject poverty and conspicuous affluence would exist side by side and those affected by the former would be painfully aware of the lifestyles enjoyed by the rich and famous. The dissonance generated by this proximity would generate crime and vice inside and outside the ghetto as the haves were preyed upon by the have-nots and as people confronting hopelessness and feeling trapped struck out at one another and/or sought refuge in drugs and alcohol. This would be an economically aggressive society wherein success was considered to be the just reward of those who had made it to the top in a boundlessly competitive marketplace. But the market would be rigged against certain sections of society whose access to the multiple avenues through which affluence could be achieved would be severely restricted. Make this a multiracial and ethnically divided society and, rather than being random, inequality would be structurally embedded and coherent on the basis of skin colour. Economic aggression would be supported by a proud military tradition and this society would be used to waging war and having a standing army ready for both national defence and international attack. A martial emphasis would be an outstanding feature of the cultural production and this would help to sustain an equation between masculinity and physical strength and domination through the application of violence. Women would have a restricted say in the political and legislative processes. Education would be structured in such a way that access and quality were linked to socio-economic status. Finally, introduce sport and assign it fewer restrictions on entry than most other areas of social life. Create a professional tier to sport and make its stars highly paid and highly visible and within this nexus make boxers the highest paid of all. In such a scenario, pushed by the ghetto and pulled by market demand, professional boxing would thrive.

The second model would be designed to produce a relatively affluent society within which the distance between the richest and poorest members would be comparatively narrow. Democracy would be at an advanced stage of development and there would be a corresponding culture of collective responsibility and civic duty. This would lead to the construction of an extensive welfare state through which the rights and needs of all individuals could be sustained and within which high-quality education for all would be prioritised. In terms of race and ethnicity, it would be a relatively homogeneous community with a small immigrant population and little correlation between deprivation and minority status. It would have an international reputation as a peaceful society and would be respected for its skills in international diplomacy, rather than its capacity to wage war. Notably, definitions of masculinity would not emphasise physicality and domination, and social and political relations between men and women would be relatively equal. Sport would be important, but it would be played in ways which evoked fairness, team spirit, collective goal-setting and proportionality. In this context there would be a low threshold of tolerance for violence in sport. In short, this would be a 'civilised society', within which there would be no appetite from below for participation in boxing and little demand from above for its professional display.

Of course, after the models were complete, our social engineer would be disappointed to learn that two societies corresponding to his designs already exist. The first, the United States, will continue to be a world leader in boxing so long as the socio-economic and political conditions sketched out above define its character. As for the second, professional boxing was banned in Sweden in 1970, when, 'after the ambitious programme for creating an advanced welfare society was approaching its consummation the conception of boxing was seen to be anachronistic' (Hellspong, 1982: 224). That this could occur so soon after Sweden produced in Ingemar Johansson the last white world heavyweight champion gives some indication of the power of the anti-boxing lobby in the country at that time. Amateur boxing has continued to exist in Sweden. Interestingly, since the late 1970s the immigrant population has expanded and there has been a relative decline in prosperity and welfare provision. There has been a corresponding increase in the popularity of amateur boxing among working-class Swedes in general and immigrant groups in particular. Moreover, the numbers of Swedes boxing as professionals overseas, particularly in the United States, have likewise gone up (Hellspong, 1982).

This only serves to reinforce the conclusion towards which this work has been building – that boxing is the cultural product of a global political economy which determines considerable social inequalities. The boxing subculture grows where poverty stands in the shadow of affluence. A version of civilisation which would not tolerate boxing could only be constructed upon shared prosperity, and if the sport is to be banned its prohibition will have to be paid for through a massive increase in payments from the rich to the poor in countries like the United States and Great Britain and Ireland, and universally, from the First World to the Third World. It is highly unlikely that this will happen in the foreseeable future. Under such circumstances, unless greed, corruption and maladministration cause boxing to collapse from within, it is to be expected that the sport will survive well into the next millennium.

Appendix. The perils of ethnography

This essay is mostly about the ethical and physical perils associated with doing ethnographic research. As a way into this subject I have chosen to 'tell the story' of how, through a combination of accidents and informed choice, I came to view ethnography as the purest form of sociological inquiry as well as to anticipate some of the pitfalls involved with this style of research.

Most of the sociology which I encountered as an undergraduate at the University of Essex was of a grand theoretical nature. The relative explanatory power of classical scholars such as Marx, Weber and Durkheim were discussed against a backcloth of multinational capitalism and international socialism. The final stages of my undergraduate education tended to be dominated by refining and understanding the competition between a small number of theoretical derivatives of Marxism. This left me well equipped to identify which theory of the State could do most to explain the emergence of and eventual repression of the Tupamaros, Uruguay's urban guerrilla movement, the topic of my final-year dissertation. In those days the fact that I had never set foot in Uruguay or, indeed, even met a Uruguayan did not seem to hinder such discourse or stop me becoming a self-proclaimed 'expert' on the subject.

As a final-year depth-study option I elected to take a seminar course on anarchism. For the most part this discussion group was dominated by familiar squabbles between representatives of various factions of the left over the role of the State, ideology and repression in capitalist and communist societies. In the midst of all this, however, there was an interlude wherein we were asked to consider actual examples of societies apparently held together without any central apparatus of authority, that is, stateless societies. It was at this point that I was introduced to the writings of the social anthropologist Evans-Pritchard, who, among other things, had made a series of studies of stateless primitive societies in Africa, particularly in central and southern Sudan. Having so recently ploughed my way through Habermas, Marcuse, Althusser and the like, I was immediately struck by the sense of local authenticity conveyed by Evans-Pritchard's writings. I admired the way in which he was able to move to theorisations on power and social relations without ever overwhelming his grounded narrative. I remember being particularly impressed by his book on the Nuer, a nomadic tribe of cattle herders, and being mesmerised by his description of the leopard skin chief and Evans-Pritchard's explanation of his role as an arbitrator among the Nuer's kinship networks (Evans-Pritchard, 1951). I reflected on my own abstracted scribblings on Uruguay and felt embarrassed by their inadequacy.

On graduating from Essex, Evans-Pritchard, classical social theorists and neo-Marxists seemed to be of equally little use to me as dejectedly I looked through the job advertisements. Three months after graduation I found myself working in a pub in north London. (What else did one do with a degree in politics and sociology in the 1970s?) The choice seemed to lie between school teaching and social work, two worthy careers, neither of which I had much interest in. I was on the verge of accepting a job with Tower Hamlets Social Services when I spotted an advertisement in *The Guardian* for volunteers to work in the Sudan. Within two weeks I was in Khartoum being briefed for my sojourn as a teacher of English in the Southern Sahara (the fact that I had not taught a day in my life and had an accent which would have graced the set of Brookside[1] did not seem to put off the Sudanese Ministry of Education).

Ten months spent in the village of Khor Taggat, ten miles outside the desert city of El Obeid, proved to be a humbling experience as I reflected on the abundance of First World existence in comparison with the pressures of life in one of the world's poorest nations. My interlude in Sudan left me with lots of time for reflection, much of which I expressed in written form, either in letters home or through entries in a daily journal which I kept. I have unearthed these 'memoirs' and patched together a section which illustrates how, even though I did not realise it at the time, ethnography became established as a key element in my own personal and intellectual development.

It was half-way through my stay in Africa, during a journey to southern Sudan, that I had one of the more bizarre experiences of my life which, for the first time, evoked echoes of my work as an Essex undergraduate. I had travelled with another Englishman overland from El Obeid to El Muglad in the most extreme discomfort in the rear of a lorry which was otherwise jammed full of half-naked Dinka tribesmen making their way from working in the peanut harvest in the north to their homes in the south.

El Muglad is in mid-west of Sudan and is one of the points were the Arab north meets the black African south. It is also one of the staging posts for the Baggara, a nomadic tribe of Arab descent, who centuries before had abandoned the camel as a means of transport in favour of long-horned cattle, which they ride in a manner curiously reminiscent of Peter Fonda on his chopped Harley in the cult film *Easy Rider*. Because my companion and I were the first whites to visit El Muglad for some time we were objects of great curiosity. We were given shelter by a government official in the only non-mud-and-straw dwelling in the town. For the first time since graduation, my university education came in handy as our host proved to be something of an expert on Evans-Pritchard, who had lived and worked in the region in the 1950s and who had written books on many of the

---

[1] Soap opera set in Liverpool.

nomadic tribes who roamed around here. We talked into the small hours about the different peoples who inhabited this part of the world, about the rift between the Arab north and the African south, and about the merits and demerits of the military regime which ruled from Khartoum. Before we left the next morning he presented me with a copy of Evans-Pritchard's book on the Nuer.

There was a slight sandstorm blowing just after dawn as we waited at the station for a train to take us further south. Sudan has only one railway line, upon which run a handful of ageing diesel engines pulling ancient rolling stock left over from the British Empire. The gauge of the track is narrow and this causes the train to travel quite slowly. I heard the train approaching, but I was not prepared for the sight of it as it emerged from the dawn's purple gloom quite close to the station. The labouring engine hauled approximately ten ancient Pullman carriages, on the roofs of which were spread what seemed to be a whole tribe of Dinka, sitting cross-legged with clusters of spears waving in the air like bulrushes on the banks of the Nile.

We had government passes which permitted us to travel 'first class', below which were three other classes, excluding the roof. I remember thinking, 'God help classes 2, 3 and 4,' as I surveyed the cramped and dusty accommodation which would house me and about six other people for the next seventy-two hours. The first-class toilet deserves a special mention. It was the size of a small telephone booth and contained a porcelain WC and a tiny wash hand-basin to which no water flowed. Tethered to the WC was a goat. Given that perpetual diarrhoea is a fact of life for First-World visitors in many Third-World countries, for the next two days the goat and I got to be firm friends, and I was dismayed when on the third day he was no longer there to share my frequent constitutionals and goat's head soup appeared on the menu handed out by the steward. (Has there ever been a worse venue for death row?) I was beginning to learn the hard way the meaning of cultural relativism. Eventually, I ate the soup.

A further surprise awaited me the following afternoon as I awoke from a nap and peered out of the compartment's slatted windows straight into the eyes of a Nuer leopard skin chief in full regalia, with a leopard's head for a crown and the rest of the pelt hanging as a cloak down the back of his otherwise naked body. It was as if he had stepped straight out of the pages of one of Evans-Pritchard's texts. My travelling companion was taken aback when I was able to explain how this figure fitted into the power structure of Dinka kinship networks. For the first time I began to think that my undergraduate education had not been a total waste of time.

This episode was not without its down side. In the six months before these events I had already contracted malaria and somewhere between El Muglad and our destination, Wau, I was bitten by an unidentified insect and became smitten with one of the thousands of tropical diseases they have yet to find a name for. During a delirious ten days I lost more than 20 lb (which, unlike now, in those days I could ill afford); according to the emergency medical team when they finally reached me I was almost dead. Luckily the drugs they gave me worked and I survived to tell the tale. While it did not occur to me at the time, the fact that I had nearly died to get the tale was part and parcel of my ethnographer's apprenticeship.

Five years later I was making another journey of discovery in a totally different context in the United States. I was on my way to a boxing club in a black and Hispanic ghetto in the self-proclaimed 'insurance capital of the world', Hartford, Connecticut. I described the setting for this field work like this:

> Below the horizon, in the shadows of the houses of corporate finance and partly hidden beneath the elevated steel and concrete network of highways, there is a wasteland of urban decomposition and social subsistence ... the down town residential showcase of nineteenth century Hartford has gradually deteriorated into its twentieth century ghetto.

In the intervening period I had revisited the theoretical and methodological debates which had informed so much of my undergraduate education as a postgraduate at the University of Connecticut. I was particularly fortunate to have taken a course under the guidance of Albert Cohen, who was a guru on delinquent subcultures. He and other colleagues who were likewise devotees of the Chicago School of urban sociology/ethnography provided me with an informed and analytical framework within which to embed the self-taught social observation and recording skills picked up in sub-Saharan Africa.

At the same time, largely inspired by work of Raymond Williams (1977) and E. P. Thompson (1968), critical theorists and researchers were beginning to turn their attention to areas of cultural production which hitherto had fallen outside the embrace of serious academic scholarship. In terms of additional empirical research the CCCS (Centre for Contemporary Cultural Studies) at the University of Birmingham took a lead in this area and much of the work it produced was at least quasi-ethnographic in style and interpretation. While in terms of clarity of prose and richness of interpretation none of this work seriously challenged the supremacy of the early Chicago School (classics such as Wirth's, *The Ghetto* (1928) or Whyte's *Street Corner Society* (1955)), texts such as *Resistance through Rituals* (Hall and Jefferson, 1975) and Paul Willis's excellent *Learning to Labour* (1977), by placing an emphasis on the social-structural and power-related elements which frame the subcultural experience, provided me with another piece of the jigsaw which would comprise the epistemological foundation for the research style which has tended to characterise my work ever since. Ironically, the final piece of this puzzle was provided by a detached theoriser, Anthony Giddens, who, in *New Rules of Sociological Method* (1976), spelled out in theoretical terms justification for the methods of the CCCS and fellow travellers.

Summarising a long and complex journey through the sociology of knowledge, Giddens argued that the critical point of social reproduction is at the moment when human agency interacts with institutional determination and that this is precisely the site where the development of social theory should begin and end. Because of the highly complex and subliminal nature of this process of social reproduction, Durkheim's (1964) 'old' rules of sociological method, that is, principles which cast the researcher at a detached vantage point from those to be studied (in their most modern guise accurately characterised by C. Wright Mills (1959) as 'abstracted empiricism'), are inadequate for accessing and making sense of the lived experience of cultural transformation. Thus, Giddens makes a strong case for hermeneutics as a philosophical foundation for empirical research in sociology, arguing that 'immersion' in structurally bounded spheres of social interaction – points of praxis once power relationships are introduced into the equation – is the most appropriate method for sociological analyses and – presumably – theoretical construction and theoretical transformation:

> The production and constitution of society is a skilled accomplishment of its members, but one that does not take place under conditions that are wholly intended or wholly comprehended by its members. The key to understanding social order is not the 'internalisation of values', but the shifting relations between the production and representation of social life by its constituent actors. (Wright Mills, 1970: 102)

With Giddens' benediction I was finally ready to set out for the field. Evans-Pritchard finally met Marx (albeit through Gramsci), and my epistemological learning curve, at least in theory, was complete.

In terms of the more practical aspects of the methodologies which inform the preceding case studies, I have drawn upon a number of qualitative and investigative strategies recommended by Douglas (1976), Lofland (1976) and Hammersley and Atkinson (1983) which require the researcher to become totally immersed in the field. It is only through total immersion that she or he can become sufficiently conversant with the formal and informal rules governing the webbing of the human interaction under investigation so that its inner-most secrets can be revealed.

However, having adopted this approach, what Giddens and many others who have written on the theory of qualitative methodology fail to point out soon becomes apparent: that is, done properly, the practice of ethnography is very time consuming, emotionally draining, extremely unpredictable and, from time to time, ethically problematic and personally dangerous. For the remainder of this appendix I intend to draw upon personal experiences encountered in formal ethnographic research settings to focus on the latter of these impediments: the ethical dilemmas and physical perils of ethnography.

Of course it is totally acceptable to undertake qualitative research in relatively non-threatening settings, for instance participant observation in a physiotherapist's clinic or interviewing retired professional soccer players in their homes. However, ethnography has a long tradition of engaging the researcher in subterranean aspects of social life which, trading upon their invisibility from the public gaze, either border on or are at the very centre of that area of social life designated as deviant by the guardians of social order. Becker's (1963) and Polsky's (1971) work with drug users and other social misfits and various scholars' work with delinquent gangs (Cohen, 1955; Robins and Cohen, 1978), would be fairly typical of this genre.

In the sociology of sport there have been several excellent studies which have required the researcher to spend long periods of time in the company of often quite violent football hooligans (Marsh, 1978; Williams *et al.*, 1984). The title of Bill Buford's book, *Among the Thugs* (1991), eloquently captures the location of this particular research role (although it can be argued that Buford's ethnography was, at best, incomplete). This title does raise some interesting ethical questions, not the least of which is how much of the guise of a thug, delinquent, sexual deviant, drug user and so on does a researcher adopt in order to get at authentic information?

In terms of my own focus, for more than a decade I have been interested in the subculture which surrounds amateur and professional boxing in various cultural settings. While boxing itself has a tenuous degree of social legitimacy, the social space which the boxing subculture traditionally occupies is usually the poorest areas of the inner city, where deprivation, crime, delinquency and violence are common bedfellows. The poorer and more degenerate a neighbourhood, the more likely it is to sustain a strong boxing tradition. In addition, in the United States in particular, it is not unusual for criminal elements to take an active interest in the goings on of the boxing fraternity. Thus, at a time when urban crime is reaching epidemic proportions on both sides of the Atlantic, if a researcher really wants to get to know the inner workings of the boxing subculture he or she has to be prepared to spend extended periods in some of the most dangerous neighbourhoods in some of the world's meanest cities, sometimes rubbing shoulders with people who regularly operate outside the law.

In reality the danger is partially real and partially a socially constructed fiction. On the separate occasions that I announced that I was considering spending extended time in a black ghetto in Hartford, Connecticut, and in the New Lodge estate of north Belfast I was strongly advised not to by friends and colleagues who had absolutely no practical knowledge of these neighbourhoods. In the first case it was the fact that I was white which, according to concerned associates, would make me stand out in a neighbourhood which had the highest murder rate in the city and where the only whites are usually armed police in squad cars. In the second case I was English, which different but equally concerned acquaintances assured me would make me a target in one of Belfast's most nationalist enclaves, in the proximity of which more than a quarter of those civilians killed in the troubles had perished.

The views of these largely middle-class and detached audiences augmented the feelings of apprehension I had when I first entered the field on both occasions. Partly as a result of listening to relatives and friends and partly because of a prepossession with my own cultural biases, I felt as if I did not belong in the location, that my incongruity was obvious to the locals and that I was sure to be attacked at any moment. In fact the neighbourhoods in question turned out to be far less threatening than my imagination suggested. The more often I visited the boxing clubs and the longer I spent in the field, the more familiar the terrain became and the less scared I was.

However, while overcoming fear is an important step towards doing good ethnography in potentially dangerous locations, fearlessness is not to be recommended. I can honestly state that from the day I began to the day I finished the two investigations my spine would tingle each time I entered the field and my pulse would not return to its normal pattern until I had put a few miles between myself and the boxing club's doors. On reflection I consider this to have been a good thing because, regardless of the inflated sense of risk experienced in my earliest days and despite the protective embrace of those about whom I was researching, these areas were dangerous places. It was vitally important to keep this in mind and be aware of the dangers at all times, otherwise the doom-filled predictions of some colleagues may well have come true.

My experience suggests that it is usually not those in whom you are interested who pose the greatest direct threat. On the contrary, in the case of my boxing studies, the managers and trainers and most of the others who drift in and out of boxing clubs have been extremely friendly and helpful. What is more, once they accept your research role they are very protective because they, above anybody else, understand the many dangers which come with hanging around ghetto environments. Ethical considerations notwithstanding, this is an important reason why being 'up front' about one's research role, particularly in potentially dangerous settings, is a cardinal principle of good ethnography. I learned that one's presence as a researcher can soon be forgotten so long as you adopt a participant role (for instance, training, helping with equipment, cleaning mouth guards, sweeping the floor and so forth). To be accepted as 'one of them' came to be very important not just in terms of access to information but also in terms of self-preservation. Along with the status of 'boxer' – or someone with a role in the boxing fraternity – comes an unofficial immunity from the vicissitudes which tend to be routine in the ghetto experience (such as gang fighting; drug dealing; car theft; and, in the case of north Belfast, involvement or confrontation with the paramilitary gangs). Thus, the closer I got to key figures in the boxing subculture and the more public these relationships became, the safer I felt.

I have three boxing-related episodes which should illustrate how simply being in settings such as these can be dangerous and can raise certain ethical issues. Ironically, the first story, which is based on experiences in the United States, relates to an event which took place in an affluent part of Rhode Island, 100 miles away from the north Hartford ghetto gym where I spent most of my time while in the field:

Late one night I had arranged to meet a boxing promoter (let's call him Cavanagh) in a restaurant on Route 1 close to the Atlantic coast in the small state of Rhode Island. He came straight from the airport having spent the day in Washington, DC, negotiating a contract for one of the Sugar Ray Leonard–Roberto Duran fights. He had the contract and who knows what else in the dark-brown leather briefcase which he held tightly in his hand as he stepped out of his

Lincoln Continental. We sat down to eat at about 10 p.m. along with one of Cavanagh's associates and chatted about the wheeling and dealing that goes on between promoters, managers and match makers in the fight game.

After the meal Cavanagh invited me to travel with him in his car so we could carry on the conversation which had been going on over dinner. It was about midnight when we left the restaurant. Cavanagh stopped at the doorway and announced that he was going back inside to use the rest-rooms. I continued to the carpark with the other dinner guest, who got into his car and drove off. On the way out we had passed two heavy-set men on their way into the restaurant from the carpark. Before Cavanagh came back the two men returned to separate cars and drove out of the carpark at speed. When Cavanagh did appear he was in a state of panic. He asked me whether I had seen his briefcase, which he said he had left by the entrance thinking I was waiting for him there. It was then that I remembered that the two strangers had not had anything with them when they went into the restaurant, but that one of them was carrying a briefcase when they came out. The chase was on!

Cavanagh jumped into his car and urged me to get in with him. We sped off down the highway in hot pursuit of the suspected thieves. I dreaded to think what we were going to do if we caught up with them and I was rather hoping we wouldn't. However, Cavanagh, who must have valued the contents of his briefcase more than his life (not to mention mine) had other ideas and he floored the Continental. Eventually the two suspect cars, a Mercedes and a Camero, came into view and as Cavanagh drew level with them he told me to lean out of the window and tell them to pull over. The famous defence at the Nuremberg trials, 'I was only obeying orders', springs to mind at this point as almost without thinking I found myself hanging out of the window of a car doing in excess of 100 miles per hour screaming to a rather sinister-looking stranger in a Mercedes to 'Pull over!'. What else was I to do? It was too late to run for cover behind my academic persona. 'Fuck you!' the Mercedes driver roared back in reply. With Cavanagh urging me on I persisted in my overtures until eventually, filling me with even more trepidation, the suspect yelled back, 'Okay, you fucking arsehole, I'll pull over and then you'll get yours buddy!'.

At the next exit both the suspect cars peeled off the highway and we followed them into the deserted parking lot of a closed shopping mall. By now my palms were sweating. Cavanagh, who is by no means a big man, got out of the car and walked towards the strangers, who likewise stepped out of their vehicles. Both were big men. One in particular I remember being very broad and weighing about 200 lb, with longish black hair and black designer stubble. He walked towards Cavanagh, who was trying to be diplomatic by saying, 'Hey guys, sorry to trouble you, but I guess none of you picked up my briefcase by mistake back at that restaurant?' to which the stranger shouted back less than diplomatically, 'You calling me a thief, you fucking arsehole? I'm not a thief I'm a fucking businessman!' He then lifted Cavanagh off the ground by the lapels of his expensive suit, slapped him across the face a few times and stuck him face forward into the trunk of his Camero, which his friend had opened, banging his head repeatedly on the inside of the boot and shouting, 'Go on, see if you can find your briefcase in there you fucking arsehole!'

At this point I was glad I had Cavanagh's car between me and the two thugs, whom I was sure I could not out-fight, but was equally certain I could out-run, assuming my legs, which seemed to have gone to jelly, would carry me. At any moment I was expecting one of them to produce a firearm. However, by now the disturbance had attracted the attention of a group of teenagers who had been hanging out in the shelter of the distant mall and who were now approaching to see what all the excitement was about. Our two assailants exchanged glances before pushing Cavanagh to the ground and jumping in their cars to speed back on to the highway.

I picked Cavanagh up, feeling slightly embarrassed that I had not come to his assistance. Even if I thought we could have out-fought them, would this have been a legitimate course of action? How far can a researcher take his participant observer's role? As it happened, both he and I knew that we were out of our depth and that it was time to call in the cavalry. With the assistance of the police we tracked down the thugs, whose cars I spotted at the back of another restaurant in the next town. The police waited outside and when our suspects went to drive off pulled them over to search their cars. Cavanagh and I observed from the shadows but one of them spotted us and, despite the attentions of the police, began shouting life-threatening insults which, after what had just happened, seemed quite plausible to me.

Although the police found nothing in the thugs' cars they believed our story. Why? Because when they called in the names of our suspects they discovered that one had recently completed a seven-year prison term for armed robbery and malicious wounding and that his colleague had no convictions but was the nephew of the local Mafia boss. I knew then that up to this point this was the closest I have ever come to being killed and that if I stuck around much longer this event might indeed come to pass! The cop asked Cavanagh if he wanted to press charges for the assault and I breathed a very heavy sigh of relief when he said that he did not, obviating my responsibility to stay around for the court case.

Laughably the briefcase did turn up much later that night when Cavanagh and I conducted a search outside the restaurant where the suspected theft had taken place. I found it hidden in a low hedge near to where the thugs had parked their cars. Obviously they had stolen it in the doorway and stashed it in the hedge when they saw me still in the carpark, hoping to come back for it some time later when the coast was clear. I thought Cavanagh was going to cry when he saw it, and to this day I would dearly like to know what was in that bag for which he was prepared to risk our lives.

An accidental encounter likewise had a lot to do with the next life-threatening research experience I was to have. While I was once more engaged in research on boxing, in itself this had nothing directly to do with the fact that I came face to face with an IRA gunman. I was carrying out field work for the BBC, who had hired me as a consultant to a production team who were making a documentary about a boxing club in north Belfast. I was also using this as an opportunity to gather information for a book about boxing in diverse cultural settings:

It was Halloween and we were filming a bonfire scene in the middle of the New Lodge housing estate because some of the young boys who boxed at the local club were having some fun with other children around a bonfire while watching a fireworks display. The New Lodge is a stronghold of Irish nationalism and is controlled by various factions of Irish republican paramilitaries. The strongest of these groups is the Provisional IRA and we had to seek permission from them in order to be allowed into the area, particularly for filming. Unbeknown to us, throughout Belfast the Provos were using the cover of Halloween to assert their authority over another republican faction, the INLA (Irish National Liberation Army), whom they had accused of being too closely involved with drug dealing.

We were filming about fifty yards back from the group around the bonfire when two hooded men stepped out of the shadows and grabbed another man who was standing watching the fire, dragging him off through our camera angle back into the shadows before disappearing around the back of a block of flats. The cameraman cast a concerned look towards the young producer, who passed it on to me. I went off to find out what was happening only to see a group of men frog marching their victim down a back alley. 'If he's lucky he'll only lose his knee caps,' I said to the producer when I came back. Just when I was beginning to think that we had not been noticed the two original hooded captors returned and came over to us. I had been living in Northern Ireland for more than ten years but this was the first time I had knowingly come face to face (or at least half face) with a terrorist.

The ring leader walked straight up to the cameraman and with no emotion in his voice commanded, 'Provisional IRA, give us the film'. Immediately the producer interceded, 'Look I'm sorry we caught you on shot, but it's not that kind of film, there's no way you could be identified, besides, we've got permission to film here.' The IRA man stared straight through her and repeated his order, this time with a little more sternness in his voice, at which the producer turned to me and pleaded, 'John, can't you do something?'

'Like what?' I thought. 'Take notes, wet myself, run?' Instead I heard myself restating her own position, while trying to sound as friendly and 'in the know' as possible: 'Listen pal, we've no interest in you, we're just filming those kids over there and as she says the film's...'. Before I could finish the sentence a rather large-looking revolver was being produced. 'Provisional IRA. Give us the fucking film!', shouted the hooded figure at the other end of the gun. 'Andy,' I said quietly to the cameraman, trying to keep the tremble out of my voice, 'give him the fucking film, now'.

We explained that this was a technical task which would have to be done back at the van which was parked around the other side of the flats. The terrorists reluctantly agreed and we were marched to the van, seated behind the wheel of which was Stan, a local hard man whom we had hired as a minder. 'Stan, can't you do something about this?' implored the producer. Stan looked uncomfortable.

Nevertheless he turned to the gunman and said, 'Come on Badger, give them a break, they're not doing any harm'. 'No names Stanley!' yelled Badger, obviously displeased that our minder had given away the fact that he had recognised him. I was none too pleased myself: the last thing I needed in this situation was for one of them to think that I could identify him to the RUC!

Meanwhile, at the back of the van the cameraman and his assistant were making heavy weather of getting the film out of the camera. It was not like an ordinary video cassette and it was highly unlikely that the IRA brigade who were taking it had the technology on hand to view it. It was never disclosed to me, but I am almost certain that a switch was worked and they gave the Provos a blank tape. Anyway, cassette in hand they melted away into the darkness. Once they had gone, Andy, the cameraman, veteran of many minor war fronts, passed around with a shaking hand the half bottle of dark rum which he kept in his inside pocket for such occasions. As I took a mouthful it occurred to me that even though in this case a gun had been pointed at me and I was pretty scared, I did not feel I was in mortal danger, unlike when Cavanagh was being shoved into the boot of the gangster's Camero in New England.

Two nights later I was ringside in a local hotel not far away from where this incident had taken place, checking on an unlicensed night of boxing to see if it would be worth filming at a later date. To my horror I recognised the man sitting at the table in front of me (an anorak hood can only conceal so much). My worst fears were confirmed when a passer-by called out, 'Hey Badger, what about ye?'. Now not only did I know the identity of an IRA gunman, but I also knew where he drank.

Once I got safely away from the place it did cross my mind whether or not I should use the confidential telephone line and pass this information to the RUC. That I did not continues to bother me and I only hope that nobody has suffered because of my decision. It had to be a matter of judgement. If I had passed information to the security forces, for reasons of personal safety there is no way that I could have continued my field work. Moreover, one of the unwritten rules of the boxing fraternity in Belfast is that politics and related events are kept outside the gymnasium. If it became known (and in north Belfast secrets are as rare as snakes) that I had used my position as a researcher under the protection of the Holy Family Boxing Club to inform on a local IRA operative, it is highly unlikely that I would have been allowed to continue my research there. The ethical rule of thumb I obeyed here is that although I witnessed an illegal event, I did not take part in it and, as such, my presence in the field did not make a contribution to that act.

The final scenario relates to field work which I recently carried out in Cuba. When this particular event took place I was hanging around the back streets of Havana trying to get a feel for the social milieu which produces some of the world's best amateur boxers. There are some who would think that even going to Cuba at a time when many Cubans were trying to escape from Castro's crumbling socialist experiment was in and of itself a perilous undertaking, particularly if one was determined to live outside of the tourists' cocoon. For the most part my experiences suggested that this view was mistaken. However, once in a while I did find myself in situations which could have got me into serious trouble with the Cuban authorities. The following extract, which is taken from my field notes, should illustrate what I mean:

Social life in Old Havana is three dimensional. In the first place there are those Cubans who live in the slums all year round and who stoically persevere with their poverty. The problem for them is that their poverty is picturesque. Falling-down, 200-year-old, Spanish colonial apartments with dejected, but white toothed Cubans at the open doors and windows offer great photo opportunities for tourists (and photo-journalists). The presence of ancient buildings such as San Cristobol Cathedral, el Palicio de los Capitanos Generales and el Castilllo de la Real Fuerza likewise has the tourists flooding in, as do more recent additions such as the Revolution Museum and the Bodigito de Medio, a bar famously frequented by Ernest Hemingway when he lived and wrote in Cuba. Thus shoulder to shoulder with Cubans who can expect to earn no more than the equivalent of $5 per week are flocks of tourists, many of whom are spending more than $100 per day (twenty times the average local weekly income).

Under these circumstances it is not surprising that the third dimension of Old Havana exists somewhere in between the stoic locals and the influx of tourists. This is Cuba's underworld: the black marketeers (*jinteros*) and varieties of prostitutes whose main aim in life is to gain access to the multimillion dollar tourist economy and profit from it.

Undoubtedly the best place to dwell within this nether region of Old Havana is the Paris Cafe, which is in the heart of Old Havana on the corner of Calle Obispo and Calle San Ignacio. This is a place where Old Havana's underworld goes when it's not working. It is no more than 200 metres from el Bodegeta de Medio, one of the city's biggest tourist attractions, but it is rare to see foreigners inside the Paris Cafe. Because it is a dollar-only establishment it is equally rare to see 'ordinary' Cubans there. It is open for twenty-four hours a day, but the best time to go is between midnight and 6 a.m., during which period many of Old Havana's characters and their entourages will pass through.

Initially, the Paris Cafe can feel intimidating to non-Cubans. There is always a heavy police presence outside the large arched entrance and an even larger crowd of locals milling around outside, either waiting for a table or simply interested in watching the social interaction taking place within. The cafe is dominated by a large hardwood bar, behind which Cuba's equivalent of a busty British barmaid serves small draughts of cheap German larger and cans of Hatuey, the almost undrinkable local beer. A small army of waiters scurry about, ferrying drinks and plates of over-done chicken and *patatas fritas* (thin fried potatoes) to customers at the ten or more small tables which take up the rest of the cafe.

The intimidating atmosphere of the place fades as I realise that I am far less accessible here than in other, more tourist-oriented bars, and that most of the clientele are here for their own good time and are not, at this stage of the evening, interested in hustling foreigners. The best place to be is at the bar, especially if you can get the bar stool close to a criss-cross wooded screen which divides the cafe from Calle Obispo. From this vantage point it is possible to watch the comings and goings of the bar as well as keep an eye on the chaotic street life of Old Havana. It is hard to avoid the impression of stepping out of one zoo and into another, however, as passers-by regularly pause at the screen to stare at the people inside the bar.

The next time I am in the Paris Cafe I am invited to join a table of young Cubans who are obviously in the midst of a good night out. One is wearing a 1994 US soccer World Cup T-shirt and we immediately have a point of common interest. His bad English and my bad Spanish dovetail perfectly and we manage to have a decent conversation. He tells me proudly that his name is Laredo and that he is named after a town in Texas in the United States. With his mop of curly brown hair and pale olive-brown complexion, Laredo looks more Greek than Cuban. He would like to visit the town which is named after him one day, he informs me with a laugh. Laredo's voice drops to a whisper as he admits that he has been in prison for two years after having been caught trying to escape to Florida. (Is there a young Cuban who is not an athlete who has not done time in the pursuit of freedom I wonder?)

Laredo is twenty-six, handsome, intelligent and very dissatisfied with his life in Cuba. The fact that he has been in prison for trying to flee the country means that he is unable to get a decent job – not that this would be worth much in terms of salary, but at least he would have some self-respect. He complains about being constantly harassed by the police and produces a piece of paper which tells me that he has had his car confiscated because he acquired it through improper channels – that is, without seeking the permission of the State, which would have been denied because of his 'criminal' record. He believes that thirty years ago the revolution was good for Cuba because it got rid of much of the corruption and injustice which had become institutionalised under successive dictatorships. However, he thinks that the revolution has now become stagnant and has failed the people, largely because Castro has stubbornly refused to adapt his view of political economy, despite radical changes in the rest of the world. Even worse, he believes that Castro's Cuba has become as corrupt and dictatorial as the Cuba of Batista. Che Guevarra could see this happening, he tells me, which is why he left to fight and die in Bolivia.

The more beer Laredo drinks the more vociferous he becomes. He insists on an anti-Castro toast and I find myself spontaneously joining him. I am uncomfortable about this in more ways than one. In my days as an Essex undergraduate I held Castro and his revolution in high esteem. While I have come to recognise the many failings of his regime I feel vaguely treacherous cheering for his downfall. Of more pressing concern is the close proximity of armed, paramilitary police, who are beginning to pay undue attention to the goings on at our table.

Laredo finishes his anti-Castro polemic and begins to entertain us with a series of conjuring tricks which he learned in prison. Salsa is blaring from the cafe's hi-fi and some people begin to dance in the aisles between the tables. A young black man approaches our table to whisper with Laredo before leaving. Five minutes later he returns and, with a policeman standing no further than three yards away surreptitiously slips Laredo a small silver paper package of what I assume to be drugs of some description. It is an ingenious pass. The dealer has the package concealed beneath his watch strap. He shakes hands with Laredo and as he does so Laredo's middle finger dislodges the drugs from behind the watch strap and flicks them into the palm of his hand. The policeman is looking, but he sees nothing. Nevertheless I think it is time for me to leave.

This final episode was in no way life threatening, but I could have easily ended up being arrested, locked up and even deported for seditious behaviour and/or drug dealing. Apart from anything else this would have seriously undermined my capacity to carry out any further research in the country and it is certain that I would have been barred by the Cuban authorities from having any kind of access to the country's elite athletes, including the boxers. However, if I wanted to get deeper insights into the general lived experience of being young in Havana I felt that it was necessary to get close to people like Laredo and his friends. As such I felt that the risks involved were worth taking, but only up to a point. Like many other people, I have seen *Midnight Express* and did not relish the prospect of spending a few years in a Cuban prison.

Conclusion

Even the everyday lives which we know so well are fraught with risks. Indeed, the routines which we establish to get ourselves through the day are, at least in part, designed to minimise these risks. We cross roads in safe places, buy houses in crime-free neighbourhoods, stay out of areas with bad reputations, associate with people we know, like and trust, and so forth. Even so, from time to time we have accidents, have our cars stolen and some of us even get mugged (recently on the way through London to do some field work in the United States I had my luggage stolen). For the most part, however, the routines which structure our day-to-day lives are constructed in ways which minimise risks, as a result of which our lives are often boring, but relatively safe. When we take the decision to undertake ethnographic research we are electing to step outside these familiar and relatively secure routines, and once we take to the field the chances of encountering threatening situations are increased.

What I have presented are a few relatively extreme examples of the kind of trouble which a researcher can encounter while engaged in ethnographic research. Of course, it is not absolutely necessary to select 'darkest' Africa, US ghettos, Irish nationalist and republican housing estates and besieged communist dictatorships as venues for this kind of work. Nevertheless, I would argue that there are elements of risk in all forms of ethnography if only because, by definition, when we are engaged in ethnographic research we are working within social and political contexts with which we do not have, at least at the outset, intimate familiarity and as such are more vulnerable within.

Furthermore, unlike as is generally the case with positivistic research designs, we cannot control the research environment. When out in the field things will happen which we cannot prevent (and neither should we seek to) and which will face us with ethical dilemmas and/or place us in physical jeopardy. When this happens, the extent to which we 'stay with the action' then becomes a question of professional judgement balanced with considerations of personal safety. Should I have refused to 'follow that car' and lose a valuable contact in the murky world of US professional boxing? Should I have 'turned in' the IRA operative and exiled myself from research in north Belfast? Was it unnecessary to share anti-Castro toasts with shady characters in Old Havana to elicit the truth about what it is like to be young in contemporary Cuba? The answer to all of these questions could have been yes or no. The fact that, in the heat of the ethnographic moment, I chose to answer no undoubtedly enhanced my credentials with those upon whom I was dependent for authentic information. I would argue that two out of three decisions could be justified on ethical grounds because I was involved in events which would have happened irrespective of my presence in the field and that I did not take a significant role in them. On reflection I now have a few reservations about my performance in the Rhode Island car chase, primarily because I was a key actor in an affair which probably would not have happened in the first place if I had not arranged to meet with Cavanagh. Also, and of greater significance, it now strikes me that taking a proactive role in the car chase went beyond the call of an ethnographer's duty.

Giddens (1976) points out – albeit from his armchair – that while in order to get close to authentic social data we must 'immerse' ourselves in a chosen milieu, there must be limits to how much we become like the people whom we are seeking to understand. We need to develop empathy with our subjects without getting emotionally tied to them. Easier said than done. As the experiences outlined herein illustrate, there is a grey area between understanding the natives and going native. A few of my own simple 'rules' might help: be up front about the research role; remember, we are not secret agents and neither are we investigative journalists, although occasionally we may borrow information-gathering techniques from either camp; neither are we *agents provocateurs* – we should not set in motion procedures which otherwise would not have happened in order to unearth interesting material; we are interested in naturally emergent (or concealed) social truths, not good stories; under (almost) all circumstances we should stay within the laws which govern the land within which we are operating. We may follow all of these 'rules' and still get caught in a flow of interaction which leads us into trouble. But, unlike scribes in the library, if we choose to work at the cutting edge of social construction, we should not be too surprised if, from time to time, we get a little dirty and a little bloody.

Bibliography

Adelman, M. L. (1980) *The development of modern athletics; sport in New York City, 1820–1870*, unpublished DPhil dissertation, University of Illinois at Urbana-Champaign.

Alfonso, G. (1988) *Punos Dorados. Apuntes para la historia del boxeo en Cuba*. Santiago de Cuba, Editorial Oriente.

Andre, M. and Fleischer, N. (1993) *A pictorial history of boxing*. London, Hamlyn.

Becker, H. (1963) *Outsiders: studies in the sociology of deviance*. New York, Free Press.

Bookchin, M. (1973) *The limits of the city*. New York, Harper Colophon.

Brailsford, D. (1988) *Bareknuckles*. Cambridge, Lutterworth Press.

Brake, M. (1980) *The sociology of youth and youth subcultures*. London, Routledge and Kegan Paul.

Brown, R. (1978) The jock trap: how the black athlete gets caught, in W. F. Straub (ed.), *Sport psychology: an analysis of athletes' behavior*. Ithica, Movement Publications: 171–84.

Buford, W. (1991) *Among the thugs*. London, Secker and Warburg.

Bunuel, L. (1972) *The discreet charm of the bourgeoisie*. London, Electronic Pictures.

Butler, F. (1986) *The good, the bad and the ugly*. London, Stanley Paul.

Calder, S. and Hatchwell, E. (1993) *Cuba, a travellers' survival kit*. Oxford, Vacation Work.

Cantu, R. C. (1995) *Boxing and medicine*. Leeds, Human Kinetics.

Clarke, A. and Critcher, C. (1985) *The devil makes work: leisure in capitalist Britian*. London, Macmillan.

Cohen, A. K. (1955) *Deliquent boys – the subculture of the gang*. London, Collier-Macmillan.

Cornwell, R. (1992) The gripes of senator Roth. *The Independent*, 28 August.

Corrigan, P. (1979) *Schooling the smash street kids*. London, Macmillan.

Curtis, J. (1986) Isn't it difficult to support some notions of the civilizing process?, in C. R. Rees and A. W. Miracle (eds), *Sport and social theory*. Champaign, Human Kinetics.

Davis, H. (1993) Winners run out on a loser. *The Daily Telegraph*, 2 December.

Douglas, J. (1976) *Investigative sociological research*. Beverly Hills, Sage.

Dunning, E. G. (1993) Sport in the civilising process. Aspects of the development of modern sport, in E. G. Dunning, *et al.* (eds) *The sports process*. Leeds, Human Kinetics: 39–70.

Durkheim, E. (1964) *The rules of sociological method*. New York, Free Press.

Edwards, H. (1981) Authority, power and intergroup stratification by race and sex in American sport and society, in G. S. Luschen and G. Sage (eds), *Handbook of social science of sport*. Champaign, Stipes: 383–99.

Egan, P. (1812) *Boxiana; or sketches of ancient and modern pugilism; from the days of the renowned Broughton and Slack to the heroes of the present milling era*. London, Sherwood.

Elias, N, and Dunning, E. (1986) *The quest for excitement*. Oxford, Basil Blackwell.

Evans-Pritchard, E. (1951) *Kinship and marriage among the Nuer*. London, Clarendon Press.

Gebler, C. (1988) *Driving through Cuba*. London, Abacus.

Giddens, A. (1976) *New rules of sociological method*. London, Hutchinson.

Gorn, E. J. (1986) *The manly art. Bare-knuckle prize fighting in America*. New York, Cornell University Press.

Guevara, C. (1996) *The motorcycle diaries*. London, Fourth Estate.

Gutteridge, R. (1974) Going, going, gone! *London Evening News*, 30 October.

Hall, S. and Jefferson, T. (1975) *Resistance through rituals: youth subcultures in post war Britain*. London, Hutchinson.

Halling, N. (1993) How the noble art has been devalued by division. *The Independent*, 18 May, p. 30.

Hammersley, M. and Atkinson, P. (1983) *Ethnography. Principles and practice*. London, Tavistock.

Bibliography

Handlin, O. (1954) *American people in the twentieth century*. Boston, Harvard University Press.

Hare, N. (1971) A study of the black fighter. *Black Scholar*, November: 2–9.

Hargreaves, J. (1986) Where's the virtue? Where's the grace? A discussion of the social production of gender relations in and through sport. *Theory, Culture and Society*, 3, 1.

Hargreaves, J. (1994) *Sporting females*. London, Routledge and Kegan Paul.

Hauser, T. (1991) *Muhammad Ali, his life and times*. London, Robson Books.

Hay, D. (1977) *Albion's fatal tree. Crime and society in eighteenth century England*. Harmondsworth, Penguin.

Hellspong, M. (1982) *The sport of boxing in Sweden. A study of the cultural environment of sport*. Stokholm, Nordiska Museets Handlingar.

Higham, J. (1975) *Strangers in the land. Patterns of American nativism 1860–1925*. New York, Atheneum.

Hobbes, T. (1968) *Leviathan*. Harmondsworth, Penguin

Holt, R. (1989) *Sport and the British*. Oxford, Oxford University Press.

Horne, J. and Jary, D. (1987) Figurational sociology of sport and leisure, in Horne *et al.* (eds), *Sport, leisure and social relations*. London, Routledge.

Huberman, L. and Sweezy, P. (1968) *Cuba: anatomy of a revolution*. New York, Monthly Review Press.

Ingham, A. and Beamish, R. (1993) The industrialisation of the United States and the 'bourgeosification' of American sport, in E. G. Dunning, *et al.* (eds), *The sports process*. Leeds, Human Kinetics: 169–206.

Ingram, W. (1995) The demise of cockfighting in Belfast, 1750–1850, unpublished paper, presented at the British Sociological Association annual conference, University of Leicester, April.

Jewell, B. (1977) *Sports and games*. Tunbridge Wells, Midas Press.

Jones, K. (1992) King's let-in clause. *The Independent*, 17 December.

Jones, K. (1995) Dark cloud over a brutal business: Nigel Benn versus Gerald McClellan. *The Independent*, 27 February.

Lardner, R. (1972) *The legendary champions*. New York, American Heritage Press.

Lefkowitz, M., *et al.* (1972) *Growing up to be violent*. New York, Pergamon.

Lofland, J. (1976) *Doing social life: the qualitative study of human interaction in natural settings*. New York, Wiley.

Lypsyte, R. (1967) *The contender*. New York, Harper-Keypoint.

MacKinnon, I. and White, J. (1995) The fight goes on. *The Independent on Sunday*, 17 October.

Macmillan, C. (1991) We have a right to dream. *The Observer*, 29 September.

Mailer, N. (1975) *The fight*. Harmondsworth, Penguin.

Malcolmson, R. (1973) *Popular recreations in English society 1700–1850*. Cambridge, Cambridge University Press.

Marsh, P. (1978) *The rules of disorder*. London, Routledge.

McCallum, J. and Kennedy, K. (1995) Still the King. *Sports Illustrated*, 83, 23: 25.

McIntosh, P. (1993) The sociology of sport in the ancient world, in E. G. Dunning, *et al.* (eds), *The sports process*. Leeds, Human Kinetics: 18–38.

McLaughlin, J. (1995) *Sport, physical education and community relations in Northern Ireland*, unpublished PhD dissertation, University of Ulster.

McMillan, C. (1991) Boxers must fight their own corner. *The Observer*, 29 September.

Michner, J. (1976) *On sport*. London, Secker and Warburg.

Mitchel, K. (1992) Sadness after the first glove affair. *The Observer*, 6 September.

Oates, J. C. (1980) *On boxing*. New York, Bloomsbury.

O'Sullivan, J. (1991) The savage pleasure of watching a man go down. *The Independent*, 23 September.

Pagnameta, P. (1995) *The people's century*. London, BBC/WGBH Productions, Episode 1, 18 October.

Pettivo, P. and Pye, G. (1994) *Sport in Cuba: the diamond in the rough*. Pittsburg, University of Pittsburg Press.

Pickering, R. (1978) *Sport in Cuba*. London, BBC television documentaries.

Plimpton, G. (1993) *Shadow box*. New York, Lyons and Burford.

Plumb, J. H. (1974) The public literature and the arts in the eighteenth century, in M. R. Marus (ed.), *The emergence of leisure*. New York, Harper and Row: 11–37.

Polsky, N. (1971) *Hustlers, beats and others*. Harmondsworth, Penguin

Powers, J. (1995) A Cuban medal crisis? *Boston Globe*, 26 March.

Price, S. L. (1995) The best little sports machine in the world. *Sports Illustrated*, 13 May.

Bibliography

Reid, J. (1971) *Bucks and bruisers.* London, Routledge and Kegan Paul.

Riordan, J. (1978) *Sport under communism.* London, C. Hurst.

Robins, D. and Cohen, P. (1978) *Knuckle sandwich.* Harmondsworth, Penguin.

Rodda, J. and Weale, S. (1994) Sporting chances. *The Guardian*, 30 April.

Rude, G. (1980) *The crowd in history.* London, Lawrence and Wishart.

Ruiz, M. C. (1980) *Teofilo Stevenson.* Havana, Editorial Orbe.

Sammonds, J. (1990) *Beyond the ring. The role of boxing in American society.* Urbana and Chicago, University of Illinois Press.

Sennett, R. (1976) *The fall of public man.* New York, Knopf.

Sheard, K. (1990) *Boxing in the civilising process*, unpublished DPhil dissertation, Council for National Academic Awards, Anglia Polytechnic, Norwich.

Shipley, S. (1989) Boxing, in T. Mason (ed.), *Sport in Britain, a social history.* Cambridge, Cambridge University Press: 78–115.

Stearns, P. (1987) Men, boys and anger in American society, 1860–1940, in J. A. Mangan and J. Walvin (eds), *Manliness and morality: middle-class masculinity in Britain and America, 1800-1940.* New York, St Martin's Press: 75–91.

Sugden, J. (1984) *Urban poverty, youth culture and the subculture of the boxer*, unpublished PhD dissertation, University of Connecticut.

Sugden, J. (1987) The exploitation of disadvantage, in J. Horne, *et al.* (eds), *Sport, leisure and social relations.* London, Routledge: 187–209.

Sugden, J. (1995) Sport, community relations and community conflict in Northern Ireland, in S. Dunn (ed.), *Facets of the conflict in Northern Ireland.* London, Macmillan.

Sugden, J. and Bairner, A. (1993) *Sport, sectarianism and society in a divided Ireland.* Leicester, Leicester University Press.

Sugden, J., Tomlinson, A. and McCartan, E. (1992) The making and remaking of white lighting. Sport in Cuba 30 years after the revolution, in A. Yiannakis, *et al.* (eds), *Sports sociology: contemportary themes.* Dubuque Iowa, Kendall Hunt: 197–207.

Sugden, J. and Yiannakis, A. (1982) Sport and juvenile delinquency: a theoretical base. *Journal of Sport and Social Issues*, 6, 1: 22–7.

Thomas, H. (1971) *Cuba, or the pursuit of freedom.* London, Eyre and Spoteswode.

Tiger, L. (1971) *Men in groups.* London, Longman.

Tompson, E. P. (1967) Time, work discipline and industrial capitalism. *Past and Present*, 38: 60–81

Tompson, E. P. (1968) *The making of the English working class.* London, Pelican.

Torres, J. (1990) *Fire and fear: the inside story of Mike Tyson.* London, W. H. Allen.

Trower, M. (1995) Human cockfighting. *XL: Sport Fitness and Health*, May: 21–4.

Veblen, T. (1953) *The theory of the leisure class.* New York, Mentor.

Virgil (1956) *The aeneid.* Harmondsworth, Penguin.

Wacquant, L. (1989) The social logic of boxing in black Chicago, unpublished paper presented at the 16th Annual Conference on Social Theory, Politics and Arts, New York City, October.

Wacquant, L. (1993) The pugilistic point of view how boxers think about their trade, unpublished paper, Russell Sage Foundation, University of California, Berkley.

Wacquant, L. (1994) *Inside the zone. The social art of the hustler in the contemporary ghetto*, working paper number 49. New York, Russell Sage Foundation.

Wacquant, L. (1995) Pugs at work: bodily capital and bodily labour among professional boxers. *Body and Society*, 1, 1: 65–93.

Weber, M. (1958) *The Protestant ethic and the spirit of capitalism.* New York, Scribners.

Weinberg, S. and Arond, H. (1952) The occupational culture of the boxer. *American Journal of Sociology*, 57: 460–9.

Whyte, W. (1955) *Street corner society.* Chicago, University of Chicago Press.

Williams, J., *et al.* (1984) *Hooligans abroad.* London, Routledge.

Williams, R. (1977) *Marxism and literature.* Oxford, Oxford University Press.

Willis, P. (1977) *Learning to labour: how working class kids get working class jobs.* London, Saxon House.

Willis, P. (1978) *Profane culture.* London, Routledge and Kegan Paul.

Wirth, L. (1928) *The ghetto.* Chicago, University of Chicago Press.

Wright Mills, C. (1959) *The sociological imagination.* New York, Oxford University Press.

Index

216

Index